The Great Thanks-giving

The Great Thanks-giving

The Eucharistic Norm of Christian Worship

by

Keith Watkins

Chalice Press
St. Louis, Missouri

Biblical quotations, unless otherwise noted, are from the *New Revised Standard Version Bible*, copyright 1989, Division of Christian Education of the National Council of the Churches of Christ in the USA. Used by permission.

Quotations marked RSV are from the Revised Standard Version of the Bible, copyright 1946, 1952, © 1971, 1973.

Cover design: Michael Dominguez

Cover Photo: D.D. Design

10987654321

BV
10.2
.W27
1995

Library of Congress Cataloging–in–Publication Data

Watkins, Keith
    The great Thanksgiving : the eucharistic norm of Christian worship / by Keith Watkins.
      p.   cm.
    Includes bibliographical references and index.
    ISBN 0-8272-1238-0
    1. Public worship.   2. Lord's Supper   3. Liturgics.   I. Title.
BV10.2.W27   1995   95-18754
264'.001—dc20   CIP

Printed in the United States of America

Contents

Acknowledgments

I gladly express appreciation to many people who have helped me think through the issues discussed in this book. My special thanks go to several who read the manuscript in earlier stages and offered me their counsel: Hoyt Hickman, Thomas Schattauer, Richard Leggett, Laura Baumgartner, Andrew Tooze, and David Kinsey who prepared the index.

It was possible to write this manuscript only because Christian Theological Seminary is such a hospitable place for scholarly work. I express my appreciation to the Board of Trustees, who authorize research leaves, and to T. J. Liggett, Richard Dickinson, Joe Jones, and Newell Williams whose administrative leadership has encouraged me along the way. My work has depended upon library resources at Christian Theological Seminary, and I express my appreciation to David Bundy and his staff.

My opportunities to work with colleagues in other churches and liturgical traditions have depended primarily upon the privilege of representing the Christian Church (Disciples of Christ) in several ecumenical contexts. I gratefully acknowledge the ways that Peter Morgan and Paul Crow have made this wider ministry possible.

Preface

Many people yearn for the renewal of worship in their churches. I know this is true because I meet so many of you in my work with pastors and musicians, other congregational leaders, and students who are preparing for ministries in the church. Some of you remember a time when your experience of God's presence was very strong and you long for that energizing power once again. Others of you have come to a deeper relationship with Christ and want to learn more about this one who has called us to be his disciples. In conversations after church, and in conferences where we are studying worship, you tell me about your hunger to learn the faith so that you can live more faithfully.

Because my main ministry for more than thirty years has been in a school where ministers prepare for their life of leadership, most of my conversations have been campus based. Yet I have also been active in other aspects of the church's life, as member and worshiper, pastor, and consultant. Talking with you in all of the settings where Christians gather, I understand how much you want the church to be alive and your ministries used by God. I share your disappointment with congregations in which the fire of the gospel has died down; and I too want to see the Spirit of God blow these embers into flames. With you I rejoice at testimonies of vitality in worship and mission.

That is why I've written this book—to speak my heart and mind to you. This book shows a professor's bias, that good practice begins with good principles. So I talk more about *what* worship is and *why* we do it than about *how* to prepare and lead. Yet the purpose of the theory is to generate worship—worship that expresses God's truth and communicates God's Spirit. (See John 4:23.)

The principles I present are based upon the earliest decades of the church's life, the years described in the New Testament. Led by the apostles, the first generation of Christians reclaimed their ancient faith in God, reshaped it in the light of their experiences with Jesus, and moved out into the world with a new spirit of joyful courage. Central to their life was the meal of bread and "the fruit of the vine" by which they remembered Jesus Christ and were reconnected with him.

This tradition that began in New Testament times has been handed down to us by many generations of faithful Christians. In each generation the received tradition has been adapted in various ways to the convictions and circumstances of the age. Yet the main outlines of the apostolic inheritance have continued. Our responsibility is to reclaim the tradition and shape it according to the needs of our own time.

We live in an especially challenging time to work for the renewal of worship. The whole earth is groaning in travail, to use Paul's words, waiting for its redemption (Romans 8:22–23). In our worship we have no choice but to describe our pain, confess our part in the world's suffering, and reach out in hope. As we blurt out this tragic tale, the details gradually fade and another story comes into focus—the story of God's suffering love in Jesus Christ. The burdens of our hearts are lifted, taken up by the suffering servant who now intercedes for us before the throne of grace (Hebrews 7:8ff).

In sharp contrast to the way it used to be, the renewal of worship in our time is drawing the separated churches together. We used to live in isolation from one another. Catholics and Protestants could scarcely acknowledge that each is Christian. Even within the Protestant family, each church made its own decisions about worship, with little regard for anyone else. Now, however, unity in Christ is more important than the ideas and habits that have kept us apart. We still worship as Catholics or Protestants, as Lutherans or Methodists or Disciples, as evangelicals or mainliners, as black or white. Yet the patterns of our worship, the contents of our liturgies, and the sounds of our music are increasingly alike.

We can experience this movement toward a common center by visiting churches that once were very different from one another, noting the patterns of what they do and listening to the words in their hymns and prayers. We can also see how much alike the worship of our churches has already become by studying the books that have been published since the 1960s. The hymnals, worship books, and other collections of materials for worship are very much alike in the form and contents of services and prayers, but varied in detail. They seek to represent the classic heritage, which all of our churches claim, adapted according to the particular experiences of each church. These books speak the ancient faith in accents that belong to contemporary English, serious but simple, and more inclusive of all the people than ever before.

Because published materials are easily available, I draw upon them generously for illustrations throughout this book. Many of us, however, worship in traditions that value and practice extemporaneous prayer rather than written prayer. These churches also participate in the movement toward the center and are very much in my mind as I write. My own church is of this type, and therefore I am aware of the characteristics of worship in congregations that develop worship locally and use prayers that are created by those who speak them. Although it is hard to freeze oral prayers long enough to take samples, I have also drawn upon this body of experience, even for the text of communion prayers offered extemporaneously.

Three factors influence us as we work to renew worship and recover a more vibrant Christian life. The first is our own experience in the church, especially in the congregations that have nurtured our faith. This experience usually creates the internal and often unrecognized criteria by which we evaluate all other patterns of worship. This experience needs to be valued for it has brought us to faith and continues, with varying degrees of effectiveness, to sustain us in our Christian lives. Part of the valuing of experience is understanding it, which includes becoming aware of its history and rationale. Valuing experience also includes discerning its strengths and acknowledging its limitations.

The second factor that influences each of us is the general approach to worship and witness in the larger family of churches with which our own congregation is related. For most of us that larger family is a denomination like Baptist or Episcopalian. For others that larger communion is a type of church such as Pentecostal or a cultural form of Christianity such as African-American. This larger family has its own characteristic convictions, cultural patterns, forms of piety, and expectations. In order to know our individual experience thoroughly, we also need to be aware of this larger family. The more we understand our tradition, the more we can represent it in the ongoing dialogue with Christians who stand in other traditions.

The third factor is the movement toward the center that has been so pronounced during the second half of the twentieth century. Larger social movements such as this take place on a continental, and sometimes global, scale; and they usually move just slowly enough that most of us can barely discern the changes as they occur. Certainly this has been the case in the movements toward the center in worship. Only when we remember back a couple of decades ago and compare what happens in our own church with what is happening elsewhere do we see how much the world of worship is changing. Nearly every church's tradition is experiencing the need to reclaim its heritage at the same time that it knows that it must move forward into a future that none of us can fully anticipate. We claim the one faith delivered long ago; and we wait for the consummation of all things in the commonwealth of God still to come. The dynamic character of this new historical moment invites all of the separated traditions to move toward one another; and it calls each of us to a way of worship that includes our own past experience but blends it into a deeper, stronger harmony of praise.

I hope that as you read this book you will be stimulated to think about your own experience and learn to speak knowingly from within the body of convictions that this experience has generated within you. I also hope that you will become more knowledgeable about the family of churches you claim as your own, and about the larger tradition that I am trying to present in this book. In order to stimulate this process, I have concluded each chapter with a section called "Encouraging the Conversation." Each of these sections presents reflective activities for remembering your experience, thinking about your family of churches, and summing up your impressions of the ideas I am presenting. I hope that you will take time for the conversation, letting the several partners speak, encouraging each to listen to the other.

Having taught for many years, I know as well as most that it takes more than a book to renew worship and fire the church for its work. But a forthright declaration of principles is part of the process; and that is what I intend this book to be. Early in my ministry a book—*Principles of Christian Worship* by Raymond Abba—helped me think about worship in the congregation where I was pastor. That book became my guide as I reached a new understanding of worship that would be faithful both to my own tradition and to the wider tradition of the Christian world; and because of that new understanding I was able to lead my congregation to reform and strengthen its Sunday service. In a similar manner may this book be useful to you.

I am grateful to many people in congregations and in classrooms across the country who have helped me develop the ideas in this book. I thank some of you who have read some part, or all, of this manuscript as it was gradually developing. Your ministry to me is one for which I offer to God my thankful praise.

For a third of a century my ministry has been centered at Christian Theological Seminary in Indianapolis. I cannot count the students who have been part of my life during these thirty-three-and-a-half years. A much smaller number of colleagues and staff have shared this life on campus. We have worked and prayed together in innumerable ways. This book is a testament to our shared life and work. My work in this context will be drawing to a close sometime soon; and I am looking forward to "an echo career" as organizing pastor of new congregations. My hope is that this new pastoral setting will provide a bracing framework for continuing the work of a lifetime that this book reports.

1

FOUNDATIONS

Most of us have a tightly focused experience of Christian worship. We know the practices of the congregation or congregations where our Christian life has taken shape and now is expressed; and we may know something of the worship in a few other churches. This sharply focused experience usually is the foundation of our convictions about worship and our evaluations of what ought to happen when Christians gather to praise God.

The tradition of Christian worship, however, is much longer, deeper, wider, and higher than the specific experiences of any one of us. This wider focus is where we begin this book in the hope that each of us can strengthen the foundation on which our practice of worship is built.

The three chapters in Part One focus upon the development of worship from the century of the apostles to our own time. The first chapter describes the remarkable degree of change that has taken place in recent years and affirms that churches once divided from one another in their ways of worship are more and more alike. The second chapter sketches the history of worship in the life of the churches, giving special attention to the way that the Lord's supper has been the generating center of Christian worship. The third chapter shows how *thankful praise* is the source of power and the standard for measuring worship and the life of the Christian community.

At every point, however, the important questions are not what the people of these other times and places have done and why they did it. Rather, the questions are these: what are we going to do when we come together to worship God? And why is it important for us to worship as we do?

1

Transforming Christian Worship

The central action of most churches is the weekly gathering, usually on Sunday, to praise God and be strengthened in faith and life. Here, in a tightly knit sequence of hymns, readings, prayers, and ceremonial actions, Christians present themselves to the God whom they know through Jesus Christ, proclaim the essential doctrines of their faith, and affirm the primary attitudes of the Christian life. Surrounding this weekly celebration of the drama of life are other acts of worship that in their own ways provide the counterpoint to the central theme. This full pattern of praise and prayer is the subject of this book. If any one scriptural text stands as keynote, it is the apostolic exhortation in the third chapter of Colossians: "And let the peace of Christ rule in your hearts, to which indeed you were called in the one body. And be thankful" (3:15). This text continues by encouraging the people to treasure the word of Christ and to sing their gratitude to God. It concludes with a powerful exhortation: "And whatever you do, in word or deed, do everything in the name of the Lord Jesus, giving thanks to God the Father through him" (3:17).

As used in this passage, *giving thanks* is ambiguous in ways that are important to this book. The word comes from the New Testament Greek verb *eucharisteo,* which means to express gratitude. One use of *eucharisteo* was to give thanks to God for food. Another was to honor deity or to praise leaders of the people. It is the word used in the instituting of the Lord's supper; and during the early decades of the church's life this word, adapted into English as *eucharist,* became the most widely used name for the distinctive act of Christian worship. When this word appears in New Testament passages like the third chapter of Colossians, it is not clear which of these meanings was the most prominent in the mind of the writer or of the hearers. Perhaps all of the meanings were intertwined so that the general

3

meaning of thanksgiving and the specialized meaning of Lord's supper interpenetrated each other.

A useful English equivalent to *eucharisteo* is *thankful praise*, which
can also describe the general quality of the Christian life and the
specifically religious act of holy communion. Christian worship is
the constant offering of praise to God; and the ceremonies with bread
and wine, remembering Jesus Christ, are the distinctive vehicle by
which the churches express their great thanksgiving.

The thesis of this book is that *the reform and recovery of eucharistic
worship is the major task for ministers, musicians, and all others responsible for preparing and leading Christian worship.* This thesis is supported
four ways. The first is a brief outline of the origin and development
of Christian worship in the early generations of the church's life, giving special attention to the service of word and table. Second, the
book offers an extended pastoral-theological interpretation of the full
service of word and table. This commentary on the service is the
heart of the book because the words, music, and actions of the liturgy are the primary expression of the Christian faith and the source
of the church's vital life. Third, the eucharistic character of baptism
and other acts of worship is presented. Finally, the book describes
the impact that the recovery of eucharistic worship can have upon
congregations, their members, and their mission in the wider world.

The Churches in This Time of Change

These years near the turn of the century and millennium provide an especially good time for rethinking and reshaping worship.
A generation ago, Susanne Langer declared that our civilization is in
violent passage, being swept from a world we cannot keep to one we
cannot yet see, when everyone is afraid (Langer 1964, 141). More
recently Stephen Toulmin has described these years as the end of
modernity and the beginning of a more humane era that he is not yet
able to name (Toulmin 1990, see especially 2-3, 161-66). Toulmin seems
to have lost Langer's fear, perhaps because he anticipates a better
future than the half-millennium we have passed through.

Although I too hope for a world in which God's purposes for
creation are completed, I find Langer's somber assessment of things
more faithful to current reality than Toulmin's. Paul's statement to
the Romans in the first century also describes our time as the twenty-
first century struggles to be born. "We know that the whole creation
has been groaning in labor pains until now" while it waits for its
redemption (8:22ff). Certainly events in our time demonstrate that
the whole creation continues to suffer. Furthermore, much of the
music and art of recent generations portray the terror and suffering
of vast numbers of people.

Whatever we think of the generation now passing from view and the post-modern culture that is pushing in upon us, all of us are swept along by political, economic, and cultural change. For everyone in these coming decades, life will be significantly different from the period of "normalcy" to which Western society, including the churches, "returned" in the two decades following the close of World War II.

The churches are caught up in the radical changes of our generation. For fifteen hundred years, Christianity has provided the central motifs for parts of Asia and Africa and most of Europe, and more recently for the Americas and other portions of the world influenced by Western culture. As the major institutional embodiment of the Christian religion, the churches have been an important, and often dominant, player in the economic and political arenas of the world. Both conditions are changing. Major tenets of the Christian faith are much questioned, and their power to persuade has diminished. Furthermore, other religious traditions and nonreligious systems of conviction compete with growing effectiveness. Churches no longer are politically protected as divinely authorized institutions; instead they are considered to be but one more public institution, with all of the ambiguities exhibited by other structures in society.

Participation in worship is therefore more problematic than it used to be. Everywhere people are ever more free to come or not to come. Their decisions are based upon the persuasiveness of the message they hear, the impact of that message upon their lives, and the value they find in church programs rather than because of political or economic expectations. Life in modern societies can be lived without reference to the gospel and its churchly embodiment; and increasing numbers of people now live away from the Christian religion of former generations.

This change is felt with special intensity by historic churches of Western society that were shaped by the ecclesial revolution of the Reformation of the sixteenth century. These churches, both Catholic and Protestant, now live as closely parallel institutions, each related to society in ways very much like the relationship that the Catholic Church alone had sustained for so many generations. Once on the road to reform, the Protestant churches increasingly became adapted to the modern world, with the result that they have become fully assimilated into the intellectual and moral system of modernity.

When the Christian faith and the cultural tradition are assimilated to each other and membership in church and civil society are virtually one and the same, the distinctiveness of the gospel is blurred. Being a good Christian is little different from being a good citizen; however, as the other-than-Christian aspects of culture and public life become more assertive, assimilated Christians are beset by growing confusion. They no longer know who they are religiously, and their level of churchly participation diminishes quickly. This sorting out has been taking place for a long time, but especially during the period beginning with the cultural explosions of the 1960s. Churches that were identified with Western culture before World War II, with its vigorous but brief Indian summer after war's end, now find their growth stunted. Until recently these churches lived in an environment protected by the alliances with culture and the political-economic system. Suddenly, however, these churches have been put outside with too little time to be hardened to the harsher environment. Much of their former exuberant growth has been killed by the harsh winds that blow in the real world.

Some of the languishing churches cannot long survive in their current form. Others, however, are developing new hardiness, with new possibilities of vitality and growth. They will never be the same as they were during their hothouse days, but their vigor will become evident and their impact upon personal and public life will grow stronger.

At the same time other churches that formerly stood outside of the established order—especially Pentecostal and holiness churches, and in the United States the Roman Catholic Church—now are showing that in their isolation they have preserved the vitality of faith and the discipline of life in Christ. Since they were reasonably free from dependence upon the principalities and powers, these churches have been largely immune from the distresses that the culture of modernity is suffering. They show a vitality that appeals to people seeking faith and meaning in life.

Unexpectedly, these churches now find themselves front runners in the race for the loyalty of the people. In some cases the vitality comes from a clear understanding of the theological center of the Christian faith, an understanding not yet diluted by the assimilation of modern rationalism. Until the second Vatican Council, the Roman Catholic Church maintained this isolation from the eroding qualities of contemporary culture, and thus maintained the central tenets of the faith more completely than did the assimilated churches of mainline Protestantism. In other cases, the vitality is expressed in the persistence of folk culture that is expressed in worship in ways that continue to be powerful energizers of the people. In still other cases, the continuing vitality is the result of the way that church and the Christian faith are linked with struggles for freedom and justice by oppressed people. In North America, African-American and Hispanic churches both illustrate this immediacy to the culture and vital life of the people. Churches affirming a strong faith, using the expressive culture of the people, and identifying with the strongest passions of their people have much to offer other churches suffering from compromised faith, tied to the culture of the elite, and driven by the need to preserve the old orders of society.

With this new prominence, however, the previously underprivileged churches now encounter the very problems that have distressed the privileged churches. The temptations of this world are ever present; and the possibilities of accommodation to culture and dilution of the gospel now threaten churches that once were disestablished just as they have threatened the churches long in the center of the Western world's life.

In this time of significant change, all of the churches face two challenges: to recover the vital center of their faith and to express that core of the gospel in the cultural forms of the world today. Only when churches are faithful to the gospel do they have a reason for being. Only when they are in touch with the people of their communities are they able to serve as agents of reconciliation between these people and the God whom Christians praise through Jesus Christ.

Recovery of the Eucharistic Center of Worship

Christian worship has taken many forms in the years since the apostles "handed on that which they had received." (See 1Corinthians 1 1:23.) In nearly all church traditions, however, the celebration of the Lord's supper has been the foundation for the other aspects of worship. For fifteen hundred years the normal act of worship in all the churches on every Sunday was the remembrance of Christ with bread and wine. Worship on other days of the week often included an abridged celebration of the sacramental meal. Weddings, funerals, and major events in social and political life also were incorporated into liturgies of the Lord's supper. Over the generations, the liturgical form of eucharistic worship evolved and differing theological understandings of the sacrament arose. Despite these changes, however, the generating nucleus of Christian worship continued to be the heartfelt praise of God given form by the ceremony with bread and wine by which the church remembered and celebrated God's redeeming work in Jesus' death upon the cross.

From their beginnings in the apostolic era until now, the ancient churches of Asia and Africa, the Orthodox Churches, and the continuing Roman Catholic Church of Europe have maintained the eucharistic center of worship. During the sixteenth century collapse of the Western church, however, the patterns of worship developed by the apostolic church and shaped by later generations were challenged. The Reformation segments of the Western church appeared to move away from the eucharistic foundation. The chief reformers tried to restructure the penitential piety and sacrificial understanding of the Mass that they had experienced in the Catholic Church, but the result of the reform movement was that Lutheran, Calvinist, and Anglican churches developed patterns of worship in which the main Sunday service most weeks of the year consisted of praise, preaching, and prayer, but without the celebration of holy communion. Weekday celebrations of the Lord's supper, and the inclusion of weddings and funerals within the celebrations of the Lord's supper became less frequent.

Even in these churches, however, worship at Christ's table continued to be the theological norm of worship. Some expressed this norm by saying that the eucharist really should be the Sunday service even if for practical reasons it was celebrated less frequently. Others supported the norm by using the periodic celebration of the eucharist as the climax to an ongoing cycle of weekly services of the word of God. In most churches of the Reformed tradition, inspired by Zwingli and Calvin, the eucharistic cycle was monthly or quarterly. In some congregations of this tradition, the cycle was annual, with a week-long sacramental season serving as the focal point for the renewal of congregational life, the occasion for evangelism, and the basis of public festivals of faith.

A radical transformation is now taking place. Churches that for generations have subordinated eucharistic worship to other forms of celebration are moving to recover the centrality of the Lord's supper in their regular weekly worship of God. The historic Protestant churches are participating in the long-delayed completion of the sacramental reforms begun in the sixteenth century so that the original purpose of the reformers is finally coming to completion. The Roman Catholic Church, which reacted to the Reformation by freezing its worship, has thawed, and significant change has occurred. The result of these changes in Catholic and Protestant churches is that the sacrament of unity around which our deepest divisions have been experienced is now becoming a table of hospitality once again.

Since the 1970s the movement toward increased frequency of communion, and also of increased importance of the eucharist to the life of churchgoers, has gained momentum. Many people remember the older schedule of quarterly communion; and now they know the pattern of eucharist every month and on special days. A large proportion of Episcopal parishes and a rapidly increasing proportion of Lutheran congregations have moved to the practice of celebrating the eucharist in a major service every Sunday. A growing number of Methodist, Presbyterian, and United Church of Christ congregations have found ways of including holy communion at one of the services every Sunday. Increasingly Christians in evangelical and pentecostal churches are also rediscovering the importance of the sacramental remembrance of God's love in Jesus Christ.

Search for Transcendence

One reason for this recovery of the eucharistic center of worship is the search for transcendence. For many generations, the churches have found their primary connection to the Divine in one of three liturgical elements. For some, the connection has been the sacrament of the eucharist in which, by Word and Holy Spirit, God uses bread and wine to unite worshipers and the living Christ.

For other churches, the primary connection has been the living Word of God in scripture and sermon. The Word of God has penetrated to the very core of human life, transforming all who hear. For still other churches, the source of transcendent power has been the Holy Spirit active within their lives. Often transported into altered modes of experience and testimony, these worshipers have known the reality of God within themselves.

One of the results of modernity is that the Bible has been denatured. For many people it no longer has authority as Word of God. By itself, the Bible seems to many to be a flawed book from an ancient past. Even when it is interpreted in strong preaching, many of these same people find the Bible interesting, sometimes helpful, but still not compelling. Their life in the church has withered because what had long been their primary mode of communion with God has drained away. This problem is especially acute because the very churches that have most depended upon the Bible as their connection to transcendence are the very churches that are most fully accommodated to contemporary culture. This commitment to the intellectual convictions of modernity in itself undercuts the traditional basis for the authority of scripture.

Yet the need for connections with the transcendent remains; with the result that many people formerly in churches of the Word of God are now shifting to churches of the Holy Eucharist or churches of the Holy Spirit, hoping to find the religious power that they are not finding in their churches of the Holy Word. At the same time, Catholic churches are rediscovering the importance of preaching as a means for bringing new energy into parish life and worship; and charismatic churches are reaching out for embodied symbolism, as offered by baptism and eucharist, that connects them bodily to the God whom they worship. Everyone, it seems, is reaching out for authentic worship in which God is truly praised, the people are built up in faith and love, and the world is enjoyed and cared for in better ways.

Overcoming Alienation

Another reason for the movement toward eucharistic worship is the result of a shifting pattern in the experience of what goes wrong in life. At the time of the Reformation, and for most of the generations since then, the classical doctrines of sin and salvation made sense to people. They could understand that what goes wrong in life is a violation of God's will. People therefore are properly classified as sinners, deserving of punishment. The story of salvation is that Jesus Christ takes on the burden of our sin, pays the penalty, thus upholding the moral order of the universe, and declares that we are forgiven. The sacraments become the instruments by which that forgiveness is experienced and witnessed to. Nevertheless, the significant change is that which the Word announces.

In our time, however, this historic view of what is wrong in life makes less sense to people. Instead, life seems to them to be meaningless and lonely. Alienation from God, the world, others, and oneself is the prevailing experience. What is needed to set things right is not a declaration that sins are forgiven so much as dramatic gestures of solidarity between ourselves and with our Maker. The isolated and powerless people need to be brought together in communities of love and transformation. Thus, the celebration of the Lord's supper makes sense. Here one of the major metaphors is community: "we who are many are one body, for we all partake of the one bread" (1 Corinthians 10:17). Furthermore, the character of this community is dramatically represented in every celebration: we meet at the foot of the cross where Jesus died for the sins of the world, stand at the open tomb where God's victory over sin and death is won, and join Christ Jesus at God's own side, where our lives are linked with Jesus' never ending intercessions for all the world (Pannenberg 1983, especially 13-49).

Commitment to Contemporary Culture

Even as their prominence in the social order declines, the churches of our time are developing a new commitment to contemporary culture. As the recovery of the eucharistic center of worship is reconnecting worshipers to the Divine, it also promises to reconnect these same people to their own world.

This intention reshapes one of the features that has been present in Protestant churches from the beginning of the Reformation. The reformers were determined that the liturgy should be spoken in German, French, English, and any other language used in daily life. Services were translated from Latin into the vernacular tongues, and the Bible was brought into these same languages from Hebrew, Greek, and Latin. Sermonic styles were popularized; and hymnody using folk material became a prominent mode for participation by the people. This commitment to the vernacular helped to shape the developing European languages and stabilized folk cultures. No wonder these reforming churches took root among the people.

Over time this commitment to contemporary modes of expression was obscured because liturgy tends to lag behind culture. Popular speech, popular music, and other popular forms of expression run at a faster pace than the churches can sustain. In part, the lag comes because ritual, by its very nature, encourages repetition and permanence. The hymns sung during one's childhood and at critical points in the life cycle become rooted in the emotional depths of one's life. They continue to be sung because they release the power of emotional life, warming the hearts and blessing the spirits of those who sing and hear the music. Many worshipers find that to set this traditional music aside in order to introduce some new thing, which has no connection to their previous experience, destroys the power of worship.

Another illustration is the way that the language of the Bible resists change. When first prepared, the King James translation adopted a form of English that was close to the way that people used the language in public life. Over the nearly four centuries since that translation was made, however, English usage has changed dramatically. Yet, despite the many new and wonderful translations of the Bible, the King James continues to command a wide following. For many people, including a large proportion of conservative Christians, the Christian faith and King James language are virtually inseparable. For a growing proportion of the population, however, these archaic forms of speech and music are barriers to participation. While traditional liturgical language is more usable than Shakespeare or Chaucer, the problems it creates become ever greater.

A second way that the commitment to contemporary culture is obscured results from the tendency of liturgy to become identified with the cultural forms favored by the elite. In part, this tendency is driven by theological concerns. If the intended audience of our worship is God the Holy One, then we are motivated to bring only the best that we can offer—our finest music, our strongest prayers, and our most carefully developed liturgies. The way we speak and act needs to be appropriate when they are done in the presence of the glorious, majestic God. The artistic tastes of the people in power become the standards for measuring all things esthetic. Theologians, who represent the intellectual elite, define what ought to be in worship. Connoisseurs of the arts establish the criteria for architecture, music, and graphic arts. The result, to use a phrase of Lawrence Hoffman, is that worship becomes sacred concert with liturgical accompaniment. It is a performance to be watched rather than an action in which everyone participates.

In Western civilization there has long been a cleavage between the culture of the elite and of the masses. It seems to be even deeper and wider now than in earlier generations. In most cities, when the symphony, ballet, or opera perform, a decent crowd can be persuaded to come. These elitist forms of artistic life, however, suffer under great financial pressure. The general population enjoys these media only a little and supports them financially in similar measure. In contrast, let a popular music group come for a concert and crowds throng to participate; and these popular ensembles seem able to generate their own support. Similarly, the "sacred concert churches" are struggling against ever greater odds for their very survival, whereas many churches that embrace popular expressive media thrive.

Neither of these obstructions of the commitment to contemporary culture can be easily counteracted. Liturgical materials have to be used repeatedly over time in order to develop power; yet there has to be movement and change or worship becomes stale. The issues of taste, suitability, and expressive adequacy do have to be considered carefully. Are some forms of expression to be ruled out and for what reasons? Are there objective standards of beauty or religious content? Does the fact that many people like something mean that this something should be used in the Sunday liturgy? Pastors, musicians, and congregants continually wrestle with these questions. Agreement on the answers to these questions is not yet in sight.

At this point, however, two things are clear. The Sunday liturgy in many of the historic liturgies is out of touch with the hearts and minds of most people today. The recovery of modes of expression that genuinely belong to the people and are alive is critically important. At the least, this recovery will include the use of modern, idiomatic language, greater movement in the liturgy, and a wider cultural range in music and the other expressive arts. In the several churches this commitment to contemporaneity is leading toward more eclecticism, especially in music. Thus churches are at the same time becoming more diversified and more alike.

A significant challenge to these churches seeking new vigor is the renewing of the Sunday assembly. More than any other aspect of their life, what churches do on Sunday maintains their faithfulness to God and demonstrates their ability to communicate with the wider community of people. The languishing of the historic Western churches is a clear indication that their Sunday liturgies are less than they need to be. In many of these churches, the more serious loss is the weakened connection with transcendence. They no longer have a powerful word from God, nor access to religious power to transform the lives of people who participate in them. These churches now need to make new connections with the transcendent power of God, so that the distinctive content of the gospel way of life is understood anew, people can experience a new sense of community, and they can be energized for their ongoing life in the world.

Just as the Sunday assembly is the theater where these losses have occurred, so this weekly gathering of the faithful is the arena in which the recovery will take place. Worship is the activity in which the miracle of revelation bursts into being. The story of God's life and work is portrayed in a highly artistic form and interpreted with the most careful of speech. The result, when all is done appropriately, is ecstatic experience of God's person and presence. Furthermore, in this theater or arena, the people are the performers. The language, music, and ceremonies provide the script and score for the people's self-presentation to God and one another. The people must be able to use the language, sing the songs, do the ceremonies; and all of these actions need to be expressed in media that excite the minds and energize the bodies of the worshipers.

The life of churches consists of more than worship; and church vitality requires that the various aspects of program, mission, and pastoral care be healthy in their own right. Yet, the Sunday assembly is the key to all others. This service provides direction, creates motivation, and maintains the coherence of the church as the community of love.

Completing the Reformation

One of the most important characteristics of the contemporary renewal in worship is the drawing together of the churches whose history and self-understanding are directly related to the Protestant Reformation. For five hundred years these churches have been sorely divided in worship, ministry, and polity, but they are now coming closer to one another in worship and ministry. The long history of rancor and isolation is well known, as is the way that this religious division has contributed to the divisions of society in the West and in other areas of the world colonized by Western institutions. Now that the cultural imperialism of these churches has been undermined, now that they have to justify their lives on religious grounds more than political and cultural, these churches are trying with new purpose to overcome the breaches that have existed for so long a time.

The churches have been coming together for nearly a century by their common ventures in life and work and in faith and order. These cooperative actions provide a common foundation for shared life and coordinated instruments for extending throughout the world the love of God and neighbor. The churches have also created councils for cooperative work. These ecumenical institutions provide systems within which the representatives of the separated churches can acknowledge one another's Christian identity and work together while still preserving their theological and sacramental differences.

What is becoming ever more evident is that another kind of drawing together has been happening at the same time that these organizational and missional activities have been taking place. The churches that have been separated from one another in their worship are now coming together again to praise God, proclaim God's word, and participate in the liturgies that actualize the redemption that God has accomplished in Jesus Christ. What is important about the rediscovery of unity in worship is its impact upon the life of ordinary Christians. Many of the other efforts to achieve unity have affected the organizational life of churches more than the internal life of congregations. In contrast, the coming together in worship has direct, ongoing impact upon people who come to church week after week and may be doing more than any other kind of uniting process to help church members move past five centuries of disunion and animosity into unity in Christ and with one another. In the past Christian disunity has been especially evident in practices of closed communion. We could preach, pray, and work together as Christians. What we could not do was eat and drink together around Christ's table. Increasingly, we can now share this meal which itself is beginning to be experienced as the sacrament of our oneness in Jesus Christ.

In both Catholic and Protestant churches a similar point of view motivates scholars and pastors, and the artists and musicians, who lead the reform. They have become aware that their traditional liturgies, service books, and hymnals are based on historical, theological, and cultural traditions that are quickly becoming archaic and obsolete. They recognize that some of their claims of distinction were created during the doctrinal wars of earlier generations and no longer make sense. To overcome the limitations of their post-Reformation positions, these leaders in the field of worship have turned again to early Christian literature, both in the Bible and in later books. They have examined again the history of worship and the theology of worship through the Middle Ages and into the sixteenth century. This recovered knowledge of the tradition has been used to critique their own customs and convictions. It has also stimulated renewed understandings of what worship can and ought to be.

Whereas the criterion for reforming worship used to be that service books and liturgies be made to conform to pure sixteenth-century models or to the books of another period considered by a church to be foundational, such is the case no more. Instead, the orientation is more toward faithfulness to the apostolic witness, appropriateness within our modern context, and trust in God for time to come. The questions being addressed are these: how can the churches that are built upon the testimonies of the apostles and martyrs praise God in the modern world? What language and dramatic forms can be used that, while rooted in the past, nevertheless belong to our own time and point toward the future?

Even though our worship today has been transformed in language, action, and meaning, there is more to be done. More than ever before the churches are becoming aware of the way that the language used for worship can distort our understanding of God's true self and oppress many of the participants in services. We can see better now than before that sinful human society rather than the holy commonwealth is mirrored in our liturgies. The coming together of the churches cannot be completed until the issues that currently divide the human family are transcended by the love of God expressed through Jesus Christ. Even in these very difficult aspects of church life, however, much progress is being made. Even where we still are divided from one another, we are moving toward a way of life more fully formed by the vision of Jesus Christ.

We still are far from overcoming the divisions that have existed for half a millennium. Yet, the contemporary coming together in worship brings Christians together in more dramatic ways than at any time since the shattering of the Western church early in the Reformation.

New Communities of Love

When the gospel was first proclaimed in Jerusalem, the response was electrifying. People heard the message in their own language, were persuaded of its truth, and accepted the message. They were baptized and became members of a community so intense that members sold their possessions to care for one another. They spent time in the temple, studying the commandments and praying. They met together day by day in their homes, breaking bread and praising God. Says the writer of Acts: they enjoyed "the goodwill of all the people. And day by day the Lord added to their number those who were being saved" (Acts 2:43–47).

The initial days of the church's life were unique and the intensity of that time cannot be reproduced in our era. What can be hoped for—and this book aims at that goal—is that many languishing churches of our time will be transformed. No longer will they be moribund societies "all reverend with the gloom of departed years"; instead, they will become new communities of love, strong in faith and active in extending everywhere the love of God and neighbor.

Encouraging the Conversation

One of my hopes for this book is that it will stimulate conversation within each reader, encouraging you to become thoughtfully aware of your own experience in worship, knowledgeable of the tradition of your larger family of churches, and acquainted with the movement toward unity in worship that this book represents. If there is to be a conversation, however, you have to bring these partners together; and the following suggestions provide ways for you to get started.

1. You can begin your part of the conversation about worship by remembering your significant experiences in worship:

- Where did they take place?
- What was happening in your life and in the world around you at the times when you most remember worship?

2. You can enlarge the conversation by identifying the larger church family that you claim as your own.

- Is it a denomination like Presbyterian, a type like evangelical, or a cultural community like Hispanic?
- What are the leading characteristics about worship in this church family you have identified?

3. Then compare:

- Your experienced conviction and the main characteristics of your church family.
- How much are they alike? How do they differ?

4. As you think about this chapter and your own experience:

- Do you see changes like those described in this chapter in the churches you know?
- Is there a growing emphasis upon the Lord's supper in churches you know?
- How would you describe the relationship between the Christian faith and contemporary culture?

2

The Historic Center
of the Church's Life

In the conclusion to his monumental book *The Shape of the Liturgy*, Gregory Dix declares that for two thousand years "the One Body of Christ has incarnated itself" by a simple ritual pattern using bread and wine. This ritual has continued while "several great civilizations and empires and innumerable lesser social groups have risen and flourished and passed away." The outlines of this ritual pattern, Dix continues, "have come down to us unchanged in Christian practice from before the crucifixion." The service of the Word comes from "Jesus' preaching in the synagogues of Galilee, the eucharist proper from the evening meals of Jesus with his disciples." These two forms of worship were united in the early years of the church's history, and this way of worshiping God fulfills "every need of every church in every age."

Jesus told his disciples that when they performed these actions with bread and wine they should do it to remember him. "Was ever another command so obeyed?" Dix asks. "For century after century," he answers, "spreading slowly to every continent and country and among every race on earth, this action has been done, in every conceivable human circumstance, for every conceivable human need from infancy and before it to extreme old age and after it, from the pinnacles of earthly greatness to the refuge of fugitives in the caves and dens of the earth." After mentioning some of the momentous events that began with the celebration of this liturgy, Dix says: "And best of all, week by week and month by month, on a hundred thousand successive Sundays, faithfully, unfailingly, across all the parishes of christendom, the pastors have done this just to make the *plebs sancta Dei*—the holy common people of God" (Dix 1945, 743f.).

This chapter outlines the process by which this eucharistic tradition became the center of Christian worship. It traces the develop-

17

ment over time and describes the pace-setting liturgies and theological writings that have expressed the recent history of eucharistic worship in the churches.

Eating and Drinking with God

The focus of Christian worship is rightly upon Jesus of Nazareth, the one whom Peter, Martha, and others identified as the Messiah, the only begotten of God. (See Matthew 16:16 and John 11:25–27.) In Jesus the monotheistic religion of Judaism took a new and decisive embodiment. Thus, the writer of the letter to the Hebrews begins by invoking God's many and various ways of speaking to the ancestors; but now, "in these last days" God speaks to us through a Son, who was with God at creation, and "is the reflection of God's glory and the exact imprint of God's very being" (Hebrews 1:1–3a). As the incarnation of God the Holy One, Jesus makes possible the extension of the faith of Abraham and Moses to the people outside of Judaism. He transforms the cultic life of his ancestors, saying "no" to its detail and saying "yes" to the basic spirit of the existing system of life in the presence of God. From the beginnings of the Jesus movement, Jesus has been the fountain from which a healing stream has flowed through the life of the church. "And sinners plunged beneath that flood," says William Cowper's hymn, "lose all their guilty stains."

All of these ways of describing the centrality of Jesus are grounded in his readiness to die and his use of a religious meal to interpret his actions. According to the accounts by the Gospel writers, Jesus came to Jerusalem as the Feast of the Passover drew near. Already he was in serious conflict with established authorities in temple and synagogue, but now that conflict became even more intense. By late in the week, Jesus had set himself on a course of action from which he would not deviate, the result of which could only be death. On Thursday evening, which in John's account began that year's day of preparation for the Passover (John 18:28), the day that the Passover lamb would be slain in the Temple, he and his closest friends gathered for their regular meal. Following traditional practice, he took up a loaf of bread, blessed God for the gift of food, and broke it to distribute among them. As he gave them the bread, he said something new that they would only later understand:

> *My body, given for you.*
> *When you do this, do it to remember me.*

After the meal, Jesus followed the traditional ceremonies with a cup of wine. He blessed God by reciting a series of God's saving acts through history. Then he passed the cup around to the people at table with him, again offering a cryptic explanation:

My blood of the covenant, poured out for you.
When you do this, do it to remember me.

Later that night he was arrested and brought to hearings before various authorities. By noon he was stretched out on the cross and by nightfall, when Jewish people would be gathering to observe the annual Passover meal, he was dead. Thus, the Passover mood of the city at the time of the crisis and Jesus' own use of sacrificial language came together. For his friends and followers Jesus was now to be understood by means of the long traditions of sacrifice and liberation. Henceforth, their liturgical gatherings would employ the metaphors of death, atonement, and salvation.

Worship through sacrifice has a history that began long before the time of Jesus, going back into the early history of the human race. The ritual destruction of valuable objects usually included several factors. Gifts were brought to the place of sacrifice to be offered to the deity associated with that place. Most common were offerings of grain or animals and birds. In most sacrificial traditions it was important that the gift be something valuable. Although details varied widely, sacrifices usually included the destruction of some portion of the gift by fire. Some sacrificial traditions, including the Hebrew, emphasized the blood that was shed. Jewish theology insisted that life itself was in the blood (Leviticus 17:11). Thus, its shedding and the resultant ritual use connected people to the source of life and offered that life back to God who was its original source. Throughout the ancient world sacrifices were also understood to be means of communion with the Divine. Just as sharing meals with other people established and maintained bonds between them, so eating and drinking with God would establish stronger connections between worshipers and the chief power of the universe. They were also seen as meals for communion with the deity. Sacrifices were done to ask forgiveness for wrong actions and to appease the offended god.

The sacrificial tradition that had developed in Judaism and was known by Jesus had become attached to Jewish understandings of their history. The ancient meaning of sacrifice as sanctifying the struggle for food was reduced in importance and the function of sacrifice as sanctifying the struggle for national identity and sovereignty became more important. This transformation was clearest in the Passover celebration. The slaughter of the paschal lamb continued at the core of the ceremony, but the retelling of the nation's central story, the solemn meal of communion, and the transmission of a way of life became the primary reasons for the festival.

So it was when Jesus met with his disciples that last evening. The traditions of their people, the important covenant that God had established with them, and the sacrificial foundation of their estab-

lished ways of worship were all present in their minds. They recited
God's wonderful work throughout their history and prayed that
God's intentions for creation and history would be fulfilled. Their
life before God and their own identity were reaffirmed.

The events of the next day brought everything into high relief.
The disciples followed the lead that Jesus had given them and developed the sacrificial motif further. From the outset Jesus' death was
seen as sacrifice. His own teachings, as remembered in the Gospel of
John, used the metaphors of sacrifice. "Very truly, I tell you, unless
you eat the flesh of the Son of Man and drink his blood, you have no
life in you" (John 6:53). The most important discussion of worship in
the New Testament, 1 Corinthians 10—14, begins with a discussion
of the issues related to sharing in pagan sacrifices, which many of
Paul's readers knew very well. Paul used their understanding of Jewish sacrifices to help his readers understand the meaning of their
communion meals around the table of Christ.

This use of the language of sacrifice dominates the book of Hebrews. "And it is by God's will that we have been sanctified through
the offering of the body of Jesus Christ once for all " (Hebrews 10:10).
The purpose of this rhetorically powerful epistle, according to the
exposition offered by Barnabas Lindars (1991), is to persuade Christians of the Mediterranean dispersion that Jesus saved them from
the sins of their past and that this salvation continues to be effective,
both in heaven with God and in their life in the world. There is no
need for them to return to the temple for this assurance of salvation.
Jesus has done once and for all what the liturgy of the day of atonement did once a year. Other powerful sacrificial language comes in
the final book of the Bible. The crowds in heaven fall before the Lamb,
singing a new song:

"For you were slaughtered and by your blood you
        ransomed for God
    saints from every tribe and language and people and
        nation;
you have made them to be a kingdom and priests serving
        our God...." (Revelation 5:9b–10a)

And later:

"To the one seated on the throne and to the Lamb
be blessing and honor and glory and might
forever and ever!" (Revelation 5:13a)

As Paul's discussion in 1 Corinthians 10 indicates, sacrificial religion was strong during his time; and this importance was true both
for Jews and other peoples of the Roman world. Even so, long before
the beginning of the Common Era, Jews had developed a second

nonsacrificial focus for their piety, the synagogue, which could be established wherever Jews lived and which did not depend upon priestly leadership. Because many Jews were scattered far from Jerusalem where the official sacrifices took place, the synagogue became increasingly important. The meditative study of the commandments became the organizing principle for much of the ongoing cultic experience of Jews in their Palestinian homeland and in the dispersion. When the temple in Jerusalem was destroyed in 70 C.E., the sacrificial system disappeared. It is true that sacrificial motifs in the annual festivals like Passover continued, but the maintenance of a priesthood, the altar, and the use of burned offerings as the core of cultic life ceased. The sacrifices simply went out, "like a fire that is not tended" (Lohmeyer 1962, 2). Thus Judaism became a religion of the word built upon the commandments and the writings.

In contrast, Christianity gave a new cultic form to sacrifice and maintained it at the very center of the church's ongoing life. This new cultic form was the eucharist, the remembrance with bread and wine of Christ's death upon the cross as a sacrifice for the sins of the world. As they participated in this meal of remembrance, their sense of Christ's living presence was invigorated, re-establishing their communion with God. This meal thus became the anchor for everything else that Christians did. It became their celebration of the new life that God had given them.

Worship on the Lord's Day

The emergence of eucharistic worship as the nucleus of the church's life may have been more circumstantial than premeditated. The confidence of the early Christians that God had acted decisively in Jesus Christ was related to epiphanies of the risen Christ. Frequent and vivid experiences in which Jesus came to the disciples are recorded in the New Testament. Several of these events occurred while the disciples were eating their meals (e.g., Mark 16:14 and Luke 24:13–43). It can be presumed that they were remembering Jesus as he had asked them to do. In those very moments he came to be with them. These times were such joy-filled events, Oscar Cullmann concludes, that they became the basis for ongoing Christian gatherings (Cullmann 1953, 14-18). These joyful Christians came together for a meal, breaking bread and drinking from the cup of blessing to remember Jesus, and recognizing him in their midst. Their excitement could not be contained. Consequently it seemed to them only right that they should continue these gatherings in remembrance of Jesus Christ. These assemblies would become the major way that they could express their unique identity.

During the early decades of the church's life, Christians of Jewish extraction continued to participate in both synagogue and temple while participating in the assemblies of the church. They followed the normal Jewish patterns for observing the Sabbath, and added their distinctive Christian remembrance of Jesus with bread and wine. The early Jerusalem church, as described in Acts 2, seems to have celebrated their festive meal daily; but the custom soon became established that the Christian meal followed the Sabbath observance each week. Thus Christians expressed their faith on the first day. It seemed right to do so because this was the day on which Jesus rose from the grave. Surely, it seemed to them, there could be no better time and way to praise God through their Lord Jesus Christ.

In time this dual allegiance to Jewish and Christian liturgies became impossible to maintain. As a result, Christians withdrew into their own assemblies and enlarged the liturgical aspects of their own activities. A service of readings and prayers derived from the synagogues came to be used as the first part of their assemblies. Then worshipers gathered around a table, with the blessing and sharing of the bread and cup. Early in the first century the full meal was observed, but before the apostolic era ended only the ritual meal was celebrated. This liturgy of reading desk and communion table became the Christian way of reciting God's saving work, the work that came to its culmination in Jesus Christ.

This process of adaptation took place in the many communities where Christians lived. The general pattern of adaptation was the same across the Mediterranean world, but the details varied from place to place. In part, the reason for variation was that worship at that time, both in Judaism and in Christian assemblies, seems to have included improvisational aspects. The outline of the liturgy and the themes to be included in the prayers were everywhere the same; but the exact wording was spoken in slightly variant phrases by each leader of prayer. In each community certain patterns developed that became characteristic of worship in that place. Thus, the different cultural regions were already slightly different from one another before Christian adaptations were made. In these regions bishops, who were the local pastors, worked out their own ways of adapting liturgical systems and language to the realities of the new era. The earliest liturgies were associated with major cities, especially Jerusalem, Antioch, Alexandria, Rome, and later Constantinople. The extensive local variation in the earliest years of the churches gradually gave way to regional patterns; distinct liturgical families emerged and continued over long periods of time.

As the Christian gospel spread, so did the celebration of this distinctive Christian rite—throughout western Asia, the northern sections of Africa, and most of Europe. In every area where Christianity took root, this act of worship became an important part of life. It became deeply interwoven into the structure of civilization in the

East and the West. Not until the rise of Islam was there any serious competition with Christianity and its eucharistic worship throughout the Mediterranean world of northern Africa, western Asia, and southern Europe.

By the fourth century of the Christian era, the shape of the eucharist was firmly fixed and largely the same across the entire Christian world even though the outline and language used in each geographical family differed from what was used in the other families. Similarly, the major set of prayers in each of these liturgies was reaching the mature form that would persist from that time forward.

Everywhere the churches were doing the same thing, which was to remember Jesus Christ and his saving work on the cross by means of the ritual with bread and wine. Yet this one thing was done with a wide range of literary and ceremonial forms, conditioned by culture, history, and the genius of local leaders.

Forward Through the Ages

As the counterpoint to this theme of eucharistic worship that has been present in all the churches is a continuing series of theological and devotional embellishments that have developed through the generations. We can better understand where the churches stand today if we trace briefly the interweaving through church history of the central theme and the embellishments.

The Meaning of the Eucharist

One way of following this evolution of eucharistic worship is to take the main ideas about the eucharist as stated in the New Testament and trace their permutations through time. Yngve Brilioth identifies these themes as thanksgiving, communion-fellowship, commemoration, sacrifice, and mystery (Brilioth 1956, 15-17). Brilioth then follows the way that these themes waxed and waned through the history of worship in the Catholic and Protestant churches. He portrays the distinctive characteristic of the Mass of the medieval Roman Catholic Church as the union of mystery and sacrifice, with a strong emphasis upon the localizing of the mystery in the idea of the presence of Christ at the central point of the service (78). The idea of thanksgiving was diminished and communion-fellowship came close to disappearing. Even though the text of the Mass continued to affirm some of the biblical ideas about the eucharist, the fact that most celebrations could neither be heard nor understood by congregants greatly reduced the value of these ideas.

The greatest contribution of the Reformers, and especially of Luther, says Brilioth, was the rediscovery of communion-fellowship.

This theme, which had been strong in Augustine's theology, had dimmed greatly in later generations, but now it "became a living element of religious experience, and a chief factor in the remodeling of worship" (Brilioth 1956, 97). Brilioth notes that Luther also retained a strong sense of mystery in his understanding of the eucharist and in the revised order for celebration that he developed. At the same time, Luther vehemently opposed the ideas of sacrifice that were part of the received doctrine of the Lord's supper.

Other branches of the Reformation developed different patterns of emphasis. Zwingli developed the ideal of communion "as a social meal in remembrance of the great fact" of Christ's death (Brilioth 1956, 162). At the same time, the sense of the mystery of union with God disappeared. On the other hand, Calvin stressed communion-fellowship not with the congregation so much as with Christ; for Calvin "the religious focus of the eucharist is union with the continually present Saviour" (167). Calvin was able to connect thanksgiving and sacrifice. As we partake of the eucharist, we become ever more aware of the blessings we receive from God, "so that we offer him the thanks and praise which are due to him" (165). Above all, it is in our daily life that this praise is due and so we give our lives to him. "This sort of oblation," Brilioth quotes Calvin as saying, "has nothing to do with the propitiation of God's wrath, or with obtaining the forgiveness of our sins; it consists simply in praising and exalting God" (166). Brilioth believes that Calvin's eucharistic liturgy was meager in comparison with his eucharistic doctrine because it failed to express the positive elements of the Reformed understanding, eucharistic praise, communion-fellowship, commemoration, and the offering of personal devotion" (178).

Two other religious families that followed after Calvin's creative work move in opposing directions. The Anglican tradition was more positive toward liturgical worship than were the continental leaders of the Reformed tradition. Furthermore, Anglicans were more conservative in their doctrinal reformulations. As a result, they developed eucharistic doctrine and liturgy that balanced these five themes more evenly than did any of the other major movements of the Reformation. Furthermore, the Anglican reformers created a liturgy that was able to carry the full range of theological and devotional qualities that the doctrine affirmed. In contrast, however, the Puritan movements emphasized the more extreme aspects of the continental reformers. Brilioth may overstate their position, but in so doing he identifies the prevailing tendencies. All is subjective, he says. "The deeper religious aspects of the rite are ousted by the idea of a glad feast of fellowship, of the communicants with one another rather than with the Lord; and even the Commemoration of the Passion has become a mere confession by the individual of his personal faith"

(Brilioth 1956, 195). The rejection of printed liturgies meant that even this way of inadvertently preserving some of the deeper qualities was not available to the Puritans.

Brilioth's analysis deals with the classical European churches and their liturgical systems. The same pattern of investigation and interpretation could be developed for churches in North America in more recent times. The patterns that were developed in the sixteenth and seventeenth centuries have continued in these churches; but the doctrinal clarity gradually has become blurred and the liturgical distinctiveness has diminished. The several systems did not become more and more alike; rather their differences became more a fact of organizational inertia than of theological and liturgical conviction. Only in the last generation have these churches begun the process of reassessing their systems, reappropriating the valuable aspects of their older traditions, and then moving deliberately toward eucharistic convergence with other churches.

A fitting objective for the churches of our time is to recover the fullness of the themes that express the meaning of the eucharist. Each theme presents an important aspect of the eucharist; and churches that emphasize some to the diminishment of others are deprived of the fullness of life with God and with one another. With the easing of tension between the churches, the reactionary mode of theological development can be set aside. We can now develop themes that need developing, no longer so concerned about the issues that for so long have put each church at odds with the others.

Theologies of the Eucharist

A second way of tracing the development of eucharistic worship through time is to follow the elaborated theological debates over the technical meaning of this sacrament. From early in the life of the churches several assumptions supported eucharistic worship, including these three: (1) This ritual connects worshipers and the church itself to Christ's death and resurrection. (2) The bread and wine are identified in some way with Christ's body and blood offered on the cross for our salvation. (3) In the eucharistic meal the risen Christ and participants in the meal are united.

Because these assumptions stand at the very core of eucharistic worship, they cannot remain unexamined. Questions are asked, sermons preached, books written, debates held, formal decisions made, dissent vigorously expressed. These topics are closely tied to the deepest religious values of human life; and therefore, their movement through generations of debate has been marked by passion. Regrettably, the debate has often done violence to the gentle savior whose life the eucharist represents. It has frequently led to division in the historical body of Christ, thus giving the lie to Paul's assertion that "we who are many are one body, for we all partake of the one bread" (1 Corinthians 10:17).

In the Western Catholic Church of the late Middle Ages, a fully developed and interlocking eucharistic system was in place. It included a juridical understanding of God and salvation that created an atmosphere of great seriousness, often verging on fear. A critical factor in the system was Christ's death on the cross that paid the penalty for sin. The sinner's connection with that saving action was achieved by the eucharistic bread and wine, which during the liturgy were believed to become the sacramental body and blood of Christ. This complex and powerful system depended upon the doctrines of transubstantiation and sacrifice that have continued ever since to be at the center of Roman Catholic understandings of the eucharist and which have been strongly contested by Protestant churches.

Transubstantiation explains how Christ is present in the eucharist in a way that is unique to that sacrament. When the doctrine arose, the intellectual and theological world used the technical philosophical ideas of substance and accidence, referring to the inward reality of a thing, that we cannot experience with our senses, and the outer reality, that we do experience with our senses. Thus in the eucharist the external appearance and character of the elements remain the same; but the inner reality is transformed. With the mouth the elements on the table are experienced as bread and wine, but with the heart they are experienced as Christ's body and blood. (For a fuller discussion of transubstantiation see the writings of Edward Schillebeeckx referred to later.)

The doctrine of sacrifice, applied devotionally to the eucharist and developed as a way of affirming the forgiveness of sins that Christ accomplished by his death on the cross, continues to be effective in many churches today. A more technical doctrine of sacrifice was formulated in the Middle Ages and preserved until our own time in the Roman Catholic Church. It holds to the idea, to use the words of David N. Power, that "the eucharist was in its essence a sacrifice, and that done in representation of Christ's sacrifice it could be offered by the minister for the forgiveness of sins" (Senn 1987, 152).

By means of these eucharistic doctrines, the Catholic Church of the Middle Ages cultivated a strong sense of penitential piety among believers. Despite Christ's atoning death, worshipers were convinced that sinfulness was still the prominent reality of their lives; and a system of repentance and restitution was for many people the defining center of the religious life. This pattern of penitential piety was directly tied to their regular participation in the Mass. Furthermore, this system was controlled by the church, administered by the priests who could use the system of fear and punishment and longing for salvation as a way of enforcing obedience to the church's intellectual and moral demands. What was required, however, was attendance at Mass more than the actual receiving of the consecrated bread and wine. Thus the pattern became attendance on Sundays and other days when church disciplines required that they be present. For many people, however, the Mass was a drama to be watched rather than a meal to be enjoyed. They would receive the elements perhaps no more often than once a year.

The sixteenth-century reformers broke this system open. Every reformer of consequence rejected the doctrines of transubstantiation and sacrifice as they existed at that time. With respect to the first of these doctrines, Luther was vigorous in his rejection of the Catholic formula but continued to focus piety upon the bread and wine. His own doctrine of consubstantiation insisted that bread and wine remained exactly what they appeared to be but that during the eucharist Christ's own body and blood were communicated to communicants as they partook of the bread and wine. Thus they truly ate and drank both the natural and the supernatural elements. Although the technical theologies differed significantly, the pieties of Catholics and Lutherans remained similar. In the Anglican reform doctrinal and devotional details differed significantly from Roman Catholics and Lutherans, yet the liturgical modifications in the Anglican reform paralleled closely those of the Lutheran reform. Not so in the Reformed tradition on the continent. The doctrine of transubstantiation was rejected and nothing was permitted to develop that could easily be mistaken for transubstantiation. The liturgical focus was effectively moved away from the bread and wine.

For different reasons, each of the Reformation churches also rejected the doctrine of sacrifice as they understood it in Roman Catholic theology and piety of the time, introducing instead what the people perceived as a new theology, the theology of the cross, of grace, of faith. The reformers insisted that what Jesus did upon the cross was once and for all; and that any talk of the repetition or reappropriation of that sacrifice diminished the significance of that event. They feared greatly that the doctrine of the eucharistic sacrifice would become a form of works righteousness in which human activity rather than the grace of God becomes the basis of our redemption.

Part of the reformers' practical reshaping of the church was to restore the sermon to its former prominence in the liturgy. Both their theology and their liturgical reform, however, accomplished more than they had expected. Now worship became focused around the Word of God spoken and heard rather than around the body and blood of Christ sacramentally present in the eucharist.

Even though the reformers rejected the theology of the eucharist that had been dominant in the Catholic Church, much of the former

piety remained in place, still based upon a strong sense of sinfulness. Popular religion tended to persist even though it had to develop new forms that were acceptable in Protestant circles. For example, the Reformed Church of Scotland rejected the Catholic holy
day called Corpus Christi (Body of Christ), but developed the custom of local sacramental seasons, sometimes called holy fairs. These
events, as Leigh Eric Schmidt has shown (Schmidt 1989), were built
around the annual celebration of the Lord's supper and were occasions for the restoration of discipline within a congregation in preparation to receive holy communion. These sacramental occasions became public festivals. While the theology and festival detail of the
Roman Catholic festival of Corpus Christi disappeared, a new festival also focusing upon holy communion sprang up to take its place.

The juridical understandings of God and salvation also continued to be prominent in the new Protestant churches. Church polity
may have opened up a little, but the general tendencies were for the
retention of a system of strong control by the churches' pastors and
other officials. These reforms, however, partial as they were, generated a long period of debate and fragmentation in the formerly united
church of the West.

We can be grateful that the history of acrimony over eucharistic
theology has entered a quiet time. There are reasons to hope that we
will finally be able to set aside the weapons of theological war that
have torn the church asunder and enter into an era of genuine peace.

Liturgies

A third way of tracing the history of eucharistic worship is to
review the liturgies that have developed over time. This approach is
especially useful in the effort to understand Catholic and Protestant
worship since the Reformation. J. A. Jungmann describes the Mass
in the late Middle Ages as "a complicated structure" in which "some
details do not seem to fit very well, like some venerable, thousand-
year-old castle whose crooked corridors and narrow stairways, high
towers and large halls appear at first sight strange and queer"
(Jungmann 1951, I, 2). Each of the reformers dealt with this castle in
a distinctive way, as Bard Thompson has documented in his classic
book *Liturgies of the Western Church* (Thompson 1961).

In Germany, Luther boarded up the parts he didn't like. This
approach is especially evident in the eucharistic prayer. Luther examined the several short prayers in the Roman Canon, rejecting them
one by one, retaining only the eucharistic words of Jesus. The result
was a eucharistic liturgy pruned of the Catholic materials that Luther
had rejected and thus made suitable for ordinary German Christians.

In Switzerland John Calvin dismantled the castle and built a new,
more modest building out of the salvaged material. The result was a

eucharistic liturgy that retained some of the language and form of the Mass but was significantly different in its overall character from the Mass that the people had previously known.

In England Thomas Cranmer remodeled the castle so that the ambiance of the old was retained while the interior spaces were significantly altered. The eucharistic prayer, for example, included phrases and ceremonies that would be familiar to formerly Catholic worshipers, but the language that may have felt Catholic expressed a radically Protestant theology of the eucharist.

In their response to the Reformation, Catholic bishops at the Council of Trent built a high fence around the castle so that nothing could change. They standardized the texts and modes of celebration among the many dioceses of the Catholic Church. For more than four hundred years Catholic worship remained fixed in its post-Reformation character.

In later generations these major post-Reformation liturgies spun off further variations. Puritan liturgies extended ideas derived from Calvin, and Methodist liturgies moved beyond the limits previously set by Anglicanism. These two liturgical families continued to develop new forms, including the Holiness movement within the Anglican-Methodist framework and the Restorationist movement of the Churches of Christ and Christian Church (Disciples of Christ) within the Reformed-Presbyterian framework. Although there are many of these later liturgical traditions, certain qualities tend to be present in all of them. First, these churches affirm and expect extensive local variation. They resist standardization, especially if the standardized forms are recommended by church authorities other than their own congregational leaders and members. Second, they are unified in their rejection of what they consider to be Catholic ideas about the Lord's supper. Third, they tend to have a cross-centered piety, as is illustrated by the importance of hymns like "The Old Rugged Cross." Fourth, these churches give greater attention to services of praise, preaching, and prayer than they do to the celebration of the sacraments.

Even among these churches, however, the older tradition of worship at the communion table is honored in memory and preserved in theology even when it has largely disappeared from the piety of the people.

Developments in Eucharistic Theology

This tendency toward splintering into ever more numerous segments is being countered in our time by the movement back to the eucharistic center of Christian worship. Even in our separation into Catholic, Protestant, and evangelical wings of the church, each with

its own subdivisions, we have held onto worship as the life orientation of thankful praise. Our separation has been sharply focused upon
our celebrations of the sacraments. These actions that supposedly
mark our oneness in Jesus Christ have demonstrated that social and
theological issues do tear us apart from one another. Just as the breaking apart of the Western church was fired by theological convictions,
so the moving back together has been energized by creative theological work, and has given rise to new liturgies for celebrating God's
gift of life in Jesus Christ.

The major fault line in the Western churches has divided Catholics and Protestants from each other. Therefore the renewal of theology and the movement to overcome separation has given major attention to bridging this chasm. Although many writers have contributed to the renaissance of eucharistic theology, two contributions
call for special notice. Each of them has reorganized the way that
people in the several churches frame their theological discussion of
the meaning of the Lord's supper. Many people in the Catholic and
Protestant churches addressed by this book have had a similar experience. When inter-church discussion of the eucharist has reached an
impasse, the introduction of these more recent theological themes
has led to breakthroughs. Serious theological discussion that had
seemed impossible suddenly became possible again.

The Theology of Mystery

The first of these breakthroughs has been associated with several people, including the Catholic Odo Casel and Protestants Rudolf
Otto, C. H. Dodd, and Gregory Dix. In an account of how he had
been affected by this *mystery theology*, as this approach to the eucharist
is labeled, Theodore Wedel characterizes it as a "pre-medieval understanding of the real presence in the Eucharist, as real presence in
action rather than in a substance" (Shepherd 1960, 6). Wedel proposes that this approach to eucharistic theology may bridge the gulf
that has existed between Protestants and Catholics since the Reformation, and in support of this hope he summarizes the sympathetic
treatment of Casel's ideas by Protestant theologian Rudolf Otto.
Massey Shepherd says of this same theology: "The *Mysterium* of
Christianity, as understood by Dom Casel, is not so much the content of the Christian revelation, to be apprehended by faith and ex-
plored by reason; it is the reality of redemption itself, the revelation
of God Himself in Christ, in the totality of his mighty acts of incarnation, atonement, and exaltation, made present, operative, and effective in us through the participation of the body of the faithful in the
cultic action of the liturgy" (Shepherd 1960, 33).

Casel's work appeared in scattered essays (Casel 1962); and later
scholars have questioned many of his ideas, especially those that in-

sisted that the eucharist was a Christian adaptation of ancient mystery religions. It is now generally accepted that Casel's historical reconstruction cannot be accepted, but that his insight into the nature of worship continues to be fruitful. Again quoting Shepherd, Casel reintroduced into Western eucharistic thought the "fertile Platonic mysticism of the early fathers" and "the spirit of Eastern Christian worship." Casel re-established the connections of worship in the Western churches with the biblical faith and "the sacramental experience of the whole Graeco-Roman world, where Christianity brought into a new creative unity the finest insights and aspirations of the Jew and the Greek" (Shepherd 1960, 33).

The vehicle by which Casel's *mystery theology* has become known to many people interested in worship is Gregory Dix's exposition of anamnesis or memorial in *The Shape of the Liturgy*. Dix states the idea this way: Memorial is "the 're-calling' before God of the one sacrifice of Christ in all its accomplished and effectual fullness so that it is here and now operative by its effects in the souls of the redeemed." Again he says: "What the Body and Blood of Christ were on Calvary and *before and after*—'an offering and a sacrifice to God for us'—that they are now in the eucharist, the anamnesis not of His death only, but 'of Me'—of the Redeemer in the fullness of His offered Self, and work and life and death, perpetually accepted by the Father in the world to come" (Dix 1945, 143, 242). Even Dix is difficult to understand; yet like Casel's, his writings communicate well at one level: he speaks convincingly of a reality experienced in and through the eucharist, a reality related both to the cross and to Christ's continuing life with God. Many people of our time who were unable to respond to mystery connected to *the change of substance* were attracted by a doctrine of mystery that *overcomes time* so that actions from the past and people of today come together.

Edward Schillebeeckx

A second theological breakthrough came by way of two slender volumes by Edward Schillebeeckx: *Christ the Sacrament of the Encounter with God* (1963) and *The Eucharist* (1968). In the earlier book Schillebeeckx addresses the general topic of sacramentality, doing so in a way that makes the topic approachable by many Christians who previously were alienated by the topic. A sacrament, Schillebeeckx states, "is a divine bestowal of salvation in an outwardly perceptible form which makes the bestowal manifest; a bestowal of salvation in historical visibility" (Schillebeeckx 1963, 15). He then affirms that Jesus is "*the* sacrament, the primordial sacrament....Human encounter with Jesus is therefore the sacrament of the encounter with God" (15).

Schillebeeckx takes another step when he states that Christ is no longer with us as immediate physical presence. Therefore another mode of sacramentality becomes active. "Christ makes his presence among us actively visible and tangible too, not directly through his bodiliness, but by extending among us on earth in visible form the function of his bodily reality which is in heaven" (41). The exposition continues to broaden when Schillebeeckx shows how the church is that extension of Christ's bodiliness, and then how specific actions of the church extend that bodiliness even further. The great value of this book is that it roots sacraments in the redemptive mystery itself rather than in the power of churchly action. It creates a basis for serious conversation among the churches which for generations have been unable to converse.

The second Schillebeeckx book deals more explicitly with the eucharist and particularly with one topic, "the unique presence of Christ in the Eucharist" (Schillebeeckx 1968, 11). His purpose is to establish dialogue both with theologians of the Council of Trent and Christians in the modern world. In this book the doctrine of transubstantiation appears prominently; and Schillebeeckx affirms the truth that this doctrine expresses while at the same time he acknowledges the problems that the wording of this doctrine presents to contemporary Christians.

In his exposition Schillebeeckx mentions terms from other contemporary theologians, including *transfunctionalization, transfinalization,* and *transignification.* Each term claims that something definitive and enduring happens in the eucharist. Whereas transubstantiation focuses the change upon the material elements of the eucharist, each of these other doctrines focuses upon another aspect of the event, such as its use of time or its function in the church and upon the believer. Although Schillebeeckx hesitates to adopt any of these terms, his constructive argument revolves around the function of signs and the importance of meanings that the signs communicate. The real presence of Christ, he says, is not directed toward bread and wine but toward the faithful. "In this commemorative meal, bread and wine become the subject of a new *establishment of meaning,* not by men, but by the living Lord *in* the Church, through which they become the *sign* of the real presence of Christ giving himself to us" (Schillebeeckx 1968, 137).

This book is similar in spirit to the mystery theology of Casel, Otto, Dodd, and Dix. It is more tightly constructed and has held up more successfully in the face of scholarly attention. Like the earlier book on Christ, this volume on the eucharist shifts the terms of discussion sufficiently that barriers to communication are breached. People who had never been able to talk across denominational lines about the central core of their Christian experience find themselves on common ground. On the solid foundation of their experience of God's grace in the Lord's supper, and surrounded by others in the family of faith, they can reach out for new ways of describing and defining what God is doing in Jesus Christ and in eucharistic celebrations.

Scholarly writing about the eucharist continues to be published; and the time is coming when other lines of investigation and exposition will overshadow the pioneering work of Casel, Dix, and Schillebeeckx. These scholars, however, blazed a trail that many will follow. Their work continues to help us find our way.

A New Era of Liturgical Development

The movement back to the eucharistic center of Christian worship has taken shape in new orders for celebrating holy communion. Although many new liturgies for celebrating the eucharist have been published since mid-century, four stand out as representative of the work being done around the world. Three were published during the 1960s and became pace-setting liturgies, with strong ecumenical implications, that opened up new possibilities for worship at the holy table. The fourth, published in 1982, represents a culmination of this liturgical development.

The Church of South India

In 1962 the Synod of the Church of South India authorized the publication of *The Book of Common Worship* (published in 1963). "An Order for the Lord's Supper or the Holy Eucharist" had developed from a rite first published in 1950, early in the life of this church that combined previously Reformed, Methodist, and Anglican church bodies. This liturgy commanded attention, in part, because there was so much interest around the world in the union itself. Another reason was that this liturgy was one of the earliest efforts to give official form to the emerging scholarly consensus about the eucharist, a consensus that could be seen in the order of its parts, the interaction of presbyter and people, and the intermingling in one liturgy of both Catholic and Protestant elements. The South India liturgy included three readings from the Bible, using a one-year lectionary. The offering of the peace of Christ throughout the congregation was featured. Congregational responses interrupted the monological eucharistic prayer. Commentators noted that this liturgy is more biblical and more catholic than its predecessors in the uniting churches. As published in 1963, the text is heavily European; and the language preserves the Elizabethan style of the King James Bible and the 1662 *Prayer Book*. As celebrated in Indian parishes, however, with music and customs rooted in Indian culture, the liturgy transcends the European characteristics that are so strong in the printed text.

The Taizé Liturgy

Developing during this same period of time, and published in English translation in 1962, was the Taizé eucharistic liturgy. Already the Taizé community was well known around the world. Founded by members of the Reformed Church of France, this monastic community sought for renewal of the church and of the larger society in which it was stationed. Taizé represented a serious venture by Protestants to use the monastic pattern previously identified with more Catholic traditions. Central in the life of such a community was the celebration of the eucharist. A full liturgy was developed, with the serious intention of expressing eucharistic doctrine that could be affirmed by Catholics as well as Protestants. The entrance liturgy was built around repentance and pardon. The liturgy of the Word included three readings and sermon. The liturgy of the table included a fully developed offertory, a newly composed eucharistic prayer after the classical model of the Roman Catholic Church, and communion by the entire assembly. The announced intention of the framers of this liturgy was to create a liturgy that is theologically complete and could be celebrated in a manner fully expressive of the meanings contained within it. They affirmed the priesthood of all believers, expressing this conviction by depicting a highly stratified community, each level with its explicit responsibilities in the liturgy. The people at Taizé made a serious and remarkably successful effort to bridge the liturgical and sacramental chasm between the Reformed and Roman Catholic Churches.

The Consultation on Church Union

In 1968 the Consultation on Church Union published *An Order of Worship for The Proclamation of the Word of God and The Celebration of the Lord's Supper with Commentary*. At that time the Consultation consisted of nine church bodies in the United States that were developing the outline for a new uniting church. These churches included Reformed, Methodist, and Episcopal church traditions, and represented churches that were predominantly white and others that were predominantly African-American. The Consultation's commission on worship consisted of two representatives from each participating denomination. In addition, observer-participants from Roman Catholic, Lutheran, and American Baptist traditions were also active in the commission's work. For about a decade this commission was the most important forum in North America for interchurch discussion about liturgy.

The COCU eucharistic liturgy was the commission's major project during those years. It was a good time to be at work. Vatican II had only recently opened new relations between Catholics and Protestants. Several churches in the United States had recently completed or were currently involved in major revisions of their eucharistic rites, and thus were interested in a forum for wider consultation. The work on this liturgy was connected to the Consultation's larger process that anticipated organic union within a decade; which meant that people were motivated to create a significant liturgy that would help their churches move toward a more complete sharing of their traditions of worship. The drafters were determined to include the eucharistic traditions of the participating church bodies, but to do so in ways that opened the liturgy to other traditions, too. It was desired that this liturgy be fully usable by the churches in the Consultation, and also that nothing in this liturgy would create theological barriers to full participation by Roman Catholic, Orthodox, or Lutheran Christians. The drafters also decided that they would use contemporary English rather than the archaic forms still used in most of the participating churches.

The resulting liturgy was widely studied, much admired, and little used. It served more as a study document and liturgy for ecumenical occasions than as a living form for the worship of congregations. On some occasions in the official meetings of the Consultation, this liturgy was celebrated in ways that demonstrated its more lively possibilities. Over a period of time it became clear that this liturgy confirmed the theological possibility of creating a liturgy that is catholic, evangelical, and reformed. It also heightened the question of the basic nature of liturgy: is it a printed text or is it a performed experience? The use of this liturgy by churches in the Consultation accented the fact that living worship is the combination of a text that is theologically strong with a performative style that is adapted to the cultural setting.

The Lima Liturgy

Nearly two decades later a fourth pace-setting liturgy was created. It was drafted for use in the Plenary Assembly of the Faith and Order Commission of the World Council of Churches, meeting in Lima, Peru, in January 1982. Although used later that year for the meeting of the Council's Central Committee and the Sixth Assembly of the World Council of Churches in Vancouver, Canada, the liturgy continues to be called the Lima liturgy. It shows characteristics that are similar to those in the Taizé liturgy and could be considered a second generation in the family of Reformed Tradition-Roman Catholic eucharistic liturgies. This order for the eucharist draws upon a wide range of ancient and modern liturgies. It also seeks to express themes that are prominent in the ecumenical convergence published in the Council's statement *Baptism, Eucharist and Ministry* that was adopted at Vancouver. The resulting liturgy is complex and verbally extended. As with the COCU liturgy, the Lima liturgy provides an experimental text that shows the possibility of theological convergence concerning the meaning of the Lord's supper. Again like COCU, the Lima liturgy has not become the rite for ordinary use by any group of Christians, even in the abridged form proposed by one of its chief creators. (For the text and an explanation of the rite, see Thurian and Wainwright 1983, 241-55).

These four liturgies are representative of the transition to a new era of liturgical creativity. In revised forms, Taizé and South India continue to be living liturgies, used as the regular pattern for worship by on-going communities of Christians. The churches that collaborated in the COCU liturgy, however, have largely left that text behind as they have moved forward to create a new generation of service books and prayer books for their respective churches. These newer liturgies, however, bear the marks of their parentage both in the theologies they express and the liturgical forms they employ.

Consensus Statements

The collaboration of scholars, liturgical writers, editors, and church leaders has led to the development of several summary statements about eucharistic worship that depict the spirit of this work. Within a two-year period two important ecumenical documents were published dealing with the faith and ecclesial life of the churches. *Baptism, Eucharist and Ministry*, published in 1982 by the Faith and Order Commission of the World Council of Churches, focuses explicitly upon the sacramental life expressed in worship. Here is affirmed the united witness of Orthodox, Catholic, and Protestant churches around the world. Because the World Council of Churches exists to proclaim and encourage the visible unity of these long-divided churches, *BEM* focuses upon the theological themes upon which they find agreement and seeks to identify places where they differ. Over the fifty-year period of discussion leading to *BEM*, theologians from a wide confessional range found themselves agreeing in much of what they believe about the eucharist. They presented the results of their labors in a concise document with the urgent request that their churches study this statement in order to determine the extent to which their churches "can recognize in this text the faith of the Church through the ages" (*BEM* 1982, x). Each church was to ask itself questions in the light of this apostolicity therein discerned; and each church was invited, in the light of its own understandings of the apostolic faith, to continue the conversation with other churches.

Churches of every kind around the world have studied this statement and responded. The broad lines of its theology are affirmed, but with many questions. The further from traditional catholic practice churches have historically been positioned, the greater has been their uneasiness with the sacramental interpretations they perceive in *BEM*. It is not clear to them that this way of understanding worship is a useful interpretation of the gospel proclaimed by the apostles. Other churches that are closer to the traditional catholic practices find that the *BEM* consensus is consistent with apostolic Christianity even though these churches may believe that at certain points *BEM* either understates or misstates the major liturgical tradition that began with the first generation of witnesses to Jesus Christ. *BEM* has probably generated more discussion about sacramental worship than has any other document in this century.

Two years after *BEM* was released, the Consultation on Church Union published *In Quest of a Church of Christ Uniting*. This statement brought to culmination the process of theological discussion and prophetic exploration that churches had conducted over a period of more than two decades. Although the range of topics is broader than in *BEM*, *In Quest* also focuses on the liturgical and sacramental life of the churches. It affirms that shining through the variety in worship practices is a common tradition of "thanksgiving for God's holy love revealed supremely in Jesus Christ" (COCU 1985, 35). The COCU consensus is clear in its assertion that "corporate worship centers in the proclamation of the Word and the celebration of the sacraments." It also affirms that "the individual believer's prayer, obedience, and service are essential components of the entire community's worship" (COCU 1985, 35). Although much shorter than the discussions in *BEM*, *In Quest* discusses worship in ways that are faithful to the catholic, evangelical, and reformed traditions that are represented in the Consultation.

An earlier document expressing the convergence concerning Christian worship is the *Constitution on the Liturgy*, published by the Roman Catholic Church in 1963. This statement of policy represented the leading edge of Roman Catholic reform generated by the Second Vatican Council. In this small book, a century of scholarly and pastoral experimentation reached a climax, and a remarkable stream of insight into worship and energy for the reform of congregational life was released into the world. The follow-up to the *Constitution* included the redrafting of liturgies and liturgical books, the creation of the three-year lectionary, and the development of a new approach to adult conversion and baptism. The decision to conduct worship in vernacular languages guaranteed that the reforms would affect the people across the world, rather than priests and scholars only. It may be that the most important result of Vatican II was that the Catholic side of the wall of isolation between that church and other churches was dismantled. Although Catholic and Protestant churches continue to exist in separation from one another, the former wall between them is but a pile of rubble between churches that now know one another and share much life in common.

From the beginning of this period of Roman Catholic reform, Protestants were caught up by these developments in the Catholic world. Quickly Catholic and Protestant scholars, publishers, and pastoral leaders collaborated in ways that had never before been imaginable or attempted. The most dramatic evidence of this reciprocal influence is that the three-year lectionary was developed by Catholics for use in that church, but quickly adopted by Protestant churches in North America. The Consultation on Church Union helped to extend the acceptance of this lectionary for use in worship and preaching, and in close cooperation with the United Methodist Church developed a "consensus version." Later, Protestants and Catholics formed the Consultation on Common Texts, and this group of scholars, editors, and publishers has developed a significant revision of the lectionary for consideration both by Protestant and Catholic churches: *The Revised Common Lectionary*, first published in 1983 and in a revised edition in 1992. Another important activity of this consortium is developing standardized contemporary translations into English of traditional liturgical formularies. The most recent edition of this work is *Praying Together* (CCT 1988). Thus, the several traditions that once worked in isolation (and sometimes enmity) are now close collaborators in a very wide range of liturgical work.

Eucharistic Hospitality

It is important to underscore the fact that these eucharistic theologies, liturgies, and consensus statements developed during a period of time when Christians had begun to participate in a widening practice of eucharistic hospitality. Long before, the churches had developed disciplines that limited access to the table to persons in good standing with the church in which the table was spread. Breaches in this good standing could be defined doctrinally, morally, and politically. If people held theological views that were seriously counter to church teaching, lived in ways that violated the church's ethical standards, or gave their allegiance to a different organizational system than the one that prevailed where they were, then they would be excluded from communion. Regrettably, a great many of the church divisions in the history of Christianity have been interpreted as serious enough that they required breach of communion fellowship.

In our time, however, there is a growing conviction among church people as a whole, and their leaders too, that the eucharistic theologies of the several churches express apostolic faith and practice; and therefore no doctrinal barriers should keep us from extending hospitality to one another. The use of excommunication as a means of enforcing discipline and agreement in church organization is also diminishing. Furthermore, the deliberate extension of eucharistic hospitality in certain pastoral situations, such as communion at the marriage of people from different church traditions, is becoming widespread. In some church union relationships, such as the Consultation on Church Union, interchurch celebrations of holy communion are encouraged in order to express the apostolic faith already shared by these churches, the one baptism that they recognize in the baptism performed in one another's churches, and the one ministry that they perceive even though the historic forms of that ministry differ widely.

This process of increased contact and extending of liturgical hospitality has also been encouraged by a significant series of bilateral discussions between churches. The Roman Catholic Church has been the most active partner in these conversations, having conducted bilateral discussions on an international level with major confessional traditions. Other bilateral conversations have also taken place between historic Protestant churches. Especially interesting is the rapprochement that has developed between Episcopal and Lutheran churches whose approaches to worship are quite similar but whose formal relations have previously discouraged eucharistic hospitality.

The fact that people from various churches received the eucharist from people outside of their own tradition has had a profound effect upon the development of liturgies and the reshaping of eucharistic practice. We learn from one another. Even more important, we have been able to see more clearly than we could in any other circumstance that each church's preferred way of understanding and conducting the Lord's supper is but one of many forms this central sacrament can take.

The work of scholars and liturgists continues, and as it moves forward Christians of many traditions find themselves worshiping together. The eucharist is positioned between God's grace expressed in Jesus Christ and our continuing life in this world. Our words and celebrations, which can never do justice to God, are also too feeble to express God's mysterious love as it comes to us through Christ, the church, and the sacraments. Yet we must speak, and therefore we do the eucharist in order to give God our thankful praise, to testify to our experience, and to invite others to share this heavenly banquet. What is radically different now is that members still separated in the many churches can cross over the divide and find once again that doctrinally and liturgically as well as spiritually, "we who are many are one body, for we all partake of the one bread" (1 Corinthians 10:17).

Encouraging the Conversation

One way to get the conversation going is to sum up, in a sentence or two, what I've said in this chapter. My intention has been to outline the process by which the earliest patterns of Christian worship gradually developed until they came to be the forms we know today. In order to fix this story in your memory, make your own summary of the main elements. Then stand back, so to speak, and think about this long and complex story. The following suggestions may help you along.

1. This chapter contrasts two traditions of worship:
   - The apostolic tradition, which defines worship by means of the Lord's supper; and
   - The reformation tradition, which defines worship by means of the proclaimed word of God.

2. Where do you and your church family stand in this spectrum?
   - Closer to the supper tradition? or
   - Closer to the sermon tradition?

3. This chapter also describes a strong movement to reclaim the Lord's supper as the defining mark of worship in churches today.
   - What signs of this coming together do you see in churches you know?
   - What evidence do you see that runs counter to the thesis of this book?

4. Have you attended services of holy communion in churches very different from your own?
   - If so, what was different from your previous experience?
   - What was very much the same?

3

The Theological Norm of Worship

Christian worship is a combination of celebrative actions by which people are gathered before God, re-established in our relations with God, and renewed as a community of faith. The dynamic center of this liturgical system is the weekly assembly—usually on Sunday—to praise God for life in Jesus Christ and with one another. Clustered around this center are several other acts of worship, including personal prayer and communal services of prayer, baptism and other rites of initiation and renewal, services of healing, weddings, and funerals.

In the long history of the church, as the previous chapters of this book have indicated, this pattern of praise has been eucharistic in spirit and form. This chapter continues the discussion by developing five ideas. (1) As orientation toward life, the attitude of thankful praise is the generative nucleus for the church's full life of worship and prayer. (2) As acts of worship, thankful praise proclaims God's redemptive love in Jesus Christ, which is the central theme of Christian worship. (3) The great thanksgiving expresses the incarnational character of the Christian faith. (4) Thankful praise provides criteria for evaluating what each congregation does week after week in its major assemblies of worship. (5) The eucharist provides the organizing principle for the pattern of praise. The sum of the matter is that the order of worship and the manner of celebration are to help the congregation become *in fact* what it already is *in principle*—the Body of Christ on earth.

The Generative Nucleus of Worship

"Generative nucleus" is a phrase taken from Carmine Di Sante's carefully drawn study of the origins of Christian worship, *Jewish*

Prayer: The Origins of Christian Liturgy (Di Sante 1991). He proposes that Jewish prayer can be likened to a series of concentric circles at the center of which is *berakah* (*blessing*), a specific form of experiencing reality and presenting self to God. *Blessing* is first an attitude about life in God's presence and second a specific formula of praise that can be said in one sentence or enlarged into an extended liturgy of praise and petition. Psalm 118 begins with a concise expression of this quality:

> O give thanks to the LORD, for he is good;
>   his steadfast love endures forever!

Similar is this brief blessing from the order of ceremonies for a contemporary celebration of the Passover:

> "Praised are You, Adonai, Sovereign of Existence,
> Who creates the fruit of the earth." (Bronstein 1982, 26)

Consider this longer form, also from a modern Jewish book of worship:

> Blessed is the Lord our God, Ruler of the universe, by whose law the shadows of evening fall and the gates of morn are opened. In wisdom You have established the changes of times and seasons and ordered the ways of the stars in their heavenly courses. Creator of heaven and earth, O ever-living God, rule over us. Blessed is the Lord, for the day and its work and for the night and its rest. (*Gates of Prayer* 1975, 577)

As the above prayer illustrates, the *blessing* expresses a specific way of linking God, human beings, and the world. In reference to human beings and the world, says Di Sante, God is their source and norm, placing them in existence and determining the "ways in which they are to achieve fruition and bear fruit." Human beings "are the interpreters of God and the world, but also the beneficiaries of these, for they are the objects of God's care and recipients of the fruits of the earth." The world is sacrament and gift, "sign of God's good will and concrete gift to human beings" (Di Sante 1991, 35). Thus God, humankind, and the world are linked together as three poles in a dynamic and healthful relationship.

People who live according to this attitude experience God's awesome presence in all aspects of life and therefore find praise constantly coming to their lips. They perceive God's rich purposes and are continually inspired to thank God for the divine generosity and to petition God that these gifts continue. Because God, people, and the world are so intertwined, people become aware of how much has been given to them and thus how much they have to share. Their prayers and religious rites are rooted in their experiences of the earth's goodness and God's love; and therefore these religious words and actions "reveal the ultimate, deepest, and innermost identity" of the things of this world, their relationship to God, and their function as a sign of God's attentiveness and care (Di Sante 1991, 41).

Di Sante shows that this attitude of adoring thankfulness is given a liturgical "carrying structure" consisting of three concentric rings. Virtually every extended form of Jewish prayer, and especially the weekly Sabbath services, uses these three elements as the means of expressing the thankful praise of God. The innermost ring is the recitation of the Shema (Deuteronomy 6:4–9), the affirmation that God is one, which Jesus reaffirmed in his summary of the law (Mark 12:28–31). The prayerful character of this recitation is signaled by the group of brief prayers that immediately surround the stating of this testimony of Jewish belief. The second ring is a group of short prayers, usually called the eighteen benedictions, in which worshipers praise God and offer petitions for themselves and their world. The third ring is the reading, proclaiming, and meditating upon the Torah in which God's character and work are described. Throughout the year Jewish worship includes festivals and special liturgies. Yet their foundation is this threefold structure of praise generated by the thankful praise of God.

Thankful praise or *eucharist* is the Christian equivalent of *berakah/blessing*. As an attitude it permeates the classic tradition of Christian prayer; and surrounded by its own liturgical "carrying structure" this attitude shapes the classical pattern of Christian worship. The Greek word means very much the same as the Hebrew term; and the fact that the distinctive act of Christian worship took this name indicates the continuity with Judaism that existed at the heart of the church's life. *Berakah, blessing, eucharistia, thankful praise* is the engine that drives Christian worship. This attitude shapes Jesus' teaching when he tells his disciples not to worry about food and clothing. The God who clothes the grass of the field will also clothe us. Thus, instead of worrying about these things and striving after them as the Gentiles do, we should trust God and strive for the kingdom of God and the righteousness that belongs to that kingdom. The theology of life explicitly stated here, as Richard H. Lowery has written (Lowery 1993), is that God's world is filled with the good things that we need, and these things will be given to us. God's generosity is the foundation for life itself; and because God is generous, the people who love God can live worry-free, generous lives. The natural outgrowth of this confidence is the combination of awe-praise-petition that is expressed in the prayer that Jesus taught his disciples. It begins by honoring the name of God and then moves through a series of petitions that express confidence in God's purpose for the world and the assurance that God's purposes will be fulfilled.

This attitude is the foundation for the combination of joy and peace in the midst of suffering that is so prominent in the writings of Paul. An especially eloquent expression of this attitude is a passage toward the conclusion of Philippians. Despite the hardships and sufferings that Paul relates in this epistle, his attitude is one of confidence and hope; and this same attitude is urged upon the Philippians. Paul sums it up by telling his readers to "rejoice in the Lord always." We are not to worry about anything, but "by prayer and supplication with thanksgiving [*eucharistias*] let your requests be made known to God." The conclusion of the matter is then stated: "And the peace of God, which surpasses all understanding, will guard your hearts and your minds in Christ Jesus" (Philippians 4:4–7).

This attitude of awe-praise-petition is much needed in the churches of our time. We need to recover the perspective toward the earth, God, and culture that is expressed by the attitude of thankful praise. Modern economic systems encourage us to accumulate an ever-increasing store of possessions; and to do so with little regard to the impact upon the natural world and other people. Now that world population has become so large and the machines for intervening in natural processes so powerful, human greed and cruelty threaten to overrun creation. The divinely given equation for life in the world is: *abundance for all and limited desire by each person equals peace, joy, and praise*. The humanly created equation for life in the world is: *unlimited desire by all and scarcity of the good things of the world equals a world groaning in travail, waiting for its redemption*. While the economic systems of the developed world are not likely going to change quickly, changes can be made in the power these systems hold over the hearts and minds of people in the churches. The attitude of thankful praise can help Christians remember God from whom all blessings flow, the earth that manifests that blessing-filled goodness of God, and the interconnectedness of the human community.

It is easy for worship to become a justification of the existing social system or a repudiation of life in the world. Neither attitude leads to good relations with God, the world, and one another. What is needed is the recovery of the perspective provided by the eucharistic attitude toward the world, for it can lead to health within each person and to the gradual renewing of the broader systems of life in which we live and work. Alexander Schmemann makes this point in an especially sharp way. Human beings have the unique position in the universe in that we are able to *bless* God for the food and life we receive from God. "So the only *natural* (and not "supernatural") reaction of [humankind] to whom God gave this blessed and sanctified world, is to bless God in return, to thank [God], to see the world as God sees it—and in this act of gratitude and adoration—to know, name and possess the world." Schmemann notes that before we are *homo sapiens* (knowers), or *homo faber* (doers), we are *homo adorans* (worshipers). Our basic definition as human beings is to be priest. We stand in "the center of the world" and we unify it in our act of blessing God, "of both receiving the world from God and offering it to God." Schmemann's conclusion is this: "The world was created as the 'matter,' the material of one all-embracing eucharist, and [humankind] was created as the priest of this cosmic sacrament" (Schmemann 1973, 5).

God's Redemptive Love in Jesus Christ

The eucharistic attitude links Christians with Jews, and also with many other peoples of the world since thankful praise, as an attitude toward God, nature, and society is as close to being universal as is any religious idea. It is good for Christians to acknowledge the universality of this foundation of worship. Yet each of the religions of the world has its distinctive characteristics. Each one develops its own way of describing reality and commanding participation by the people in the rites and ceremonies of the religion. So too with the church. The distinctive message, as phrased in the traditional language of John's Gospel, is this:

"For God so loved the world that he gave his only Son, so that everyone who believes in him may not perish but have eternal life." (John 3:16)

This faith that animates the church was first proclaimed by the apostles, embodied in the congregations they established, and collected in the writings that have become the New Testament. Thus, the prologue to the Epistle to the Hebrews begins by affirming that "long ago God spoke to our ancestors in many and various ways by the prophets." Now, "in these last days," the writer continues, God has spoken "by a Son" who is "the reflection of God's glory and the exact imprint of God's very being" (Hebrews 1:1–4).

Even before the New Testament scriptures were written down, however, the church was gathering around the communion table, offering its faith and life to God in prayer. Although we do not possess the earliest prayer texts, it is possible to assume continuity in the liturgical tradition, which means that the faith expressed in the eucharist texts is another way, in addition to scripture, for us to understand the gospel as it first was heard, believed, and lived in the Christian community. An illustration is the "Anaphora of Addai and Mari," which some scholars date as third century and consider to be perhaps the oldest eucharistic prayer text known to the church today. (See Deiss 1979, 157-63.) This prayer is addressed to the Lord who is sometimes God, the majestic Lord and creator of the universe, and sometimes Jesus, who clothed himself in humanity and gave new life to humankind. Central to this faith tradition, expressed in the eucharist and extending from apostolic times until our own, is the conviction that God was working in Jesus Christ to bring salvation to the people. The prayer praises God who:

> ...created the world in accordance with his graciousness
> and those who dwell in it in accordance with his kindness.
> He saved mankind in accordance with his mercy,
> he has filled mortal men with his great grace.

The prayer continues, addressed now to Jesus Christ:

> You exalted our lowliness,
> you raised us up when we had fallen,
> you brought our mortal nature back to life,
> you forgave our sins.
> You justified us when we were sinners,
> you enlightened our minds.
> Our Lord and our God,
> you conquered our enemies,
> you gave victory to our frail, weak human nature
> through the abundant mercies of your grace.

This section of the prayer concludes with a doxology:

> For all your helps and graces to us,
> we offer you praise, honor,
> gratitude and adoration,
> now and always and forever and ever.

The next section of this prayer intercedes for the people of the church, the inhabitants of the world, and the people celebrating this service. Once again, there is a concluding doxology:

> With open mouths and faces unveiled
> we present you with praise and honor,
> gratitude and adoration
> to your living, holy, and life-giving name,
> now and always and forever and ever.

Other eucharistic prayers, ancient and modern, also focus on God's saving work in Jesus Christ. This salvation is built upon God's love that is affirmed as the source of creation and the leading characteristic of God's continuing relationship with the world. The salvation that God accomplishes through Jesus Christ consists of three dimensions: (1) justification, which is salvation from one's sins; (2) liberation, which is salvation from oppression; (3) and perfection, which is salvation from the limitations of this life for the fulfilment in the age to come. These themes were present in Judaism, expressed repeatedly in the Hebrew Scriptures, and incorporated by Jesus into his movement. They continued in the early Christian community and became leading motifs in the Greek-language writings that the church developed in its early years.

Other themes also appeared in the long history of Israel and the Christian movement. After all, the full life of humankind, as well as everything from this world and the next, have always been suitable topics for religious reflection. Much of this theological and ethical heritage also came to be included in worship. As the range of ideas expands, however, the organizing center becomes ever more important. Which ideas explain it all and give power to the people in their relations with God, with one another, and with all the world? The eucharistic tradition claims that at the center is the mystery of God's saving love expressed in the life, death, and glorification of Jesus Christ and communicated to his friends and followers through the sacred meal at Christ's table.

The result of God's saving work in Jesus Christ is that the estrangement between God and humanity is overcome. The painful separations within the human community are bridged so that people who otherwise live in isolation from one another may now live together in peace. Because of God's saving work we are given power to extend the love of God and neighbor in all that we do.

This central theme of the gospel, portrayed so vividly in the eucharist, can be interpreted by means of a statement drawn from an essay by Frederick Herzog. The purpose of worship is that the church *may grasp the crude shape of what God has done in Christ* (Shepherd 1963, 98-127). The most important idea in this statement is that *in the life and work of Jesus Christ GOD was doing something for us.* Paul states the idea with great simplicity and eloquence in his correspondance with the Corinthian church. All who are in Christ, Paul asserts, are a new creation. "Everything old has passed away; see, everything has become new!" Paul continues: "All this is from God," who reconciled us to God's own self through Christ. No longer does God hold our trespasses against us because "for our sake" God made Christ "to be sin who knew no sin, so that in him we might become the righteousness of God" (2 Corinthians 5:16–21).

The later history of Christian doctrine continues this line of thought. The questions that made the ancient doctrinal debates so impassioned were these: Who is at work in the salvation ascribed to Jesus Christ? And by what power does our salvation come? Definitive answers were given to that question in the resolutions of ancient councils of the churches and in the ecumenical creeds. These answers were also embedded in the eucharistic prayers of the churches, as is illustrated by the prayer of Hippolytus: "We render thanks to you, O God, through your beloved child Jesus Christ, whom in the last times you sent to us as a savior and redeemer and angel of your will" (Jasper and Cuming 1987, 35).

A second idea in Herzog's sentence is the crude shape. The meaning of this phrase is implicit in the Corinthians passage cited above. The central story in the Gospels recounts the tragic career of a man who lived obscurely most of his years and then flashed briefly into public awareness. After an extended period of ministry with his people, with a growing response from all who heard him, Jesus found himself embroiled with public authorities representing both civil and religious institutions. When the final confrontation came, he was given *pro forma* hearings before hostile officials, and then turned into a political scapegoat. As one official put the matter: "It was better to have one person die for the people" (John 18:14b). After several hours of torture, he was executed by crucifixion—a physically cruel form of death made even worse by its public exposure and shame. Although the Gospel accounts of this story use subdued language, the grim plot line of the narrative is clear and the crudeness of human life is revealed. In this story the long history of human sin, abasement, cruelty, suffering, and broken hopes comes into view once again. Instead of being the continuing chronicle of futility, however, this time the tragedy bursts open in hope. In the midst of shame and suffering, God works to transform humankind and all creation.

One more term can be factored from Herzog's statement: *to grasp*. Worship is a complex process of communication. It includes the subtle interweaving of time and eternity—past, present, and future. In worship the ancestors and the current generation speak to one another. God and humanity converse. The dramatic narrative of God's will for the world and the subplots of individuals and communities are interwoven. By its very nature, this complex process of communication can barely use ordinary speech from the worlds of science and history. It is more art than discursive prose. We who participate in the communicative process reach out with all of our senses to take hold of the message as best we can in order to understand and obey it. Even the most didactic aspect of worship, scripture readings and sermons, can outline the shape of God's work but cannot give its full detail. The melody is bequeathed us in the biblical accounts. What we do not have in scripture is the theological and social harmonization that supports the melody and provides its depth. To shift the musical metaphor, the Bible gives a score to be read, but music needs to be performed in order for people to experience it. The worship service is the performing that allows us to experience the message of God in Jesus Christ that the scriptures proclaim.

We can see this process being set in motion in the upper room before Jesus went out to die. In his cryptic words to his disciples, he gave them the key:

My body given for you.
My blood of the covenant poured out for you.
Do this to remember me.

Earlier he had told them: "Where two or three are gathered in my name, I am there among them" (Matthew 18:20). He spoke of himself as the living water that would quench thirst forever (John 4). Again, on the day of the resurrection itself, two disciples leaving Jerusalem were joined by a stranger; and when they broke bread remembering Jesus, the stranger was revealed to them as their risen Savior. Resurrection stories in the Gospels indicate that in the ceremonies with bread and wine, used to remember Jesus, an ever-widening band of disciples came to understand what had happened in Jesus Christ, and they experienced salvation in his name. Their worship thus was their faith-interpretation of a sordid, shameful history. They discovered, to use another of Herzog's phrases, the "meaning in meaningless" which is the heart of the gospel.

The Christian faith includes a complex set of ideas about God, the world, and humankind; and a fully developed ethical and moral system for life. All of these ideas are suitable for celebration and elaboration when Christians gather. The value of eucharistic worship is that it helps the church keep all of these ideas in perspective. When our assemblies are focused on the communion table, and the liturgy of praise and remembrance conducted there, we remember what is supposed to happen when the faithful gather to worship. In the liturgy we enter into the story of God, but God also enters into our story. Worship acknowledges the tragic character of life; but it also proclaims hope and gives us cause to believe that God's future is better than our present. All of this is cast in the form of thankful praise; or using the language of the epistle to the Hebrews, worship is our "sacrifice of praise to God" (Hebrews 13:15). In our worship we bring to God our bodies given to God and one another as our spiritual worship (Romans 12:1).

Incarnational Worship

The final sentence of the previous paragraph could just as well be the first sentence of this paragraph and section of the chapter. Another value of eucharistic worship is that *it binds spirit and body in a strong, enduring union.* The interpenetration of spirit and body has been a major theme throughout the history of Christian thought. Creation itself can be understood as the forming of a body that God's own inner life may be expressed; and God is experienced in and through our contact with this world, much as our spiritual knowledge of one another is by means of bodily relations.

This emphasis upon spiritual communication through bodily form accounts for major elements in the liturgical life of Judaism and early Christianity. From early times Jews believed that God is one and that this one God transcends our understanding and earthliness. For much of their history, Jews maintained a shrine for this mysterious God—a darkened sacred space, with a throne that the unseen God was thought to occupy. To emphasize even more that their God was never seen, Jews rejected the making of pictures or statues of their God. Their sacred stories told of hearing God speak; but with only few exceptions, such as Moses, even their heroes never saw God. Even Moses did not see God directly when he received the divine commission to lead the people out of slavery. On that occasion God revealed the divine name to Moses, but not the divine face or form. Yet God did use bodiliness: God spoke to Moses and God's glory was emblazoned in a bush that flamed but did not burn.

One occasion in Moses' leadership when this distance between God and the people was reduced was the time when God gave the Israelites the covenant and its laws. Moses took his closest advisors and seventy of the elders onto "the mountain of God." There they saw the God of Israel, and "ate and drank" (Exodus 24:9–11). At this beginning of the Jewish religious tradition, a meal was the means of communion with God. The use of a meal as communion with God can also be seen in the sacrifices that were central elements in Jewish religion from earliest times until the destruction of the temple in 70 C.E. The offering of gifts to God took several forms, each with its own set of purposes. Important to the system as a whole were ritualized meals in which portions of the sacrificed commodity were consumed. In this way worshipers and the God of Israel came into relationship with one another. The connection between the spiritual and bodily aspects of this ancient religious system is demonstrated by the psalms in the Old Testament. They constitute some of the most spiritual religious expressions in human history; yet they represent the piety of worshipers in the temple where animal sacrifices were the central ritual.

This religious tradition also believed that communion with God took place in the affairs of daily life—in the politics, economics, and ethics of human affairs. As the legal codes in the first books of the Bible indicate, religion was an earthy matter. The people expressed their life with God by what they ate and wore; and by how they conducted their bodily relationships with one another. What is even more important is their conviction that in these same bodily actions, God came to them.

This emphasis upon the bodily experience both of revelation and response is sometimes described by the phrase incarnational religion. The natural world takes on a sacral dimension. For humankind the world is the mode of God's self-disclosure. Just as two friends encounter each other spiritually by means of their bodily contact, so we encounter God spiritually through the contact of our bodies with God's self-revelation through physical forms. The incarnational understanding also means that God is real to us even though God always remains behind the veil of understanding and full knowledge.

For Christians the incarnational understanding of religion comes into its highest form in Jesus Christ. In this person, fully human as all of us are, God was "pleased to dwell." In the first chapter of his Gospel, John develops this idea in a way that has become foundational for the church ever since. He begins by telling of the "Word" that was with God in the beginning, and an active agent in creation. This Word was with God, says John, and "was God." Later in the same passage, John states that this "Word became flesh and lived among us, and we have seen his glory, the glory as of a father's only son, full of grace and truth" (John 1:14). Through this one, Jesus Christ, whom we describe as God incarnate, we meet the one true and living God.

This emphasis upon meeting God in physical form has important implications for Christian worship today. At the core of the religious quest is the desire to be connected to the world's center of meaning, purpose, and energy. People need to understand what life is all about, to have a reason for their lives, and to be empowered to live according to these purposes.

Herein lies our problem. God is elusive; and our efforts to reach for spiritual contact with the Great Spirit leave us uncertain. The basic question is this: how can I know when I have encountered God? One answer is when our emotional life is overwhelmed and we enter into altered states of consciousness. The pentecostal experience expresses the fullness of this way of encountering God. For many people, the pentecostal way of meeting God is possible, satisfying, and repeatable.

Many other people, however, do not readily experience religious ecstasy. Perhaps their emotional structure or cultural formation is not compatible with this kind of experience. Or, their theological convictions may establish barriers to pentecostal religious practice. For these people, incarnational religion offers an alternative approach to experience with God.

Body-centered worship uses a powerful set of personal dynamics. Emotional energy is generated in the deepest levels of personal being. This energy is directly connected to the most elemental of human processes—making love, giving birth, nurturing children, facing danger, growing old, dying. These processes are experienced individually, but they are inescapably social. They bind us into com-munities—into families, tribes, and larger social units. In order for the communities to be strong, and thus able to perform their needed functions for the well being of the individuals within them, this same dynamic energy also has to be invested in these communities. Yet the communities cannot by themselves generate this energy; it comes only from the inner life of the persons within them.

Ritual is the process whereby the vital energy of personal life is connected to the values, procedures, and requirements of the group. The ceremonies use substances and perform actions that evoke the strongest of personal emotions. For example, the shedding of blood is part of most of the elemental activities in which human beings engaged. Thus ritualized references to the shedding of blood sum-mon the emotions that are generated in those basic activies of hu-man life.

The ritual also proclaims the foundational stories of the commu-nity; and it shows how the emotions of persons can become the emo-tional energy of the community. The values of the group and its de-mands upon its members now take on qualities similar to those that support us in our lives as individuals. When persons participate in ritual, the power of love and emotional strength generated in their inner life now rises to the surface and becomes part of the life of the group. Because this transfer takes place, people are prepared to honor the community, serve it, even suffer and die on its behalf. All of this they have to do if the group is to survive. Because the rituals have invested the community's demands with powerful emotions, then people willingly yield themselves into its care and control. The ritual converts what is obligatory into something desirable.

The eucharist is this kind of powerful ritual action. It uses bread and wine as the emblems of human flesh and blood. The emotional intensity is increased when worshipers are invited to eat and drink these elements. The effectiveness of the ritual is found in the transfer of emotion, for this ritual meal generates in individual worshipers many feelings that are transferred to the central beliefs and expecta-tions of the group. The strength of God's love is demonstrated by God's willingness to be sacrificed for us. The urgency of our response is revealed by the price that was paid for our redemption. The possi-bility of new life in this world and the next is guaranteed by the completeness of God's identification with humankind in its sinful-ness.

Most people do not have to choose between pentecostal and sac-ramental religion, for both kinds of self-transcendence are likely to be included in powerful moments of religious experience. Yet most people are likely to incline one way or the other, either because of factors in their personalities or because of social conditioning. Since both kinds of self-transcendence are common to humanity, many people are likely to find an alternating current in their religious life, sometimes moving toward the ecstatic, sometimes toward the bodily. The eucharist is one of the poles for this alternation of religious energy. But whichever condition applies, worship focused upon the "sacrament of Christ's body and blood" is a major way of communicating between God and God's people.

Several implications result from the incarnational understanding of worship. One is that the liturgy focuses explicitly upon physical elements and physical actions. Even though much of the service consists of words and music, it comes to its climax when the physical objects of bread and wine are displayed, broken and poured, and eaten.

A second implication is that bold metaphorical language is employed. A seventh-century hymn extends this invitation:

Draw nigh and take the Body of the Lord,
and drink the holy Blood for you outpoured. (*Hymnal 1982*, 327)

The eucharistic hymns of John and Charles Wesley show this same power of bold metaphor. "Who shall say," asks a hymn by Charles Wesley,

how the bread his flesh imparts,
how the wine transmits his blood,
fills his faithful people's hearts
with all the life of God!

Even "angels round our altars/ bow to search it out in vain." The hymn continues to express the wonder of God's gift of life and the impossibility of understanding how it comes about in the eucharistic meal. The hymn concludes:

Let us taste the heavenly powers, Lord, we ask for nothing
    more,
thine to bless, 'tis only ours to wonder and adore. (*UMH*,
627)

A third implication is that incarnational worship requires bodily action by worshipers. The eucharistic elements, and the ceremonies surrounding them, are to be seen and heard. Even more, they are to be smelled and touched and tasted. Not only do the bread and wine call for physical interaction between the people and these objects, but physical interaction between the people is also summoned. It is difficult to share a meal, even a highly stylized ceremonial meal, without becoming attached to the other participants in the feast. Thus eucharistic worship calls for people to move around, to touch one another, to become bodily connected in order to experience spiritual union.

Criteria for Evaluation

The eucharistic character of worship provides a set of criteria that can be used to evaluate worship in a congregation. (1) Are the stories of God's creating love revealed in all of life and the story of God's redeeming love manifested in Jesus Christ told clearly, provocatively, and persuasively to the mind? (2) Is the ritual that embodies these stories performed dramatically, faithfully, and in an emotionally compelling way? (3) Does the full combination of services in the congregation's life connect people so that they experience themselves as Christ's body in the world?

Worship tells the story of God's creating and redeeming work, the work that reaches its definitive form in Jesus Christ. Everything in the Sunday service needs to unfold from that central message. When people leave the church on Sunday, it should be with a renewed sense of their relationship with the God who is revealed in Jesus Christ. Not only must the story line itself be clear; the order of worship itself needs to express that story and invite the full participation of congregants. In some congregations the order of the service is confused so that the preeminence of the eucharist is compromised. In contrast, the classic order is strong and clear—introduction, scripture and sermon, intercessions, offering, great thanksgiving prayer, the breaking of bread, and communion. When done with devotional fullness this outline sharpens the sense of what is being done. The climax to the service comes with the people of God eating and drinking together with God and one another. This order is direct and simple. What sometimes happens, to the detriment of the service, is that the parts are mixed up in their order, and the service becomes too elaborate. The challenge to ministers and musicians alike is to revise the order and select the devotional adornments so that the service moves clearly and vigorously from its proper beginning to its climax at the holy table.

An important consideration, as one evaluates the pattern of worship in a congregation, is the tone and texture of worship. Herzog warns against "glory" in Christian worship, by which he means "awestruck wonder" without sufficient awareness of the "shamefulness of the cross" (Shepherd 1963, 115). Perhaps a more likely failure in churches today is a certain kind of "joy" in Christian worship, an experience of exhilaration in the Spirit without the remorse that comes from reckoning with our sinfulness and its effect upon the heart of God. Another failure in the tone of contemporary worship is optimism, which is the proclamation of hope without facing the evidences all around us that the earth and the history of its inhabitants are lurching toward disaster. Wonder, joy, and peace are appropriate results from participating in the worship of God; but their power for us is directly related to their foundation in the story of God's love for us expressed in God's self-abasement in Jesus Christ.

The tone of worship can also be compromised by triviality in the story that it tells. The desire to make worship relevant to daily life leads some congregations to deal with the incidental frustrations that mar daily activity and also to sidestep the more fundamental disruptions in well-being that are caused by the major aspects of life and death. Worship becomes a therapy session rather than being the performance of a dramatic tragedy that explains life and provides the understanding that we depend upon in order to cope with that life. In contrast, the problem in the worship of other congregations is the unrelieved gloominess of tone. Such services tell of the pain and suffering of humankind, and of the pointlessness of life. Or they condemn worshipers for their sinfulness and relegate them to perpetual hopelessness. God's harshness becomes the leading edge of the message; and worshipers are terrorized by the story.

When the eucharistic norm is made operative, however, these violations of worship are moderated. The service tells the story of God's love that shines through the divine justice. It proclaims God's mercy that promises forgiveness. At the table with bread and wine, the signs of God's identification with humankind in their suffering, the possibility of new life is made real.

Some liturgies are damaged by the strong emphasis upon exhortation. Everything seems calculated to convince people that there is something that they ought to do. Different motivations can be offered: God loves you, and therefore you have to…; you are a sinner, and to make amends for your sinful actions, you need to…; the world is in such desperate condition, and you are so wonderfully blessed; therefore, your obligation, and the way to an easier conscience, is for you to…. Sometimes these ideas are conveyed directly in sermons. They may also be implied in more subtle ways throughout the liturgy. The problem is not the assumption that faith in Jesus Christ should take shape in how we live. Rather, the problem is that the goal of worship becomes telling people how to live (and urging them to live that way).

The eucharistic norm for worship leads to a different emphasis. The liturgy declares God's work and portrays God's character. It prompts gratitude and confession—gratitude because of God's generosity, confession because worshipers recognize how much they fall short of deserving the love that God offers. The conclusion is a renewed commitment to give our lives to God—but now the motives are different and stronger. No longer is the reason for our good works our fear of God's wrath or our sense of duty. Instead we gladly serve because of the exuberance of life that God gives.

Whatever the problem in the tone of a service, the theological norm presented in this chapter can lead to transformation. God's love and justice are seriously portrayed. Human sin is straightforwardly acknowledged. The disarray of the world, partly because of human action, is recognized for what it is. Yet God's compensating actions are also portrayed and praised. God is called upon, urgently, to come to our aid, forgiving and renewing. New hope for the future is blown into life. The people who come to worship, numbed by contemporary life or unwilling to face its pain, are sensitized, braced, and healed. They leave worship alive, fully cognizant of life's difficulties, and ready to re-enter the world on the side of God.

They make this re-entry both as individuals and as members of a strong, vital community of faith, for as Paul says, "we, who are many, are one body in Christ, and individually we are members one of another" (Romans 12:5). In the places where we live—our homes, workstations, schools, recreational sites, places of human service—we become manifestations of Christ to the people we meet. What many of them will know of God's love and of the church's life is what they will encounter in us individually. We are always very much on our own to speak and act as Christ's alter egos in these places. Yet, we are never by ourselves, for the full life of the church goes with us. We can do what we do because we are always with others who have been called into being by the love of God that forgives, renews, and redirects.

The Organizing Principle for All Worship

If worship is always to be eucharistic in spirit, must it also use the celebration of the Lord's supper as the primary rite for Sunday worship and for other occasions when the congregation assembles in the presence of God? Or can the congregation's liturgical system as a whole be eucharistic even though other rituals are celebrated much of the time? To put the question another way: can the doctrinal core of eucharistic worship—God's saving work in Jesus Christ and our joyful response—be separated from the ritual with bread and wine, or do doctrine and ritual inescapably go together?

One answer to these questions is especially clear in the worship of the Roman Catholic Church. Every Sunday service is the celebration of the Mass (the Catholic Church's name for the eucharist), and weddings, funerals, holy days, and public religious events usually include the Mass. Indeed, so constant is this practice that a service without eucharist stands out as the exception requiring an explanation. So complete is the dominance of the eucharist in this church's pattern of praise that it has become the expectation of priests, members of religious orders, and the more devout among the people. For them daily celebrations of the Mass are the major element in their devotional life before God. Even in this church, however, additional forms of worship also are conducted. Especially prominent is the pattern of daily prayer based on the psalms that has been used in the monastic communities since their beginning in Egypt in the latter part of the third century. Most Roman Catholics, however, do not attend daily Mass, nor do they participate in the daily psalm services of the religious communities. Their devotional life varies widely, and rarely can it challenge the preeminence of the Mass in their church's worship.

A radically different answer is given by members of the Society of Friends who affirm that the purpose of the outward sacraments is most fully accomplished by a religion of inward centering upon God and the religious transformation of ordinary affairs of life. Thus every meal between "friends," eaten in thankfulness, is a celebration of our life in God. Ritual eucharists are unnecessary when every meal is the breaking of bread in remembrance of God's love bestowed on us in Jesus Christ.

Most churches stand between these two extremes. Some are much like the Roman Catholic side of the spectrum in that the eucharist is celebrated often, and hovers behind the scenes even on occasions that do not include an explicit celebration of the Lord's supper. It is common in these churches for one of the Sunday services—increasingly the principal service—to be the eucharist. In other liturgies, especially those for holy days and for weddings, the eucharist is often the framework for the congregation's worship. Other services are understood by ministers and many of the people of these churches to be auxiliary to the major element, which is the service in which the word of God is proclaimed in sermon and the people's thanksgiving over bread and wine is offered back to God. In these churches, the living center of their full liturgical system tends to be the experience of salvation in Jesus Christ. The other themes appropriate to Christian faith and life are seen as clearly subsidiary to the eucharistic center.

In other churches, however, the celebration of the eucharistic ritual has declined in prominence and the doctrinal and devotional core of eucharistic worship has diminished. Two tendencies can be seen in these churches. One is that congregations function as communities of ethical discourse and the other is that they become communities of pastoral care. Although both elements belong to the gathered life of churches, to make either one the central element leads to the decline of ecclesial strength.

The emphasis upon ethical reflection and action came into prominence with the rise of the social gospel movement in the late nineteenth century. The central message is the "kingdom of God and its righteousness," derived from Jesus' example and built upon a long tradition that faith in Jesus Christ leads to active witness in the world. Too often, however, this emphasis upon what Christians should do deteriorated into what James A. Smart long ago called "the suffocating fog of moralism." Here was an emphasis upon what we ought to do, with the clear implication that we are able to do it. This kind of message included an implicit doctrine of human progress in life and it minimized the seriousness of the sin that compromises the efforts of even the best intentioned people. As ethics and morality became the practical center of worship week after week, the foundation upon which the Christian life depends tended to disappear. Increasingly the life that people were exhorted to live no longer could be sustained, because it was finally a religion of duty and dependence upon self rather than a religion of gift-giving, built upon God's love for the world expressed in Jesus Christ.

The emphasis upon ethical instruction and exhortation has waned, but its place has been taken in many churches by the religion of pastoral care. Again, an important aspect of the Christian community is being expressed. People do find that faith in Christ leads to a life that is able to cope with all of the unsettling aspects of human existence; and in worship that care of God is manifested in ways that are tangible and sustaining. Yet, this emphasis easily leads worship to become therapeutic rather than doxological. That is to say, rather than focusing upon God's majesty and the radiance of God's love for the world and for us the worshipers, the therapeutic model focuses upon our needs and upon the resources that can help us meet those needs. As with the religion of moralism, the religion of therapy cuts us off from the source of health and healing, which for Christians is the action of God that helps us recognize our own responsibility for our plight and proclaims the good news that in Jesus Christ all things can become new.

Still other churches focus sharply upon the theology of salvation that I am calling eucharistic, but do so with worship that rarely celebrates the eucharistic sacrament itself. Their precedent, in part, is the preaching of apostles like Peter who led the people on Pentecost to accept God's salvation in Jesus Christ. Three thousand responded in faith to that day of gospel preaching; and although they were baptized, there is no evidence that they completed their day by celebrating the Lord's supper. That same chapter of Acts, however, does mention that "day by day…they…ate their food with glad and generous hearts, praising God and having the goodwill of all the people" (Acts 2:46–47a). Although this passage refers to a daily fellowship meal, the emphasis is upon breaking bread. The conclusion that many interpreters draw is that the passage refers specifically to the Lord's supper in its early form when it included a full meal. (See Bruce 1990, 132.)

A major distinction between mainline and evangelical churches can be seen at this point. In their adoption of ethical and therapeutic approaches to worship, and thereby losing the eucharistic center, the mainline churches have lost their religious power. By retaining the doctrinal center of the eucharistic tradition—that God is at work in Jesus Christ to save us from our sins—the evangelical churches continue to be in the power stream of the Christian faith.

Yet the experience of the mainline churches is instructive for many of the people who are attracted to evangelical alternatives. Services of the Word, even when they stay close to scripture, can lose the sharpness of focus upon God's saving work in Jesus Christ. What has happened to many Methodist, Presbyterian, and Congregational churches can also happen to Churches of God, Nazarene churches, and Baptist churches. Although they may phrase their ethical instruction somewhat differently, and offer pastoral care in a different mode, evangelical churches can also drift into moralism and therapy, to the loss of the saving faith in Jesus Christ. Furthermore, even doctrinal clarity may satisfy the mind without ministering to the embodied heart of the worshipers. Even though they may hear the message of salvation, worshipers may not experience it in such a way that their lives are transformed.

One of the primary values of the eucharist as ritual with bread and wine in contrast to eucharist as doctrine in the spoken word is that it is so resistent to change and interpretation. It is a ceremony rather than a speech. Its elements are prescribed and not easily changed. Its connection to Jesus' is strong; and its concentration upon the central features of Jesus' life is unflinching. No matter what the leaders of the service say, this ceremony ties them to certain events in which God revealed the purpose of creation and reaffirmed God's determination that this purpose will be fulfilled.

The eucharistic attitude is to be the generating nucleus; and for this to happen the eucharistic rite—the church's great thanksgiving—needs to be the primary form of worship for congregations.

Encouraging the Conversation

Again, I invite you to sum up this chapter in a sentence or two. Write it down somewhere. Then compare it with my summary that appears below. Do you find that you have read the same chapter that I think I wrote?

Here are further suggestions to encourage the conversation about worship that I hope you are conducting within yourself:

1. This chapter invites you to think about the entire set of celebrative actions that a church does—its regular worship services, its prayer meetings, baptisms, weddings, all of the rest.

- Make a list of the worship events in your church.
- Then think about what it is that makes them worship—rather than education or some other kind of appropriate church activity.

2. Think about these celebrative actions as a coordinated system.

- Can you discern an energizing center that holds them all together in one coordinated system?
- Is it the attitude of thankful praise as described in this chapter?
- Or does some other quality bind them together into one system?

3. Eucharistic worship, according to this chapter, combines the tragic story of life with confident hope because of God.

- What would you have to do in order for these ideas to mark worship in your church?
- What would be the impact upon your church and its members if the kind of worship described in this chapter were to be the normal practice?

My sentence is this: *Thankful praise generates the church's full cycle of celebrative actions and serves as the criterion by which we measure all that we do in worship.*

THE SERVICE OF WORD AND TABLE

Part Two is a new phase in this book. It offers a detailed exposition of the service of Word and Table that, as previous chapters have indicated, is the church's principal act of worship. These chapters are really the heart of the book for they show how the church's classic order of worship articulates the central themes of the Christian faith.

Chapters 4 and 5 are closely connected. One of them describes the shape of the service, the sequence of major actions that carry the church's harmony of praise. The other focuses upon public prayer, which is the most important *language* in any service.

Chapters 6 and 7 also are tied together. One gives a description of the *Service of the Word*, the first half of the Lord's supper; and the other describes the *Service of the Table*, which is the second half. Each of these chapters offers a theological and pastoral commentary upon the pattern of words and actions by which we present ourselves to God in worship.

This section of the book is climaxed by chapter 8 which, focuses directly upon the *Great Thanksgiving Prayer*. Here in a highly compressed set of words the church praises God for life and salvation; and worshipers offer themselves to God as their spiritual worship.

By this oft-repeated service of worship, the churches proclaim what they believe and invite worshipers into this faith. The celebration of the Lord's supper is the church's kindergarten, by which infants in the faith are brought to readiness to live for the God whom Jesus reveals. This liturgy is also the church's university in which older Christians are led to an ever-deepening sense of relationship with God and responsibility for the world.

4

The Shape
of the Liturgy

The eucharist, as Gregory Dix has made clear, is an *action* (for Jesus said do this), with a *meaning* given by Jesus himself (for the *recalling* of me). The action is performed by the shape of the service, the sequence of major parts, and the meaning is expressed in the eucharistic prayer (Dix 1945, 238). This way of describing a liturgy implies that the order of worship is important in its own right; and that importance needs to be accented. By focusing attention upon the order, we highlight the active character of liturgy; for despite the prominence of speaking, worship is primarily something that people do together. We *honor* God. We *read* and *listen* to God's word. They *intercede* for the world. Worshipers *bring* gifts, *pray* over them, *eat* and *drink* in communion with God and one another. Just as the list of characters in a drama presents them in the order of their appearance, so the order of worship arranges the actions in their proper sequence, with the result that the drama unfolds in its right order. Furthermore, the players—in this case the members of the congregation—know when to come in and take their places on stage. Order sustains the plot. Were it not for this ordering mechanism, worship would be a cluster of separate actions rather than a coherent process by which a group of worshipers moves toward the realization of its corporate identity.

Furthermore, the shape of the service—its order—is one of the primary modes of theological continuity in all the churches, over time, and around the world. Even though the language, gestures, and theologies of worship may differ, the persistence of form in worship provides a significant degree of unity among the churches. The order of worship conveys the implicit meaning of the rite, the meaning that is the foundation for all explicit expressions in words. If people continue to follow the same social procession of actions, they will be united to a significant degree even though there is much that differs in what they say and how they conduct their liturgies.

The Skeleton of the Service

"No matter what the denomination from which they come," John Kirby says of eucharistic liturgies published in the decade of the 1960s, these Catholic and Protestant liturgies "tend to have the same content, though the order may vary slightly and the particular stress of each order may be different." In general, Kirby continues, "they consist of two or three bible readings followed by a Sermon, a Confession of Faith, Intercessory Prayer in litany form, and then the Eucharist in four swift actions of taking, blessing, breaking, giving." He observes that this movement toward consensus is so far advanced that "it is sometimes difficult to tell from the worship to what denomination the worshipers belong" (Kirby 1969, Introduction, n.p.)

Since the 1960s, a significant group of newer eucharistic liturgies has been published in which this similarity of form is even clearer. One writer describes this unity in worship by saying "that what we have seen develop in recent years (at least as far as the Eucharist is concerned) is simply a single 'neo-Western rite' which happens to exist in a number of slightly different recensions" (Fenwick 1991, 45). One of the clearest examples of this "single" rite was published in the 1979 *Book of Common Prayer* of The Episcopal Church, although with a statement that this order is not intended for use at the principal Sunday or weekly celebration (*BCP* 1979, 400-01):

> The People and Priest
>> Gather in the Lord's Name
>> Proclaim and Respond to the Word of God
>> Pray for the World and the Church
>> Exchange the Peace
>> Prepare the Table
>> Make Eucharist
>> Break the Bread
>> Share the Gifts of God

Even with brief explanations under several of these lines, the outline is brief, direct, and clear. Its climax is the meal at Christ's table.

Another example is "The Basic Pattern of Worship" published by the United Methodist Church (*UMH* 1989, 2). Four divisions are listed in large type:

> Entrance
> Proclamation and Response
> Thanksgiving and Communion
> Sending Forth

The two middle divisions are more important and more extensive than the first and last. *Proclamation* consists of the opening of the scriptures through reading, preaching, and other forms of expression. *Responses to God's Word* include "acts of commitment and faith with offerings of concerns, prayers, gifts, and service for the world and for one another." *Thanksgiving and Communion* provide for eucharistic services and for services without communion. In services with communion "the actions of Jesus in the upper room are re-enacted:

> taking the bread and cup,
> giving thanks over the bread and cup,
> breaking the bread, and
> giving the bread and cup.

A similar outline is offered in contemporary Presbyterian liturgies. The Presbyterian Church in Canada offers a service with four major divisions (*Word and Sacraments* 1987, 20):

> Called to Worship
> The Word Proclaimed
> The Word Made Visible [or] An Offering of Thanksgiving
> The Dismissal

The third division is similar to the United Methodist pattern in that it shows how worship can always follow the pattern of the eucharist even on Sundays when communion is not presented. Every Sunday can follow the same pattern and regularly reach its climax in joyful remembrance of the reconciliation made available by God in Jesus Christ. *The Presbyterian Hymnal* (1990) presents an outline of the "Service for the Lord's Day" that includes four major divisions:

> Assemble in God's Name
> Proclaim God's Word
> Give Thanks to God
> Go in God's Name

The third division is presented in two forms, the full service of the eucharist and a prayer of thanksgiving concluding with the Lord's Prayer (*PH* 1990, 12).

What sense are we to make out of this similarity of form? Is it a case of imitation, one church copying another? Does tradition have a binding force that controls imagination and inhibits new developments (as Kirby implies in the essay referred to earlier)? Or is the similarity of form caused by something inherent in Christian worship? Are there theological reasons for the pattern of entrance, liturgy of the Word, liturgy of the Table, and dismissal? Each of these explanations can receive the answer "yes."

A serious form of mutual influence has certainly been at work.

Since scholars, writers of liturgies, and publishers meet frequently in an interlocking group of consortia and academies, they consult both formally and informally. This process of conversation and consultation does move toward ever greater similarity in the prayers, hymns, and liturgies that these people develop for their respective churches. This influence, however, should not be called imitation. Despite the compatibility of the several streams of development in our time, the individuality of the various churches continues. Even though the *Lutheran Book of Worship* was published in 1978 and the Episcopal *Book of Common Prayer* in 1979, these two books of traditionally liturgical American churches continue to be quite distinct from each other. There is no possibility of doubting which is Episcopal and which Lutheran.

This similarity in the shape of the liturgy runs deeper, however, than the contemporary process of collaboration can account for. The sequence of actions that is to be found in the new liturgies is the same structure that is to be found in the classic liturgies bequeathed us from antiquity. It can be seen in Justin Martyr's outline of Sunday worship in the second century. The ancient liturgies, such as St. Mark's in Egypt, have this same outline, although the devotional elaboration obscures the simple shape of the rite. In the West, the Roman Catholic Mass was built upon a simple and direct outline remarkably similar to those listed above. The liturgies in the Reformation churches continued this same pattern of things. This record of virtually unbroken continuity of the outline for Christian worship certainly has had a conserving effect upon each new generation.

The value of this liturgical continuity is that generation after generation of Christians is shaped by a similar symbolic system. The revelation of God in Jesus Christ, as witnessed by the apostolic generation, continues to be alive in every succeeding generation that participates in this liturgy of remembrance and expectation.

One weakness of this unchanging character of worship is that the central symbols may become so identified with a specific set of cultural forms that the symbols lose their power. Perhaps this failing has developed in European and American cultures. Another weakness can be seen when the Christian faith is introduced into cultures where it has not previously been known. Old ways of worship may not be supple enough to incorporate experiences that are radically different from those of earlier generations. So in African villages, as reported by E. E. Uzukwu, "the received (missionary) Christian body of rituals were ineffective symbols which, though repeated, manifestly did not carry life beyond themselves" (Uzukwu 1991, 105). In both cases, the challenge is for worship to do two things at once: to express the gospel in its universality and to ground it in the specific forms of human culture.

After making his negative critique of traditional Christian worship in Africa, Uzukwu makes his positive contribution to the subject of ritualization, and in so doing he provides the strongest reason possible for continuity of the shape of the liturgy. He affirms that in Africa as everywhere else "eating and drinking together are the most striking gestures of human communication" (Uzukwu 1991, 110). He then develops a line of thought that is crucial to this chapter, and to the book as a whole. In the eucharist "the produce of the land which nourishes humankind, while remaining what it is (terrestrial food), is given a supplementary value (as conventional sign)….The depth of the eucharistic mystery is such that the self-gift of the Christ to his church creates in the context of eating and drinking a relationship of mutual assimilation."

Reduced to its most elemental condition, the central act of Christian worship is a social meal, a gathering of friends to share food and drink. The structure of the ritual, as boldly outlined in the new liturgies, provides for the *coming together* of the guests at the banquet (the entrance rites), the *telling of the story* that binds them together (scripture, sermon, and prayerful response), and then the *sharing of the feast* (offertory, eucharistic prayer, and breaking bread together). When the banqueting is finished, all are *blessed and freed* to go their separate ways.

The conclusion to this discussion of unbroken sameness in the shape of the liturgy is that custom and conviction intertwine. The traditional order does its work efficiently and powerfully. It provides the social form by which God creates and recreates the church as body of Christ; and this same liturgy provides the church its most effective means of realizing and celebrating this life.

The Liturgy as the Story of Human Life

Families and other close-knit communities share more than food when they break bread together. As they eat and drink with one another, the people at table talk about their activities and the wider ranges of their lives. The sharing of food and drink becomes the occasion for the interpenetration of life outside and life inside the home and encourages communion among the members of the household. Similarly, the eucharistic meal is a dynamic process that connects life in the world and life in the intimate community of the church. This way of understanding the eucharistic liturgy can be outlined as follows on page 68.

The table talk at communion, the dramatic narrative unfolded around the table, consists of the interweaving of two subplots. The more prominent is God's story, which tells of the Holy One who called time and space into being, gave shape to heaven and earth, and filled

Part of the Liturgy   Godly Connection   Worldly Connection

Part of the Liturgy	Godly Connection	Worldly Connection
INTRODUCTION Praise Confession	Summons the people and sets the stage for the dramatic action /	
SCRIPTURE	Portrays God's character and work, and renews the commandments of God. \	
SERMON	Interprets this > Applies > Projects > Word of God.	
THE PEOPLE'S PRAYER	Intercedes < Gives thanks < Selects from < and submits. and complains. daily life. /	
OFFERING	Converts the broad range of ideas expressed in the prayers into a highly condensed action, namely the offering of our bodies as a living sacrifice. \	
GREAT THANKSGIVING PRAYER	This offering is united with Jesus' own offering of himself as suffering Savior who intercedes for us at God's side; all is presented to God in thankful praise, with the request that the Holy Spirit renew Christ's life and the power of the Spirit in us. \	
THE MEAL	God receives the offering; eats and drinks with the people, and they with God and one another. \	
CONCLUSION	> The people return to their lives in the world with clear ideas and renewed power.	

the world with everything animate and inanimate. This magnificent story proclaims God's watchful care over the beautiful creation, a care so constant and so connected to God's own self that every continuing moment of time and existence can be understood as the outpouring of God's own life. The disruptive events that complicate this story, providing its dramatic intensity, are acts of human sin. Beginning with the first man and woman who together constituted the image of God, the people of this world break away from the Holy One who gives and sustains their life. Their sin leads to the distorting of history and the derangement of the natural world, consequences that God could not and cannot tolerate and still stand for what is beautiful and just. The story continues by stating God's condemnation of sin and God's ceaseless efforts to call humanity back to their intended way of life.

The story reaches its high point in Jesus of Nazareth, whose life is fully identified both with God and with humankind. In this Jewish peasant, the varied strands of God's story are knit together. God's commitment to the moral order of the universe is portrayed and God's power over all that would destroy is demonstrated. The story reaches its climax with the reconciliation of all who have been alienated from one another, and especially with the restoration of relationships between God and humankind.

It is significant that this dramatic narration of God's story takes place at a banquet table. Indeed, God does give the world to be the means of communion with God and the source of enjoying God forever. The Garden was given for food; but sin began when the gift of food was misused. In ancient times, sacrificial meals were central in the ongoing relationship between God and the peoples, expressing both the basis of communion and the means of overcoming estrangement. Biblical portraits depict the final phase of God's story as the gathering of the peoples of the world to a great banquet in heaven with God as host.

The lesser story at the communion table belongs to the people who have gathered there. David Power makes this point when he states that "the composition of the eucharistic prayer is impossible without the effort that goes beyond the reading of the Scriptures to the active remembrance of a community. It draws the remembrance of Christ into its own story and submits its own story to the remembrance of Christ, in the confidence that this proclaims an abiding presence and an unfailing promise" (Senn 1987, 246). Although the details vary widely from one worshiping community to another, the main outline of this human story is very much the same. It is built around the four "common ventures" of life, as Elton Trueblood entitled them many years ago: birth, work, marriage, and death. Each of these activities is common to all humanity and happens to us in our individuality; yet each depends upon our life in community.

For all people, as individuals and in their communities, the life story takes the form of tragedy. Susanne Langer speaks of "the tragic rhythm" that marks all creatures who live in "the movement from life to death." She continues: "Unlike the simple metabolic process, the deathward advance of their individual lives has a series of stations that are not repeated; growth, maturity, decline. That is the tragic rhythm" (Langer 1953, 351). Even though societies continue on, generation after generation, individuals and the lesser institutions and communities within a society come to their death. All potentiality is ended; and the knowledge that such is inevitably our lot engages us in this tragic rhythm. This recognition of tragedy is consistent with the Christian doctrine of death and resurrection. Jesus' own life demonstrates how death ends all things. His resurrection shows that even this tragedy is now incorporated into the eternity beyond tragedy that is God's intention for all things. So Christians know that they must die and with their death all is finished. This tragedy does not destroy us, however, because we anticipate that we too will enter into that further reality in which death shall be no more.

Every artistic creation creates a form that imitates life and uses that form to reveal what life is like. Thus a tragic drama abstracts from the patterns of human life a characteristic human action, intensifies that pattern, and follows it to its completion, which is "the final relinquishment of power" (Langer 1953, 356). In similar fashion, the people who gather at the communion table tell the tragic story of their own life. We pick and choose the significant experiences, arrange them in order, and then offer them to God. In so doing, we unite ourselves to Jesus Christ who died because of the very sinfulness that gave rise to death. We also yield ourselves to the God who raised Jesus from the dead and sends the Holy Spirit to give comfort and hope.

The tragic story at a particular gathering for worship does not tell the human story in general; instead, it tells the version of the story that this particular people experience, remember, and seek to understand. Necessarily, the story includes lament against God and one's enemies and the confession of human frailty and sin. The culmination of the recital comes when all is offered to God in the conviction that nothing can "separate us from the love of God in Christ Jesus" (Romans 8:39).

The clear witness in scripture is that the ambiguity and injustice of human life continue. Try as we might to force God to explain why life is this way and to ameliorate our struggles, God does not explain. The one thing God does, however, is come near and in the strength of this Godly presence we grow strong and can leave the sanctuary to return to the world.

The variable parts of the liturgy, and especially the sermon and the congregational prayers, provide the fullest opportunity for telling the congregation's story. The details told in the variable parts of the liturgy provide an interpretive context for experiencing the parts that do not change. The same set of words in the eucharistic prayer will mean different things depending upon the contents of other parts of the service. Even so, it is possible for the eucharistic prayer itself

to become a specific part of the telling of the story. A powerful example is the prayer that David Power uses to illustrate his thesis.
The people ask, "How, O God, can we sing your song in an alien
land?" The presider continues:

> We are surrounded by death all day long.
> Our old leave this life without dignity,
> our sons and daughters have no dreams but those of
>   destruction,
> our children have no future.

Even the remembrance of Jesus Christ is colored by this somber
assessment of life in our time; and the salvation that God grants is a
salvation that overcomes the particular kind of distress that contemporary people experience (Senn 1987, 251).

Principles of Development

The plot line of a good story or drama can be stated in a few
sentences; but what makes the telling interesting is the detailed development of that compressed idea. So too with worship. The outlines described earlier are utilitarian and unadorned. The stories of
God and the worshipers that are told in worship can also be summed
up in a few sentences. Once in while, worship needs to be done in as
compressed a manner as possible. Most of the time, however, the
liturgical drama needs to be developed in considerable detail. The
adventures of God and the people have many variations and their
telling calls for the nuanced dramatic presentation. The model for
the eucharist, which is the church's family dinner, ought not be the
hurried snack before rushing out to the evening's activities but the
leisurely gathering at someone's birthday or on a holiday.

Services of worship can be direct or indirect and simple or elaborate. Directness refers to the logic of development. Does the service
move from beginning to its climax and conclusion in straightforward
manner, without deviation or wandering? Or does it follow a wind-
ing course, moving in and out, backwards and forwards, gradually
coming to its finale? Both kinds of development can be supported
on dramatic and psychological grounds. Furthermore, the history of
worship abounds with examples of services that are undeviating in
their linear development from beginning to end, and of services that
are much more complex in their internal logic.

Currently published liturgies, and this book too, give the clear
preference to directness. One reason to support this emphasis upon
linear development is that it keeps the liturgy focused upon its dominant elements. When the logic of the liturgy moves the congregation
unswervingly forward, the congregants are more likely to remem-

ber why they have gathered than when the action is confused. Furthermore, they can more easily tell when they have completed their purpose for coming together.

Direct movement also maintains a specific relationship between the parts. For example, when the sermon always precedes the bringing of gifts to the table, then it is clear that the sermon's purposes include preparing the people to do their part of the liturgy. If the sermon concludes the service, as it does in some liturgies, then it can no longer assist congregants to be ready to perform their functions in the service.

Again, directness in the sequence of actions encourages efficiency in the use of time. Like movies, dramatic performances, and athletic events, worship should take as long as it needs to. Even when each item in a service is interesting, however, the attention span of congregants begins to waver when they sense that the service isn't going any place. After a while, they grow weary of wandering even when the landscape is interesting.

Directness matches the predominant cultural characteristics of most worshipers today. Although they will enjoy a little diversionary movement in the liturgies of social process, the action needs to come quickly back onto the main track, or their interest will wane and their willingness to stay for the event will disappear.

Simplicity and elaborateness refer to a second characteristic of liturgy and other social processes. The outlines discussed earlier in this chapter illustrate the eucharistic liturgy in simple form. Each of its parts, however, can also be done in fuller and more detailed ways. An example is the reading from the Bible. One lesson can be read, with no introduction or congregational response. More elaborate ways of reading scripture result from increasing the number of passages read and surrounding the readings with devotional activities. A psalm or hymn can be sung sung between them. The Bible can be carried in procession before the readings and treated with signs of reverence or respect. Other devotional details can further adorn the reading of the Bible. The directness of the liturgy is not affected, but the rate of movement certainly is changed as the elaboration of the liturgy takes place.

There are several reasons why liturgy tends toward elaboration. The fullness of ceremony and text provides for the full expression of each action. The dominant parts of the liturgy are given settings that enhance their specific qualities. The added detail provides expressive materials so that the emotional color and mood of the service comes out more fully. The fuller detail provides the means for the people to participate—with hearts, voices, and bodies. Worship is the action of a group of people, and it takes time and effort to meld the individuals into a cohesive group that can act in concerted fashion. Again, the elaboration of the liturgy is part of the means for accomplishing this purpose.

The degree of elaboration is determined, in part, by cultural expectations and social patterns. In most Catholic churches today, sermons usually are not more than eight or nine minutes in length, whereas in some evangelical churches the norm would be thirty minutes or more. Most congregants in white mainline churches begin to fidget after an hour in worship, whereas in most black congregations services ordinarily last at least an hour and a half. In all of these illustrations, the variations in elaboration are determined more by cultural experience than by theological or liturgical principles.

Elaboration can take place for other, less desirable reasons. Just as it is easier to add items to household stock or books to a professional library than to take away from them, so it is easier to add new things to a service than to take away existing items. Thus the tendency is for worship to become more and more complex. One sees this tendency at work on special days like Easter. The regular parts of the service continue; but to them other special items are added. A service that ordinarily is reasonably simple can without one's notice become swollen.

A tendency to simplify the order of worship is evident in new books published by churches that have traditionally focused upon the eucharist. Services are less elaborate than they once were. In some other churches, where worship traditionally has been rather simple, the tendency is for liturgies to become more elaborate than they formerly were. Again, cultural factors are at work. Although people are ready to indulge in extended festivals on rare occasions, the tendency is to prefer events that get on to the business at hand rather quickly and more forward with little delay. For most of us, that is the way it needs to be with Sunday worship, including the celebration of the eucharist. The liturgy needs to be full enough that it can genuinely be called celebration. It needs to be spare enough that we can move through it with full attention and unflagging energies. The challenge to people who plan and lead worship is to establish that balance between simplicity and fullness of detail.

One final point needs to be made concerning the importance of the shape of the service. When the sequence of actions is right and strong, then creative imagination can go to work. The order of worship provides the support for artistic development. Consistency in structure and creativity in expression go hand in hand. One illustration of this fruitful relationship is the large number of musical settings of the Roman Catholic Mass. Because the text is stable, composers can work in the confidence that the music they compose can be used again and again. A second illustration is the proliferation of prayers and other liturgical materials that have developed around the three-year lectionary. As writers and publishers have become aware of a stable pattern for worship, which lectionary-based services are now providing, they have been encouraged to develop an ever-expanding body of material for pastors and musicians to use.

Encouraging the Conversation

By now you know that I place a high degree of importance upon the shape of the service. It makes a difference how the several parts are strung together. My suggestion is that you jot down your theology of the order of worship; and then that you summarize in a few lines what you take mine to be (see below). Of course, compare the two.

Other activities that could encourage the conversation include the following:

1. Outline the major actions in the service that is celebrated in your church most Sundays.

- Is it direct or rambling?
- Is it simple or elaborate?

2. Compare this outline with those described in this chapter.

- How are they different from each other?
- How are they alike?

3. Suppose that you could determine the order of worship in your church.

- What would that order be?
- Why would you arrange it that way?

4. Does your experience confirm or question the claim in this chapter that our life story takes the form of tragedy?

Instead of giving you a new sentence on my theology of the order of worship, I refer you back to the second paragraph of the chapter. I can't say it any more succinctly than this.

5

Praying
the Liturgy

Soon after the second Vatican Council, the phrase "praying the liturgy" began to be used. This idea—that the entire service of worship is a prayer that the church offers to God—came as a surprise to many Catholics and as mystification to many Protestants. Catholics had been accustomed to using their time at Mass as the occasion for doing personal devotions while the priest conducted the formal liturgy in a low voice in Latin. Protestants understood prayer to be the deliberate, verbal presentation of ideas to God; for them a worship service ordinarily included prayers, but to call the service itself a prayer hardly made sense.

Gradually, however, the idea is taking hold. The entire service of worship—the hymns, readings, prayers, and even the sermon—are addressed to God. These several parts of the liturgy are the melodic themes that became a grand chorus of praise, confession, and intercession raised up to the throne of God. The current reforms of worship, in most Catholic parishes and in a growing number of Protestant congregations, are changing Sunday worship from the time for personal devotions in the presence of others to the occasion for corporate, public prayer. While a service *includes* prayers, it is more important to remember that the service itself is a prayer, the means by which the people present themselves to their God.

For God's Sake and for the World

The theological issue underlying the discussion is this: for whose benefit is worship done? Are the words and actions of the liturgy done for God's enjoyment and benefit? Or are they done for the enjoyment and benefit of the congregation? If the service is pointed toward God, then the liturgy as a whole can be called prayer; but if

75

the service has as its primary purpose the instructing and inspiring of the congregation, then prayer is an inappropriate title for the event. Older expositions of worship used the terms *objective* and *subjective* for these two ways of understanding a service. Objective worship is done for God's sake; subjective worship is done for the people's sake. Although this distinction seems clear, these two intentions cannot be as neatly isolated in real life as they are in textbooks. Objectivity and subjectivity overlap, and this intertwining of qualities can be expressed in a metaphor: worship is an *open letter* addressed to God, but with the full expectation that the congregation will hear and respond to the message. The people are instructed and inspired by the very process of giving their heartfelt consent to the words and actions that the liturgy offers to God the Holy One. This double action is intensified in sacramental worship. Both baptism and the eucharist are actions in which the church offers God its prayer praise and worship. Yet these liturgies are also the arena of God's action upon the church. The bread and wine of holy communion, for example, convey the people's praises to God; but they also bring God's gift of the saving life of Christ to the congregation.

The emphasis upon worship for God's sake is based on the conviction that God enjoys companionship with the people who pray, much as parents enjoy companionship with their children. The picture presented in Genesis 3 shows God walking in the garden at the time of the evening breeze looking for someone to talk to. The communion sacrifices in Israel's history provided a continuing way for God and the people to continue their friendship despite the disruptions caused by sin. Indeed, the sacrifices are called "a pleasing odor to the Lord" some fifty times or more in the Old Testament and this metaphor stands behind another dozen passages in the New Testament. The psalms are filled with the language of communication of the people with God, with the primary emphasis upon the benefits for the people. Yet hints also appear of the benefits to God. "What profit is there in my death?" asks Psalm 30. "If I go down to the Pit, will the dust praise you? Will it tell of your faithfulness?" In Psalm 104, the singer proclaims:

I will sing to the LORD as long as I live;
    I will sing praise to my God while I have being. (verse 33)

The passage reaches its climax with this exclamation:

May my meditation be pleasing to him,
    for I rejoice in the LORD. (verse 34)

Scripture encourages us to believe that prayers influence the way that God acts. Jesus told his disciples: "Ask, and it will be given you; search, and you will find; knock, and the door will be opened for you" (Matthew 7:7). Luke prefaces this instruction with an illustration from life, of a friend who finally opened a door to a midnight caller not because of friendship but because of the caller's persistence (Luke 11:5–13). Scripture does not explain why prayer works, nor how God responds. It repeatedly affirms that God's way of participating in events of the external world is influenced by what we say in prayer. Prayer in public worship depends upon this same confidence, for without it these utterances would be empty and deceptive.

Prayer also affects the relationships between the people who pray, God, and the world of nature and history. In part, what is achieved is the direct and effective communication between those who pray and the One to whom they pray. As Romans 8 and Matthew 6 make clear, God knows our hearts even before we understand ourselves. Still we are to pray, for the relationship between us and God reaches its potential only when our inarticulate groans and secret desires are formed into the images and ideas that words command. As we become aware of ourselves, as we are pointed by our prayers toward God, both the strength and clarity of understanding between us and God are increased.

This communication between earth and heaven also leads to changed behavior on the part of the people who pray. Their own values are gradually altered, their attitudes reformed, their actions directed toward new purposes. Consequently, the structures of nature and history are affected as a direct result of God's influence, through prayer, upon people.

Prayers Within the Liturgy

Although the *liturgy* as a *whole* is prayer, the liturgy also consists of *prayers* that are the building blocks used to construct services of worship. These prayers function in three ways. Some are structurally *dominant*; others are part of the liturgical *dialogue* between the worshipers and God; and others express the *devotions* of the people.

Dominant Prayers

In each liturgy one or more prayers are dominant, *stating explicitly the meaning that is implicit throughout the liturgy*. Examples of this kind of prayer include the prayer over the water in baptism, the prayers of blessing in weddings, the committal prayer in the burial rite, and the eucharistic prayer in the Sunday service. In each of these prayers the people address God with words that sum up what the congregation intends the service as a whole to mean. These prayers are dominant in much the same way that some mountain peaks dominate the ranges in which they stand.

This very dominance creates high expectations for these prayers, whether they are prescribed in service books or developed by the leaders of worship. Their content, form, and style need to be consistent with the liturgy in which they are set. In order to do their proper work, for example, the prayers over bread and communion wine bring together the worshipers' remembrance of God's saving work in their lives, their faith that God will continue to work in their lives, and their joyful surrender to God. Communion prayers ask that the sacrifice of praise and thanksgiving brought by the church be received and blessed and that the church receive in return Christ's own life given for the world.

These expectations of the dominant prayers in a liturgy determine their contents. Because the churches are united in their main ideas about the gospel and about the importance of worship in the life of the people, then the churches are likely to intend to do the same things when their people come together to worship. Although the choice of words may vary widely, the main content of these several prayers will tend to stay very much the same. In these dominant prayers, leaders of worship are obligated to say what the churches want to have said. In fact, one reason why many churches prescribe the exact contents of prayers to be said is the conviction that these words, so important in the relations between the people and God, ought not be left to chance or to the spirituality of one person alone. Even in churches that authorize local leaders to develop the language of these prayers, that liberty does not allow them to move far from the core of theological meaning traditionally expressed in these prayers.

Dialogical Prayers

Prayers play a second function: *they are the congregation's part of the continuing dialogue with God.* To use another metaphor, they are impulses in the alternating current of worship. God speaks; the people answer. God speaks again; the people respond anew. This alternating current can be illustrated with prayers in the service of the Word. It is common practice to begin with what is often called a prayer for illumination. This prayer asks that God enlighten the minds and hearts of the worshipers that they can understand and respond to God's word as it is proclaimed. The psalm response that ordinarily follows the first reading continues the congregation's prayerful response to God who has spoken to them in the reading. Just as human conversation consists of the rapid interchange of sentences and paragraphs, but rarely of long soliloquies, so the churchly conversation with God uses brief declarations that express what the people want to tell God.

The churches have usually encouraged a wider range of ideas and language in these dialogical prayers than in dominant prayers.

These brief prayers can be shaped by the season of the year, the conditions at the time the service is conducted, the attitudes of congregation and leaders, and the prevailing ethos of the church. In some traditions these dialogue prayers can be extemporaneous even if dominant prayers ordinarily must be prayed according to the official texts.

Even with this freedom, however, dialogue prayers are also constrained by their place and function in the service. The conversation between God and the people is an orderly one. Adoration, confession, instruction come early in the service. They are followed by the identification of human needs in the life of the world, the renewal of salvation, and rededication to the work of God in the world.

In some liturgical traditions, certain of these dialogue prayers are assigned to the ordained minister who presides over the service as a whole. Thus, they are referred to as *presidential prayers*. In other liturgical traditions, these prayers are assigned to leaders of the service other than the presiding minister. The churches differ from one another concerning which prayers belong to the presiding minister and which can be said by others. Behind this idea stand two concerns. The first is that the worshiping congregation is a publicly constituted group of people rather than a collection of individuals. The corporate character of the assembly is illustrated and fostered by the presence and appropriate functioning of persons who preside. The second is the belief that some parts of this dialogue of prayer deal with such important aspects of the conversation with God that only the most fully certified leaders of the church should be entrusted with them.

Devotional Prayers

A third function of prayers in the service is that they can serve as the devotions of the worshipers, serving as *vehicles for expressing the religious life*. Persons come to the liturgy with various experiences of God and of life, and with various needs and strengths. They hope to bring these parts of life together in a patterned way. In short prayers, the partially perceived segments of experience are more fully comprehended and controlled. Examples include prayers of confession and the prayers of the people that often include the opportunity for impromptu participation by congregants.

If the dominant prayers are basically acts of the community as a whole, prayers of this third type are very close to being prayers of individuals. Therefore, these prayers use language that helps worshipers remember experiences and clarify ideas. Even though persons come to church ready to offer themselves to God in prayer, they rarely are clear concerning the elements from life that ought to become the content of their praying. The words of the public prayers are adequate for use in worship when they bring this transition from diffused readiness to focused attention. If all persons in the worshiping congregation are to be helped in this way, prayers have to be kept sufficiently general that all persons can recognize themselves in them; and yet be specific enough that the real life experiences come to mind as people pray.

Even though these public prayers grow out of immediate life experiences, language needs to be consistent with the occasion and with the dignity of persons in the congregation. Prayers offered when we are alone, or in the family, or with a small group of prayer partners permit complete candor before God because the relationship of trust among the people is present; and because this focus is intended to be individual and personal communion with God. In the Sunday congregation, however, a different set of guidelines exists. Public worship is performed by the congregation, which is the body of Christ, and these prayers are, first, the public honor of God, and secondly, the opening of the Christian's life to God and the world.

This thoughtfulness concerning public language is especially important when the words are put in the mouths of the worshipers. Leaders of a service know in advance what the liturgy says. They can select and edit their own language, and they have time to prepare themselves to speak the public words that the service gives them. The people of the congregation, however, have little of this control. They arrive at the church and are given the words they are to say. Often there is little time for them to review the liturgy, with the result that their first acquaintance with the text is when they say it in public worship. Worshipers deserve respect, which means that the texts given to them need to be phrased so that worshipers can speak them without violating their own sense of worth and integrity before God and one another. The people who prepare and lead worship sometimes use services as opportunities for consciousness raising. The objective is to shock congregants into awareness of God's will and the implications of that will for their lives. While this arousal of Christian conscience is a necessary part of the program of a church, prayers in the Sunday service of worship are not the appropriate time for this activity.

Naming God in Liturgical Prayer

A close and continuing relationship exists between the prayers that Christians offer, the beliefs we confess, and our experiences of God. Both in daily life and in worship, we experience the mystery of God's coming to us in steadfast, self-giving love. These epiphanies of the Divine inspire the hymns, sermons, and prayers of the worshipers; and they express the basic convictions of the churches. These liturgical expressions serve as vehicles by which assemblies of worshiping people bring together, organize, and project the fleeting episodes of their experiences with God. In this way the elusiveness of their religious life is overcome. The God who seems to live in the shadows comes out into the light. Thus, one way to discover how people experience God and what they believe about those experiences is to watch and listen to them as they pray. By their ideas expressed in words and actions during the liturgy, worshipers reveal their God, their self-understanding in relationship to God, and their convictions about what constitutes the good life. By their posture, gestures, and bodily style during worship, they demonstrate the seriousness of their relationship with the God whom these prayers address.

The theological focus of Christian worship is revealed in the traditional structure of public prayer.

- *Addressing God* — The classical form of liturgical prayer begins by addressing God. The names and descriptions used to address God show how the churches have experienced the Holy One.

- *Communing with God* — The body of liturgical prayer consists of blessings, laments, intercessions, and submissions to God's will, all of which manifest the churches' understanding of life lived in communion with God.

- *Concluding in the Name of Jesus* — The prayers are concluded in the name of Jesus Christ, often using formulas that sum up the dynamic relations between the persons of the triune God.

Thus, every full liturgical prayer text is a snapshot of the Christian faith. The very form of the these prayers can form the faith of those who pray them.

The Ancient Names of God

From the beginnings of the faith, several names for God have been prominently used in Christian prayer. One family of names was drawn by the earliest Israelites from the religious culture of ancient times. The name was *El*, which, like the English word *god*, served as a general word for divine being and as the proper name of one god in particular. The god *El*, known to Canaanites in the earliest period reported in the Old Testament, was "old and wise, a mild and merciful god," called "father of humankind" and "creator of all created beings" (Mettinger 1988, 67). Ordinarily in the Old Testament *El* is part of a compound name, suggesting that in their understanding and worship of this God the Israelites were both similar to and distinct from their Canaanite neighbors.

One of the compound names is *El Shaddai* (Exodus 6:2–3), usually translated *God Almighty*. Another compound form is used in phrases such as "the God of my father" (Genesis 31:5) and "the God of your ancestors" (Exodus 3:13). In his study of the divine names with an *El* component, Mettinger shows that these two ideas were closely linked and he then draws several conclusions. This divine name probably comes from a Babylonian word that means *mountain* rather than *powerful one*. A related idea appears in a second *El* compound, *El Elyon* (Genesis 14:18–22), that is ordinarily translated *God Most High*. The biblical expressions most often used with God known as *El Shaddai* refer to divine blessings. The God known as *El Shaddai* bestows that blessing to the family and its lineage through the generations (Mettinger 1988, 72).

It is especially interesting to note this emphasis upon the God of the ancestors. This God is related to persons rather than to places; and this relationship is close. Hebrew names like Eliezer use a form of God's name and suggest, says Mettinger, "that it was possible to speak of one's god as a close relative" (Mettinger 1988, 57). This understanding of God and the ancestors displays similarities with ideas that are widespread in the traditional religions of Africa and Native Americans. In these religious systems, the ancestors continue to be very much involved in the ongoing life of the community, and especially of members of their families. God, or the gods, are part of this spiritual reality that both transcends and interpenetrates this life.

God is the English word corresponding to *El*; and this ancient title continues to be prominent in Christian prayer. The contemporary collects published in the Episcopal *Book of Common Prayer* use *God* as the primary divine name some twenty-eight times. Sometimes the name stands by itself; and sometimes it is modified by a descriptive word or phrase such as *merciful*. In the prayers of the day in the *Lutheran Book of Worship*, *God* is the primary address some twenty-four times. *God Almighty*, still the favored translation of *El Shaddai*, is used in the collects of the *Book of Common Prayer* some thirty-two times and in prayers of the day in the *Lutheran Book of Worship* about thirty-three times. The *Book of Worship* of the United Church of Christ provides several sets of prayers (*BW* 1986, 476ff.) for use in worship. The name *God* is used some forty-four times and *God Almighty* appears nine times. In the United Church of Christ set of materials, no other title for God is used more than once. Many prayers modify God's name with descriptions of the divine character or activity, thus providing a strong sense of variety throughout this material. Nevertheless, the oldest and most general name for God continues to dominate these prayers that set the stage for the Sunday assembly.

A second set of titles in Christian prayer is drawn from a name that became the distinctive Hebrew way of referring to their God.

This name consists of four Hebrew letters that are very much like the English letters YHWH. In the Hebrew script of the Bible, only consonants are written, but it is assumed that with vowels inserted the consonants of the divine name could be spelled out as *Yahweh*. In the Old Testament this name appears some 6800 times. In most translations, however, readers are unaware of this name. The reason is that from well before the time of Jesus, devout Jews did not pronounce this name. They would use some other term such as *The Name* or *Heaven* to stand for YHWH. The most common of these substitutions was the Hebrew word *Adonay*, which means *Lord*. It has long been the custom in English translations to print this substitution for YHWH in capital letters. Thus, when the eye catches LORD, the Hebrew standing back of it is YHWH. This name was the one that God announced to Moses at the burning bush. Scholars continue to debate the origin of this name and its meaning. The conclusions continue to be that it is derived from the Hebrew verb *to be*, and it means something like "I shall be with you." (See Mettinger 1988, 42.) This name of God is sometimes rendered in English as *I Am*. Although this name may have been known earlier, it comes into prominence at the time of Moses and continues thereafter.

The YHWH-Lord tradition is part of the background of New Testament language concerning Jesus. He too is called *Lord*, and in a few instances Jesus calls himself *I Am*. The most prominent of these is recorded in John 7—9. In this period of his ministry, Jesus seems consciously to be describing himself with a term that Jews identified with their God YHWH. Therefore, the people took up stones to kill him for blasphemy.

YHWH is by far the most common divine name in the prayer literature of the book of Psalms. The Lord is also very much a part of the traditional language of Christian prayer, although with some ambiguity. It is not always clear whether the reference is to God, "the great I Am" (to use a phrase from the hymn "What Wondrous Love Is This"), or to Jesus Christ. In contemporary worship books, however, the frequency of this divine name is much less than for the two names already discussed. The contemporary collects of the *Book of Common Prayer* use *Lord* some fifteen times and *Lord God* once; while the *Lutheran Book of Worship* uses *Lord* seven times and *Lord God* eleven times. As a matter of policy, the UCC *Book of Worship* avoids gender specific language for God, and in keeping with this policy does not use the title *Lord*.

The third way that traditional Christian prayer has addressed God follows the example of Jesus. Here, the title *Father* is dominant. In conversation and teaching, Jesus frequently referred to "my Father." Consistent with this practice, he also addressed God as Father when he prayed. The long prayer presented in John 17 is an extended example of this practice. Other speakers or writers in the New Testament continue this identification of God as the Father of Jesus Christ. Thus, in introductions and conclusions to his epistles Paul refers to "the God and Father of our Lord Jesus Christ." (See Romans 15:6 and 2 Corinthians 1:3.) Jesus and the apostolic writers also identify God as the Father of the disciples and other believers. In one of his most tender statements to his followers, recorded in Matthew 6, Jesus assures them that "your heavenly Father" will forgive your sins and provide your food. Paul frequently refers to this same God, sometimes with the phrase "our God and Father" (as in 1 Thessalonians 1:3), sometimes with "God our Father" (2 Thessalonians 1:1). A third variation of phrasing refers to "the Father" without possessive pronoun. The effect is to use *Father* as a more abstract title for God. So Jesus says that "no one knows the Son except the Father," and that "no one knows the Father except the Son" (Matthew 11:27). Both in the Gospel of John and in epistles of John, this same construction is commonly used. "See what love the Father has given us..." (1 John 3:1).

Although much less common in the Old Testament than in the New, *Father* as a title for God does appear in earlier Jewish prayer material. *Father* is a term used for the covenantal God of Israel. An especially strong example of this usage is in Isaiah 63. In this passage of national lament, the preacher cries out, declaring that "you are our father" and therefore should not stand aloof. The passage reaches climax: "You, O LORD, are our father; our Redeemer from of old is your name" (Isaiah 63:16b).

It is no surprise that Christian prayer has included *Father* as one of the titles used in public prayer to address God. Despite the dominance of this title in the New Testament witness, however, *Father* did not become the dominant form of address in Christian prayer. In most liturgical traditions, and for most of the time since the church began, *Father* has been less widely used than *God Almighty* or *Lord* (YHWH). (One easily accessible illustration of this fact is *The Macmillan Book of Earliest Christian Prayers*, edited by F. Forrester Church and Terrence J. Mulry.) In modern liturgical books, *Father* continues to be less commonly used than other classical titles for God. For example, in the collects of the *Book of Common Prayer*, *Father* is used only seven times and in the Lutheran prayers of the day only four times. A collection of prayers from a church that stands outside of the collect tradition shows a similar distribution of titles for God. In a collection of 154 invocations, opening prayers, and collects published in 1953 for use by the Christian Church (Disciples of Christ), *Father* is the primary name for God in thirty-six of the prayers, only one fourth of the total. In many of these prayers *Father* is paired with a second title such as *Almighty God*, and in one of these prayers God is addressed as "eternal parent, our father-mother God" (Osborn 1953, # 318, 240).

In contrast to the prayer tradition described above, another practice has developed in some evangelical churches. Here, the most commonly used title for God is *Father*. It may be that prayer forms in these churches are directly influenced by the prominence of this title in the New Testament. Whatever factors moved the early church to give greater prominence to the other names of God seem not to be operating in these churches. Because it is common in churches, where public prayer is usually extemporaneous and impromptu to name God frequently in a prayer, the prominence of the title of *Father* is often overwhelming. So too in some of the pastoral materials developed in a Roman Catholic framework.

Naming God in the Eucharist

The ancient eucharistic prayers over the bread and wine show considerable variety in the titles used for God. Hippolytus (early 3rd century) begins with the wonderfully simple "We render thanks to you, O God, through your beloved child Jesus Christ" (Jasper and Cuming 1987, 35). Another ancient prayer, from the Liturgy of Saints Addai and Mari, uses *Lord* as the dominant name of God. From a similar background is a prayer called the Third Anaphora of St. Peter (Sharar). The initial salutation is to "God our Father, Lord of all" (Jasper and Cuming 1987, 46), but throughout the rest of the prayer *Lord* is the one name of God that is used. The Liturgy of St. Mark, however, uses a more complex salutation: "I AM, Master, Lord, God, Father Almighty" (Jasper and Cuming 1987, 59). In some ancient eucharistic prayers, *Father* is used in phrases that are connected with Jesus, as in the Egyptian anaphora of St. Basil: "Father of our Lord and God and Savior Jesus Christ…" (Jasper and Cuming 1987, 70). The Liturgy of St. James offers an elaborate prayer of praise addressed to "you, the creator of all creation, visible and invisible, [the treasure of eternal good things, the fountain of life and immortality, the God and Master of all]." Later the prayer addresses God as "King of the ages and [Lord and] Giver of all holiness," and then later "O God and Father" (Jasper and Cuming 1987, 91).

The ancient Eastern traditions reach their fullest expression in the Liturgy of St. John Chrysostom. The text of the prayer addresses God: "For you are God, ineffable, inconceivable, invisible, incomprehensible, existing always and in the same way, you and your only-begotten Son and Your Holy Spirit" (Jasper and Cuming 1987, 132). Later in the prayer *Lord* is used as another way of addressing God. In the concluding doxology, God is named "the Father, the Son, and the Holy Spirit."

In the Western tradition, however, another pattern became ordinary practice. In the traditional Mass of the Roman Rite, the priest begins the prayer by addressing God as "O Lord, holy Father, almighty eternal God" (Jasper and Cuming 1987, 163). Variations of this language continue in some of the liturgies of churches that came to life during the Reformation. An important example is the *Book of Common Prayer* of 1549 in which these same three titles of God appear. Similar language can be found in other traditional English language liturgies.

In modern liturgies a wide range of prayer language is used in the eucharistic prayer. In some of the texts, phrasing is similar to the threefold naming of God that is so common in the Western liturgical tradition. At the same time, other language is becoming common. Two modern Lutheran liturgies in Europe use phrases like "Lord of heaven and earth," and "Lord, our God, Ruler of all…" (Thurian and Wainwright 1983, 136-42). The title *Father* also is used, but at a later stage in the development of the prayer. A modern prayer from the Reformed Church of France is offered to "O God of love and holiness, our Creator and our Father" (152).

A modern Episcopal prayer speaks to "God of all power, Ruler of the Universe" (165). A prayer from India addresses God as "O Supreme Lord of the Universe" (189); and a prayer from the Church of Christ in Thailand is prayed to "Eternal God, Creator of the Universe" (197).

Striving to Be Faithful

This brief survey makes it clear that in eucharistic prayers God is addressed with considerable variety. The historic names of God appear, sometimes in their original simplicity, often intertwined with other titles and descriptions of the Divine. No one name of God predominates, even in this prayer that stands at the very center of Christian and churchly identity. *God* and *Lord* are more prominent than is *Father*; although *Father* is used more prominently in eucharistic prayers than in the briefer collects and prayers for the day.

Two factors account for this variety in the names of God. The first is the desire that liturgical language express the character of the liturgy in as adequate a way as possible. When God is being addressed and when the theme is gratitude for what God has done, then it is difficult to find the right language. The tendency, therefore, in these prayers is to use all of the names, adding in a few descriptive words and phrases. Elaboration comes in the effort to be expressive.

A second factor is the need for prayers to be theologically adequate. From early times the churches have debated the nature of God and the nature of Jesus Christ. The ecumenical councils and the classical creeds were among the outcomes of these debates. A careful reading of successive generations of eucharistic liturgies reveals a serious interest in the theological import of these prayers.

The trinitarian formula in the closing doxology may be one of these efforts to use the liturgy for purposes of indoctrination and discipline.

One reason for variety in the way that God is addressed is that no set of names or descriptions can express all of God; nor can any set of words, even the ecumenical creeds, guarantee that the God to whom we pray is the one true God of Israel and the new Israel. Thus we reach out with the names that help us be confident. Furthermore, we use these names in a framework that overcomes confusion or ambiguity.

There is a growing interest in the churches in finding a wider range of names and titles of God that are suitable for public prayer in the eucharistic liturgy. At this point, however, we encounter a basic question: what is the relationship between the Bible and liturgical language? With respect to the naming of God, are we bound by what the Bible tells us; or are we free to develop an every-widening range of names as our experiences with God continue to change? Even if the worshipers were to stay with biblical language in public prayer, the range of titles and descriptions of God is wider than most people use in their prayers. Thus an intermediate step for everyone is to consider the enrichment of their liturgical language by increasing their use of the names and descriptions of God found in the Bible.

In contrast, many people today believe that prayer language can move beyond the forms given in scripture. They cite the tradition of corporate prayer in the church's history to show that language influenced by specific cultures has been incorporated into liturgical prayer from ancient times. Thus, the argument continues, there is good precedent for the churches to continue seeking out new ways of addressing God.

When the door is opened for experience to suggest the language of prayer, then it is especially important that worshipers maintain the distinction between personal prayers and public prayer. Our personal language of friendship and intimacy is something to be shared only in the immediate circles of close relationship, but not in the more public aspects of life. So, too, with prayer. The ways we speak to God in the privacy of our devotions can be much more direct, intimate, and imaginative than the things we say to God when all the world is listening in.

The next paragraphs are written on the assumption that the language for public prayer does need to expand beyond the biblical and ancient traditions. One way to do this is to use *God* as the central name, but to enrich the descriptive phrasing. Although this way of naming God is deeply rooted in the churches' liturgical traditions, it is more actively used today in the brief prayers of the service than in the eucharistic prayers. Some of the most interesting and inviting of these descriptive terms are offered in lectionary collects published by Janet Morley (1988). Among her titles are these: *Hidden God; Vulnerable God; God of terror and joy; God our mystery; God our security* (Morley 1988, 12, 16, 19). In her eucharistic prayers, Morley moves in a different direction, using *Wisdom* as the central name for God. In each prayer, she augments the name with further descriptions of God's actions: "Eternal wisdom, source of our being, and goal of all our longing"; "O eternal Wisdom, we praise you and give you thanks because you emptied yourself of power and became foolishness for our sake"; "O Eternal Wisdom, we praise you and give you thanks, because the beauty of death could not contain you" (36, 38, 42). This language is highly expressive and thus points us to the mystery of the triune God. It draws upon the feminine imagery of Wisdom from the Old Testament, joining that to the self-emptying imagery of the Word-made-flesh of the New Testament. All of this is affirmed to be the direct activity of God in the world. This language is as provocative in its theology as it is expressive in its religious power.

Another approach to broadening the language used to speak to God is illustrated in *Kol Haneshamah*, the prayerbook of the Federation of Reconstructionist Congregations and Havurot (*Kol Haneshamah* 1989)]. The editors follow a pattern that is common in prayerbooks of Sephardic Jews. A shortened form of the divine name is used— Yah, the last syllable of "hallelu-Yah," a word which means "praise Yah." With each occurrence of Yah, the editors also present another name for God along with it. Earlier prayerbooks used "the thirteen attributes of God," but the editors of *Kol Haneshamah* have enlarged the list. A few verses from Psalm 29 illustrate this approach to prayer.

Give to YAH/THE ONE WHO IS, you so-called gods,
give to YAH/THE INDIVISIBLE glory and strength!
Give to YAH/THE UNSEEN ONE the glory of the divine
        Name,
worship YAH/THE ANCIENT OF DAYS with holy orna-
        ment.

Other names in this same psalm include: THE UNENDING, THE ONE WHO CALLS, THE REVEALED ONE, THE TRUTHFUL, ETERNAL LAW, THE ALL-KNOWING (*Kol Haneshamah* 1989, 44).

Still another approach is to use *Trinity* as a name for God. An ancient precedent is a text attributed to Patrick of Ireland (c. 372-466).

I bind unto myself today,
the strong name of the Trinity
by invocation of the same,
the Three in One and One in Three.

A modern set of general prayers uses a similar approach: "Blessed Trinity, One God, Source of our Salvation; Uncreated Trinity, Encountered through history, One God; O Splendid Majesty, Most noble Trinity, One God; O Blessed Trinity, One God, Host to all our sorrows" (Smallzried 1964, 8, 20, 26, 33). This way of naming God, however, obscures the distinction between Father, Son, and Holy Spirit that the doctrine of the Trinity has sought to maintain. It uses an abstract term to name God, and thus separates us from God during the act of prayer rather than leading us directly into the very life of God.

The churches currently are in an experimental mode, with the language of prayer as one of the places where experimentation is most active. Already the experience of Christians outside of the formal Sunday liturgy of the Lord's supper is coming into the new worship books. It is likely that as experience continues to grow, even more variety will emerge in the formal liturgies for celebrating the eucharist.

The Two Polarities of Liturgical Prayer

After God is named, liturgical prayers become the congregation's conversation with God. Therefore, the prayers express a wide range of sentiments from the congregants. Most aspects of human experience can be included in these prayers so long as they are phrased suitably and understood to be within the sphere of God's will for life in the world. These many kinds of experience can be organized around two sets of ideas.

The first polarity consists of *thankful praise and lament*, both of which are prominent elements in the psalter. "My heart is steadfast, O God," Psalm 108 begins. "I will sing and make melody." A reason is given for this glad exclamation, this praise of God: "For your steadfast love is higher than the heavens, and your faithfulness reaches to the clouds" (verse 4). Many of the psalms outline the ways in which the goodness of God is experienced. Several occur in Psalm 107. God turns parched land into springs of water, lets the hungry live, and gives the people a fruitful yield from their crops. God raises the needy from their distress and protects them from their enemies. Because God saves the people from their distress it is but right that they thank God for these wonderful works, offering God their thanksgiving sacrifices (Psalm 107:21–22).

The opposite pole to thankful praise is lament. Thus Psalm 109 begins with a cry of pain. "Do not be silent, O God of my praise." The reason for the outcry is this: "For wicked and deceitful mouths are opened against me, speaking against me with lying tongues." Elsewhere in the psalms other troubles are outlined, including: hunger, loneliness, despair, humiliation, defeat in battle, sickness, and death. Sometimes the language is unrestrained, as in the prayer by an afflicted person in Psalm 102: "Hear my prayer, O Lord; let my cry come to you.... .For my days pass away like smoke, and my bones burn like a furnace" (verses 1, 3). It is rare that we know any of the autobiographical detail that gives rise to these cries, yet the expressiveness of the language draws all readers into the depth of the pain. In every generation worshipers recognize their own experience in these laments.

The second set of poles in liturgical prayer are *confession and intercession*. In some ways, and especially in its tone, confession is parallel to lament. Each aspect of prayer acknowledges that things in life are not going well. Lament, however, is the prayer in the face of the many experiences that seem to fall upon people undeserved. In contrast, confession is the acknowledgment that what happens to us is deserved because of what we have done. The classic expression is Psalm 51:3–4:

> For I know my transgressions,
>   and my sin is ever before me.
> Against you, you alone, have I sinned,
>   and done what is evil in your sight,
> so that you are justified in your sentence
>   and blameless when you pass judgment.

Such a prayer moves quickly to intercession, first for forgiveness. "Create in me a clean heart, O God" (verse 10a). The climax is the petition: "Restore to me the joy of your salvation" (verse 12a). Intercessions are not limited to the restoration of oneself to companionship with God, although this theme is prominent throughout the book of Psalms. These psalms used as prayers often call upon God to make the fields produce their crops abundantly, for the political fortunes of the people to prosper, and for the people to enjoy long life. Psalm 144 provides an example: "May our sons in their youth be like plants full grown, our daughters like corner pillars, cut for the building of a palace." This same psalm continues: "May our barns be filled, with produce of every kind," and then the prayer refers explicitly to sheep increasing by thousands and tens of thousands and the cattle being heavy with young. "May there be no breach in the walls, no exile, and no cry of distress in our streets" (Psalm 144:12–14).

The mode of expression in these intercessions is closely akin to praise. The requests mentioned above are prefaced with these words: "I will sing a new song to you, O God" (verse 9a), and followed by this exclamation: "Happy are the people to whom such blessings fall; happy are the people whose God is the Lord" (verse 15). The confidence in God's response is so great that the intercessions overflow with the joy of the anticipated fulfillment. Forgiveness can be asked because God has forgiven and promises to forgive again. Life's basic needs can be requested because God is interested in human well-being, including such simple things as food and shelter, and assures the people that once again they shall receive all that they need.

These four dimensions of prayer indicate that the entire life of worshipers is lived within the surrounding presence of the eternal God. A contemporary prayer from Australia, modeled after Psalm 139, expresses this theological sense of life:

> Help us to look for you, and to find you,
>   in the life we live and the work we do.

> If we take a drive up into the distant ranges, you are there.
> If we tram our way into the milling crowds of our city's main
>   street,
>   you are there.

> If we ride the lift to the topmost floor of our tallest building,
>   even there shall your hand lead us
>   and your right hand hold us.

> If in the dead of night we feel deserted and depressed,
>   the darkness cannot hide us from you,
>   for all times and places are your habitation.

> You are God, and we are your people;
> so hear us, O Lord, as we pray for ourselves.
>   (Falla, 1981, 140-41)

In the Name of Jesus

From the apostolic era onward, Christian prayer has consistently been offered through Jesus Christ. Paul is one example. "I thank my God through Jesus Christ..." (Romans 1:8). After encouraging the Colossians in their preaching, praying, and singing, he concludes: "And whatever you do, in word or deed, do everything in the name of the Lord Jesus, giving thanks to God the Father through him" (Colossians 3:17). The writer of 1 Peter encourages the readers "to be a holy priesthood, to offer spiritual sacrifices acceptable to God through Jesus Christ" (1 Peter 2:5).

With few exceptions the full body of Christian public prayer thereafter has followed a similar pattern. The formularies have varied, from a simple "through Jesus Christ," to somewhat more elaborate forms such as "through our Lord and Savior Jesus Christ," to highly elaborated conclusions. One of the most common of these developed conclusions is trinitarian in form: through Jesus Christ your Son our Lord, who lives and reigns with you and the Holy Spirit, one God, now and for ever. Even prayers that explore new ways of addressing God conclude with a reference to Jesus, as does the following example from the UCC *Book of Worship*: "we praise and give thanks to you, Eternal Presence; through Jesus Christ we pray" (*BW* 1986, 112).

Lying back of this tradition are four intentions. The first is to affirm Christ's identification with God. Ordinarily liturgical prayer is not addressed to Jesus Christ; yet the godly character of Jesus has been part of the Christian perception of Jesus. By including Jesus in the conclusion to every prayer, this recognition of Jesus' transcendent character has been maintained. A second reason for the Christological conclusion to prayer is to be clear in identifying the God to whom the congregation is praying. The one addressed in Christian prayer is not a generic god, a friendly and creative presence somewhere, but rather the One God whom Jesus embodied, represented, and revealed. A third reason for the Christological conclusion is the Christian sense that it is presumptuous to pray in our own strength. "All have sinned and fall short of the glory of God" (Romans 3:23). Yet Jesus has come to re-establish peace between sinners and God. Because Christ intercedes for us, we dare to approach the throne of grace. In our own strength our prayers are weak; but when they are added to Christ's intercessions on behalf of the world, these prayers take on power.

This chapter has been written for occasions when worship is explicitly Christian. Therefore traditional Christian prayer forms have been described and recommended. On some occasions, however, these traditional forms need to be modified. Christians are sometimes invited to pray in settings that are interfaith or secular. In these settings it is appropriate that all prayers be rooted in the affirmations that are widely shared among the congregants. Because the doctrines and liturgical forms that are exclusive to each of the participating religions need to be minimized, Christians will not close their prayers in the name of Jesus.

In their own churches, however, when Christians gather to worship, it is right that they close their prayers in the name of Jesus Christ who, after all, is their way of being related to the One God.

Encouraging the Conversation

We don't know how to pray as we ought, says Paul (Romans 8:26), and the Spirit comes to link our hearts with the heart of God. Prayer, therefore, can be the unpremeditated pouring out of one's inner self to the Holy One. Yet, as this chapter elaborates, prayer is also a thoughtful presentation of a congregation's life and commitments to God. One way of considering these aspects of prayer is to note the differences between your personal prayers and the prayers that are offered in church on Sundays:

- How are they alike?
- How are they different?

Listen to the prayers that are offered in your church; or look back over the prayers you have offered in public.

- What names of God are used?
- What suggestions do you have for leaders of prayer?

One way to extend the range of your prayers is to choose a title for God that you currently do not use very much. Then think devotionally about the qualities of God and your relationship to God that these titles imply. Prepare prayers that express these ideas; and use these prayers as part of your devotional life.

6

Service
of the Word

The first half of the eucharist is often called "the service of the Word" because it features the proclaiming of *the biblical words from God* so as to reveal *the Word of God made flesh*. This part of Christian worship is rooted in the regular service of the synagogue, which was one of the most important elements of Jewish life for Jesus, the twelve disciples, and the earliest Christian communities. Worship in the synagogue combined the praise of God with devout and systematic study of the law and the prophets. This devotional use of the scriptures grounded the people in their religious tradition and taught them to love God and neighbor with heart, soul, mind, and strength.

From the beginning the churches linked their modified synagogue liturgy to their eucharistic remembrance of Jesus Christ, with the result that the service of the Word came to be understood as preparation for their distinctive sacrifice of praise. By the second century other liturgical acts, such as baptism and ordination, could occasionally take the place of the standard service of the Word. Even on such occasions, however, the sacred writings were read and interpreted, and all of the activity was surrounded by a rich tapestry of prayer.

Since the sixteenth century, Protestant churches have used services of the Word, without the eucharist, as full acts of worship and as the pattern of the liturgy for ordinary Sundays. The majority of their members experience these Word-based services as the standard rather than the eucharist-based services that have been the norm throughout the longer history of the church and across the widest spectrum of its life. The purpose of this book, however, is to describe worship that is shaped by the earlier and more universal tradition in which the service of the Word is bound to the celebration of the Lord's supper. Each aspect of worship reaches its full potential when Word and Sacrament are conducted as the two acts of one drama of thankful praise.

Whether linked to the service of the Table or free standing, the service of the Word usually consists of four segments. The *entrance rite* combines adoration and humility, the two natural attitudes of worshipers toward God. The *reading of the Bible* anchors the service in the historic record of God's self-revelation and describes the ways that Judaism and Christianity took shape in the light of this revelation. The *proclamation*, which usually takes the form of a sermon, shows how God continues to act in ways consistent with divine actions of long ago. The proclamation prepares the people of the congregation to do their part of the liturgy that takes place around the table. The *response to the Word* completes the first half of the service. It may include congregational affirmations and ceremonies of commitment. Sometimes the initial elements of "the service of the Table," such as the offering, become part of the response to the Word. These four segments are tied together and surrounded by hymns, psalms, anthems, and instrumental selections that energize the spoken texts and enliven the ceremonial actions of worship.

On most Sundays, this fourfold service of the Word is conducted in the sequence described above. On these occasions, the sermon is the dominant element, and the service is usually keyed to the Christian calendar. In our time, as in the ancient church, a different liturgy may be used as the first part of the eucharist. An especially good example is the baptismal liturgy. When conducted with fullness, baptism includes its own entrance rite and reading of scripture. The sermon, however, may be abridged so that there is time for the full baptismal liturgy, and the seasonal emphasis may be modified in order to lift up the meanings associated with baptism or the other special liturgy of the day. When this special liturgy is finished, the service continues with the regular eucharistic liturgy at the offertory.

The Word as Paradigm

Our understanding of the service of the Word is increased when we remember the paradigmatic way that "the Word of God" has functioned since Luther and the beginning of the Protestant Reformation. The early reformers did more than recover preaching as a major component in worship. They seized upon "the Word of God" as the central metaphor of God's work, self-disclosure, continuing presence, and authority. "Word" thus took on much of the meaning that previously was distributed throughout the sacramental and ecclesial system of the Catholic Church. This broad use of the Word included God's speaking in creation and through the prophets. The reformers were well aware of the prominence of the Word in the

Gospel of John (especially in chapter 1) and the way that the Word was identified with Jesus. Word was also used to refer explicitly to the Bible and preaching, two liturgical events that consisted primarily of words.

In the Catholic Church at the time of the Reformation, the primary mode of participation in worship was through the eyes. Worshipers could hear very little, but there was much to see. Buildings were ornate, the liturgy itself was ceremonially graphic, and the body and blood of Christ were visually present in the transubstantiated elements lifted high for the people to behold. In contrast, the reformers developed worship in which participation was through the ears. In some of the Protestant churches serious efforts were taken to eliminate most visual symbolism in churches, with the result that aural dimensions of the liturgy were made even more important. This emphasis upon hearing seems to have been culturally appropriate because many of the people responded powerfully to the liturgies that featured preaching and singing. In these Protestant churches services based on hearing the Word increased while services based on seeing the Body of Christ diminished in importance in the normal churchgoing of many people.

Three problems developed in this Protestant emphasis upon Word. Like all other metaphors, Word can be given greater value than it deserves. No matter how powerful, each metaphor conveys only part of the wider reality that it summons to mind; and even that part which is conveyed comes with distortion. Second, powerful metaphors like Word tend to obscure other effective metaphors. Thus, as Word increased, metaphors such as Body of Christ tended to decrease. The result was an unnecessary and unfortunate diminishing of the foundation for religious experience in Protestant churches. Third, the metaphor *Word* tended to be understood as *words*. Thus the biblical text itself and sermons were ascribed a revelatory power that rightfully belongs only to the Word in its more generalized sense. Furthermore, those who spoke these words, especially in sermons, tended to escalate the value of their words. When cast into sermons, human words suffered a kind of transubstantiation. Protestants found themselves moving toward idolatrous use of one metaphor much as they accused Catholics of doing with another symbol.

Currently, this Protestant distortion of the Word of God is being corrected. In many churches that previously had given so high a priority to the Word, words are now considered less trustworthy than once was the case. Protestants are coming to understand that they need more than words in order to experience the Word of God.

A second correction is occurring within Catholic theology and liturgy. Beginning with Vatican II, official statements affirm that Christ's real presence is given to the church not only in consecrated bread and wine, but also in the liturgy as a whole, and in the reading of scripture and the preaching of sermons. Catholic teaching continues to give highest value to Christ's presence in the eucharist; yet the recognition of presence elsewhere in the liturgy and the increased emphasis upon liturgical preaching mean that Catholics are now describing the Word in ways that the early reformers would have found congenial.

A third development is that cultural life may once again be moving away from the aural and toward the visual as the primary mode of participation in worship. This aspect of our time, as Nathan Mitchell presents it (Mitchell 1982, 383-89), has important implications for worship. It is commonplace to note the preeminence of television and film in contemporary life. Both as art and as media of communication, these visual patterns predominate over radio and print media. Thus liturgies that depend upon hearing are contrary to the general tendency of our time; and liturgies that depend upon seeing are becoming important once again. The matter can be taken one more step. It can be argued that visual communication is even more fundamental to ordinary human behavior than is aural communication—that seeing and being seen is more crucial to identity than hearing and being heard. If this assessment is correct, then to continue insisting upon the Word as the primary form of worship moves against the modes of experience and understanding that mark the people of our time. By recovering a more visual liturgy Protestant churches can recover a way of worship that is responsive to currently dominant aspects of human psychology.

The Service of the Word in Detail

The Entrance Rite

The beginning of any social drama—including services of worship—influences much of what happens thereafter. The beginning ceremonies identify the participants and determine their roles; they also project the meaning and mood of what will follow. Therefore, the beginning of a ritual needs to be planned carefully and conducted skillfully.

Churches start their celebrations of the eucharistic services of the Word in several ways. On festive Sundays and holy days, the liturgy begins with extended music and ceremony, indicating the dramatic nature of the occasion. In other services, especially on week days, the eucharistic liturgy is brief, with little music at the beginning. In some churches, it is common for the people to prepare for worship by a song service in which they are gathered into a community of common purpose and praise. Even with these variations, the purposes for liturgical entrance rites are few in number. (1) The entrance

rite brings the people together and constitutes them as a congregation. (2) The entrance rite declares the theological foundation for what
is being done. (3) The entrance rite is the congregation's first addressing of God in the service. These three functions can be accomplished
by several combinations of words and actions, as well as by music
and other forms of artistic expression. What is important is that those
who prepare and lead the entrance rite understand its purposes and
arrange the liturgical elements accordingly.

The congregation is constituted, in part, by the sheer fact that the
people come together at one time and in one place. As they gather,
they may acknowledge one another's presence by gestures such as
shaking hands and words of greeting. The forming of the worshiping congregation, however, requires more than this coming together
in one place. Even though they are in the same room with others,
people may continue to be isolated from those around them. The
people in a service of worship can be a collection of individuals, each
intent upon his or her relationship with God, rather than a unified
group of people bound together by a single purpose.

The assembled people take an important step in their movement
toward becoming a congregation when leaders assume their various
roles. Leadership focuses the attention, energies, and actions of a
crowd; and this is so whether leaders are formally designated or arise
spontaneously from the group. These leaders may be understood by
several analogies: as presiding officer over a meeting, as host at a
dinner, as master of ceremonies, or as parent in the family. In each of
these models, the leader helps the group to function by organizing,
inviting, challenging, instructing, and harmonizing. Without leaders, it is virtually impossible for a group of people to act as a unified
body; with leaders, their life together comes into focus and becomes
effective.

In most services, the first leader to become identified is a musi-
cian who plays piano, organ, or other instrument. This music announces that the service is beginning and suggests the mood of what
is to follow. It is common practice for other leaders of the service to
enter the worship room in a deliberate manner. Sometimes they move
directly to the liturgical center from a nearby entrance. They may
walk down the aisle through the congregation to their respective
places. They may move as a procession during the opening music of
the service. When a group of singers is formed into a choir, this group
ordinarily joins the procession. Even the congregation may be invited to join in the joyful march around and through the church, as
though they were a band of Hebrew pilgrims singing a psalm of as-
cent as they approached the House of the Lord on Mount Zion (See
Psalms 120—134.) The movement of the people is a clear sign that
this event is participatory rather than a spectator sport; and it helps

to generate within them the readiness to do their parts of the service fully and energetically.

The first words spoken in a service also contribute to the formation of the congregation. Usually these words are spoken by one of the designated leaders of the service. It is right that these opening words address God, honoring God and invoking the divine name upon all that follows. An example is this beginning to the holy eucharist published by the Episcopal Church:

Celebrant: Blessed be the one, holy, and living God.

People: Glory to God for ever and ever.

This same source provides other examples, including:

Celebrant: Holy God,
              Holy and Mighty,
              Holy Immortal One,

People: Have mercy upon us.
              (*Commentary on Prayer Book Studies 30,* 1989, 59, 60).

Sometimes the congregation is addressed at the beginning of the service, with the strong encouragement that they join in worshipping God. One example is this salutation taken from 2 Peter 1:2:

Grace and peace be yours in abundance
in the knowledge of God and of Jesus our Lord.

Some worship leaders use a "pre-worship" time of greeting, instruction, rehearsal, and warm-up in order to get the congregation ready to participate in the liturgy that is soon to begin. The tendency is for leaders to talk too much, especially during informal (and often unplanned) times of preparation. Thus, if this kind of introduction is used, it should be planned with great care and managed in a highly disciplined way. If well done, such periods can tone up the congregation so that it is poised, ready to go, when the service begins. If not well done, these periods of pre-worship distract attention from God and give the impression that worship is a casual affair. The result is that the casual introduction limits the possibility of a powerful beginning of a dramatic engagement with God.

In some traditions the opening words include a text spoken responsively by leader and congregation. These longer texts are usually keyed to the season of the church year or to another theme that is being featured in the service. In all of these beginnings, the leader and people are clearly identified and begin their participation in the service. Together leaders and people declare the theological foundation of the words and ceremonies that follow.

The entrance rite usually includes congregational singing, most often in the form of a hymn. In some liturgies, this hymn serves primarily as the music to accompany the procession of leaders into the service and as a means of uniting the people; but does not contain a text that is essential to the service. After the leaders have taken their places, a shorter text is recited or sung.

The two most widely used are "Lord, Have Mercy" and "Glory to the Father" ("Gloria Patri"). The "Gloria Patri" is one of the few brief acclamations known by heart in Protestant churches, and therefore it continues to be widely used, usually in an archaic translation ("Glory be to the Father, and to the Son, and to the Holy Ghost") and sung to one or the other of two musical settings. The practice of having the congregation sing a brief acclamation of praise is good, but the limited range of texts and tunes needs to be expanded. One source is the final stanzas of hymns, which often summarize the praise of God that has been expressed in the hymn. An example is the final stanza to the well-known hymn "Come, Thou Almighty King."

> To thee, One in Three
> eternal praises be, hence evermore!
> Thy majesty may we in glory see,
> and to eternity love and adore.

Other texts that can be used at this point in worship are built around the ancient word of praise, "Alleluia!" This text is simple; and the musical settings range widely from soft popular religious music to medieval chant.

In other liturgies, however, the hymn is an important element of the service, serving as the major mode of praising God. Usually, the hymn of praise addresses God, the first person of the Trinity, but occasionally the hymns address Jesus Christ or the Holy Spirit. One group of hymns that have been especially prominent at this point in the liturgy are trinitarian in form. The first stanza of one of these hymns begins "Come, thou almighty King, help us thy name to sing." The second stanza continues with "Come, thou incarnate Word...our prayer attend." Stanza three is parallel: "Come, holy Comforter, thy sacred witness bear." The concluding stanza, as mentioned earlier, ties it all together: "To thee, great One in Three, eternal praises be, hence evermore."

The natural companion of praise in the opening segment of worship is penitence. The people who acknowledge God and the moral excellency of the Holy One of Israel quickly become aware of their own sinful lack of moral excellency. With the prophet long ago (Isaiah 6:1–9), they recognize themselves to be people of unclean lips and lost. Some liturgies express this quality with a plea for mercy so ancient that its original Greek text continues to be widely used:

> Kyrie eleison (Lord, have mercy upon us).
> Christe eleison (Christ, have mercy upon us).
> Kyrie eleison (Lord, have mercy upon us).

Another way of expressing penitence is with a prayer in which the congregation confesses its sin, understood both as the sins of the individual congregants and as the sinfulness of the congregation as a whole. This prayer may be prefaced with the request by the leader that the people join in this prayer, and it is usually followed with a brief declaration of the gospel promise that in Jesus Christ our sins are forgiven.

In some services the confession of sins is part of the movement from the Word to the Table. This was the placement given it by Thomas Cranmer when he introduced English into the Latin Mass of sixteenth-century England. It continues in this position because worshipers find themselves aware of their need to confess after hearing the Word of God; and only after this confession do they feel themselves ready to move closer to the Table where God's forgiving grace is manifested so clearly and persuasively.

Most entrance rites include a brief prayer at this point that sums up what has already taken place, forms the conclusion to the entrance rite itself, and sets the stage for the reading of the Bible.

> O God, prepare the soil of our hearts
> so that as your Word is sown
> through reading and preaching
> it may take root, mature,
> and come to harvest in the life of the world.
> Through Jesus Christ, the sower of the seed.
> Amen. (*Thankful Praise* 1987, 35)

Entrance rites vary widely and express differing ideas about the congregation in relation to its leaders, about the congregation in its relation to God, and about the nature and function of worship. Despite these differences in content and understanding, entrance rites perform similar functions: they constitute the assembly, declare the central themes of worship, and begin the process of coming into God's presence. (For further reading see Finn and Schellman 1990, 53-92, and Bartow 1988, 55-66).

Reading the Word of God

Although most churches agree that some portion of the Bible ought to be read in worship, questions soon come into the picture. How much of the Bible should be read? How should portions be selected? How can the devotional quality of this part of the service be increased? What is the relationship between reading from the Bible and preaching?

Some liturgical traditions answer the question about the relationship between the readings and preaching by stating that the public reading of the Bible should always be accompanied by preaching about the text that has been read. Seventeenth-century Puritan writers, whose ideas continue to influence many American churches, referred to scripture lessons without preaching as the "dumb reading" of the Bible; and they opposed the practice. Their own way of doing things was to read aloud the brief portion of scripture that would be "opened" in the sermon. The selection of texts for preaching was done systematically by most of the preachers, and ordinarily included moving week by week through books of the Bible so that over time extensive portions of the scripture were expounded to the congregation in the framework of worship.

This approach to reading and preaching, which is referred to as the *lectio continua* (continuous reading), continues to be recommended by some scholars in the field of worship and preaching. In the final chapter of a book on the history of worship in the Reformed tradition, one of these writers reminds readers that *lectio continua* was practiced in the church of New Testament times and in following generations, and that it was recovered in the pastoral practice by leaders of the sixteenth-century Reformation. He then concludes that "nothing could have a more salutary effect on preaching than the regular systematic preaching through one book of the Bible after another." He mentions briefly that such preaching has to be done "in a sensitive way, with a recognition of the capacity of the congregation," and then notes that "after several years of using the *lectio continua* the congregation will discover itself to have learned an amazing amount of Scripture" (Old 1984, 172).

Another way of connecting the reading of scripture and preaching is for preachers to decide what they are going to preach on and then to select a text that goes with it. Whereas the use of the *lectio continua* means that the biblical text itself helps to determine what will be read and influences the contents and forms of sermons, this second method means that nearly the entire responsibility for selecting passages for reading and preaching rests upon the preachers. Although many pastors exercise this responsibility with great care, the practice is so easily abused that the wisdom of such a way of relating scripture and sermon needs to be questioned.

Another approach to the relationship of reading and preaching holds that the Bible has its own place in the order of worship irrespective of the sermon for the day. Consequently, decisions about which portions of the Bible to read are made according to principles inherent either in scripture itself or in the liturgy. Most churches that hold to the Bible's independence in worship use a table of readings called a lectionary in order to select passages of scripture to be read each Sunday; and this table is often referred to as *lectio selecta*. This practice is rooted in ancient Jewish customs and developed in the early church. (A full description of this background is found in Werner 1959, 50-127; see also Interpretation 31 1977.) For centuries the lectionaries used in Roman Catholic, Lutheran, and Anglican churches provided two readings for each Sunday and holy day. One of these readings was from a Gospel and the other was taken from another part of the New Testament. These tables provided readings for one year and were repeated year after year. The result was that a very limited selection of the Bible was read in the congregation's hearing. Because preaching was usually linked to the readings in this table, the impact upon preaching was also significant. Preachers tended to focus upon a small portion of the Bible in selecting the themes for their sermons.

During the 1950s churches began processes that would lead to new worship books. One of their goals was to revise their lectionaries, and several projects were under development. The most extensive of these processes was an international effort of the Roman Catholic Church that resulted in a three-year table of readings for celebrations of the Mass on Sundays and major festivals. As scholars in other churches became aware of the scope of the Catholic program, they concluded that this new three-year lectionary could become the foundation for work in other churches, too. As a result Episcopal, Lutheran, and Presbyterian commissions set aside their own lectionaries in preparation, adopted the Roman Catholic three-year lectionary in general, and made adaptations that would fit that table to their own calendar and liturgical principles.

Much of the conversation that led to these decisions took place during the 1960s in meetings of the Commission on Worship of the Consultation on Church Union. Consequently, the impact of these discussions of the lectionary soon spread to other Protestant churches. Later, the Consultation on Church Union published its own consensus variation of this lectionary. By the later 1960s one or another variation of this three-year lectionary had been adopted in North America by Anglican, Lutheran, Presbyterian, Methodist, Disciples, United Church of Christ, and United Church of Canada commissions. Further development of the three-year lectionary on behalf of these churches was undertaken by the Consultation on Common Texts, an ecumenical consortium of North American churches. Its work in a revised form is published under the title *The Revised Common Lectionary* (1992).

In any of its variants, the three-year lectionary provides three readings for each Sunday service of worship. The climactic lesson comes from one of the Four Gospels. In Cycle A (the first of the three years), most of these readings are taken from Matthew, generally following the development of that book. In Cycle B, the readings are drawn from Mark, and in Cycle C from Luke. It is important to note that this *lectio selecta* exhibits characteristics of *lectio continua* discussed earlier in this chapter. (Cycle A begins with Advent in 1995, 1998, and 2001; Cycle B begins with Advent in 1996, 1999, and 2002; and Cycle C begins with Advent in 1997, 2000, and 2003.) Selections from John are interspersed throughout these three cycles, especially during the season following Easter. The middle reading is usually drawn from the epistles or other New Testament books. Again, the pattern is to read through each book, omitting portions of lesser usefulness for public reading. The first reading for each day is usually taken from the Old Testament. The original pattern of the three-year lectionary, followed by most of the later variations, is to select from throughout the Hebrew scriptures, choosing texts that in a thematic way connect with the gospel reading. One of the characteristics of *The Revised Common Lectionary* is that an alternative pattern for Old Testament readings during the summer has been offered in which narrative sections of Old Testament materials are read in course. During Cycle A attention is given to Abraham and Moses, during Cycle B to David, and during Cycle C to the prophets.

Some churches require that the lectionary be followed strictly, with all three readings being read. These same traditions are likely to require that the liturgical reading begin and end exactly as each selection is cited in the lectionary. Other liturgical traditions allow pastors and local assemblies to determine how many readings to include; and to exercise their own judgment concerning the length of the readings. Despite these variations in usage, churches in North America are now more united in their liturgical use of the Bible than they have ever been before.

The lectionary is organized around the church's traditional calendar of holy days and seasons, with the high points at Christmas and Easter. Even so, many of the readings have little explicit connection to the events and themes of the Sundays of the year. Furthermore, the doctrinal or thematic connection between the three readings in each day's list may be slight. They stand side by side, each one providing a glimpse into the mystery of God's self-revelation.

These sets of readings for a service can often add up to thirty or more Bible verses, a quantity that challenges the ability of modern congregations to hear and understand. Partly to help congregants listen and understand, and partly to highlight the importance of the readings, fully developed liturgies surround the readings with a set of devotions—brief prayers, songs, and ceremonies—that highlight the importance of these readings from the sacred writings of the faith. The prayer for illumination has already been mentioned. A hymn stanza, such as the familiar text by William How, can be used in a similar way:

O Word of God incarnate, O Wisdom from on high,
O Truth unchanged, unchanging, O Light of our dark sky:

we praise you for the radiance that from the hallowed page,
a lantern to our footsteps, shines on from age to age.

Or this text by Tobias Clausnitzer, a seventeenth-century Christian:

Blessed Jesus, at thy word
we are gathered all to hear thee;
let our hearts and souls be stirred
now to seek and love and fear thee,
by thy teachings sweet and holy,
drawn from earth to love thee solely.

From ancient times, churches have used portions from the Psalter between the liturgical readings of scripture. This tradition is continued in the responsive readings, often from one of the psalms, that have been common practice in many churches. The Old Testament psalms, however, were intended to be sung rather than said; and recent hymnals and books of worship are developing ways for contemporary congregations to sing these texts rather than to say them. Some churches have developed brief verses for the congregation to sing, such as this text from the *Lutheran Book of Worship*:

Alleluia. Lord to whom shall we go?
You have the words of eternal life.
Alleluia. Alleluia.

The Proclamation

The solemn reading of the Bible is usually followed by a contemporary proclamation of the Word of God. The history of Christian worship has witnessed great variety in the form of this proclamation, from a brief comment on one of the texts to elaborate lectures on a theme suggested in one of them. In recent generations preaching has most often been associated with Protestant churches, but some of the great preachers of all time, including Chrysostom and Augustine in the ancient world, and Savonarola and John Henry Newman in later times, have worked in Catholic traditions.

Throughout the history of the churches, preaching has been one of the major forms of teaching the Bible, the Christian faith, and ethical principles for life. Many of the theological books that have shaped Christian faith and practice began as sermons in the Sunday assembly. Even in the framework of eucharistic worship, preaching has functioned this way. An especially interesting example is the New England Puritan preacher, Edward Taylor, who was pastor for a lifetime in a remote Massachusetts community. Twice during his long ministry, he developed extended series of sermons for use on communion Sundays, which in his congregation came about every six weeks. In these sermons, he developed a theology of Christ and redemption that is theologically persuasive and poetically powerful. Clearly, the eucharistic setting of these sermons was for him the incentive to increase the attention he gave to preaching (Taylor 1960 and 1962).

In addition to being a form of teaching, preaching is also a way of persuading the heart to believe the gospel. Ideas and feelings are both necessary if preaching is to accomplish its liturgical function. This dual criterion is as important on eucharistic Sundays as on any others.

The greater the emphasis upon the teaching function of the sermon, the greater is the tendency for sermons to stretch out in length. A contrary pressure, however, comes from our culture. People quickly become restless; which means that most preachers feel the need to "be brief about it," to use a phrase that became the title to a book on preaching short sermons (Young 1980). There is no easy resolution to this tension, and each preacher needs to find ways of reaching a satisfactory middle ground.

Whether short or long, sermons in the context of eucharistic worship are marked by three characteristics. First, *they are grounded in one of the scripture readings for the day*. Each of the readings presents some aspect of God's self-revelation and its implications for creation. Preachers identify that act of God and in their sermons bring it out clearly so that all can see it for themselves. In their sermons they also show how the God who acted that way long ago continues to act in our time.

The second characteristic of preaching in communion services is that *it focuses upon the reconciled life with God made possible through Jesus Christ*. This characteristic narrows the range that would be possible if only the first characteristic were observed. Many of the themes in scripture are appropriate as the basis of serious Christian teaching, including the teaching that takes place in sermons. When done within celebrations of the Lord's supper, however, every theme needs to present the new life that comes to congregants from God through Jesus Christ.

The third characteristic of preaching in eucharistic services is that *it prepares congregants to do their part of the liturgy*. Already, the congregation itself has been participating in the liturgy, by singing hymns, joining in prayers, and being attentive to all that is happening. Following the sermon, however, their participation becomes more extensive, reaching its culmination as they offer their sacrifice of praise and thanksgiving and then eat and drink together in the communion meal. It can be assumed that congregants come to the service intending to do their part and generally ready to do it. The sermon, however, renews their understanding of who God is and who they, the people, are. The sermon proclaims God's promises, thus re-establishing their motives for acting, and declares God's expectations, thus teaching them how they are to live.

Every liturgical sermon should prepare the congregation for its proper action in the service, whether that action be praying, making an offering, or performing other ceremonies of commitment. When the intended participation is in the eucharist, then the sermon needs to end in ways that lead easily to the sacramental culmination of worship. This sharp focus in the conclusion of sermons makes it possible for the sermon as a whole to range broadly over the territory of Christian thought and life. On most occasions, preaching in eucharistic worship does not need to emphasize eucharistic doctrine, but can offer the full counsel of God, showing how all of the promises and commandments reach their completion in the life, death, and glorification of Jesus Christ. (An especially useful treatment of liturgical preaching is *Week In — Week Out: A New Look at Liturgical Preaching*, by David E. Babin 1976.)

This combination of wide range and sharp focus is also present in the calendar that is used with increasing fullness by Catholic and Protestant churches. "The whole church year," says Odo Casel, is "a single mystery...which is brought to us each Sunday." He develops this idea by saying that "the redemption, which reaches its height in the sacrifice of the Cross and the glory of the church which goes from that resurrection, are mystically carried out and brought to the faithful." Even though the calendar expresses one idea, that idea is expressed with great variety. Unity does not mean uniformity, says Casel, for "the more single an idea is, the deeper it is and the more powerfully it fills the mind: so the fullness of its conception seeks an outlet in a variety of rites" (Casel 1962, 68, 69).

Illustrations of this combination of unity and variety can be found in the two major events in the calendar—Christmas and Easter. In each of these seasons, God's complete identification with Jesus Christ is the dominant idea; and God's desire that we be reconciled to God's own self is the central message. Yet these two festivals highlight different aspects of this mystery. The one focuses upon incarnation—God with us; and the other focuses upon reconciliation—God for us. Similarly, other days in the year proclaim other facets of the full mystery. Each day brings us fully into the mystery of God's self-disclosure while at the same time highlighting but part of it.

The doctrinal and ethical range is especially wide during the long season following Pentecost and Trinity Sundays. The calendar itself makes few demands upon those who plan worship and preach sermons. Even so, the liturgical expectation is the same, that the theme for the day always be articulated so that it leads the congregation to its proper action around the holy table.

The three-year lectionary is now widely used as the foundation for preaching, but two problems with its use need to be mentioned. Some sermons give the impression of being a few quick comments on one of the scripture readings for the day. These sermons may have the advantage of being brief, and often they highlight one aspect of the scriptural text nicely. Unfortunately, they also give the impression of being superficial and casual. It is not clear that these homilies adequately take advantage of the opportunity to teach the Christian faith. A thoroughly prepared homily can be a wonderfully strong liturgical element, but preachers too easily offer their brief homilies without that kind of thorough, informed preparation.

A second problem is that some preachers try to address all three readings in their sermons. Each reading is given a thumbnail exposition; and then the preacher tries to show how the three are thematically related. Rarely does the effort succeed. The thematic possibilities are greater if the Old Testament and Gospel lessons are dealt with than if the epistle is included since a typological connection between the first and third readings was one of the guiding principles in the formation of the three-year lectionary. Even so, preachers will ordinarily work with one of the lections each week in developing their sermons.

The Congregation's Response

The final segment of the Service of the Word is the Response of the People, and it often includes the reciting of one of the historic creeds, extending the invitation to discipleship, and offering the prayers of the people. Together, these liturgical actions complete the proclamation of the Word of God and prepare the way for the actions that take place around the communion table. These liturgical actions usually include music. Some of the texts are sung, and the participation of the congregation may take place by their singing a hymn. Instrumental music is often used in this portion of the service.

The statement of faith most often recited in celebrations of the eucharist was developed in the ecumenical councils of the fourth and fifth centuries. It is ordinarily referred to as the Nicene Creed. This way of summarizing the Christian faith was introduced into the eucharist as part of the church's doctrinal struggles to define Christ's nature. In Africa and Asia, the first version of this creed was used by Monophysite leaders (in the late fifth and early sixth centuries) to express their commitment to the theological decisions made at the Council of Nicea (325 C.E.) and their opposition to the modifications made later at the Council of Chalcedon (451 C.E.). In Europe, the later version of the creed was introduced into the eucharist late in the sixth century as Arian Christians accepted the orthodox Catholic faith. Finally, in 1014 Pope Benedict VIII made the creed part of the Roman Rite on Sundays and major feast days (Shepherd 1950,

70-72). Whereas the reciting of the Christian faith in creedal form is one of the basic elements of the baptismal liturgy, the use of one of the creeds is part of festive elaboration rather than basic to the structure of the eucharist. Instead, the declaration of faith that is basic to the eucharist is the Great Thanksgiving prayer itself.

Some contemporary worship books suggest modern statements of faith. From *A New Zealand Prayer Book: He Karakia Mihinare o Aotearoa* comes this affirmation:

You, O God, are supreme and holy.
You create our world and give us life.
Your purpose overarches everything we do.
You have always been with us.
You are God.
You, O God, are infinitely generous,
good beyond all measure.
You came to us before we came to you.
You have revealed and proved your love for us in Jesus Christ,
who lived and died and rose again.
You are with us now.
You are God.
You, O God, are Holy Spirit.
You empower us to be your gospel in the world.
You reconcile and heal; you overcome death.
You are God. We worship you. (*NZBW* 1989, 481)

When recited in the eucharist, the Nicene Creed or other affirmation of faith honors God by describing what God has done for the salvation of the world. It calls upon the congregants to renew their baptismal vows to Jesus Christ and thus display their religious identity. Since the fourth century, Christians in every time and place have been united by the faith that the creed articulates; and its inclusion in the eucharist has been understood as a testimony to that unity.

The invitation to discipleship is a contemporary expression of a recognition that has been part of the church's life from the beginning. A worshiping congregation contains confessed, baptized Christians and others who have not yet responded fully to the gospel's call. In some periods of time and some traditions, the people who are only beginners in the journey to faith are dismissed from the service at this point. In other traditions, seekers are invited to respond to the gospel call, confess faith in Jesus Christ, and prepare for baptism. The invitation does just what the title of this segment implies: following the example of Peter on Pentecost (Acts 2), the pastor urges hearers to repent of their sins, confess their faith in Jesus Christ, and be baptized for the remission of their sins. Usually a hymn will be sung to provide the framework for the invitation and response.

The prayers of the people are also part of the response to the Word of God. Whether offered by one person on behalf of the congregation, offered in a litany or responsive form, or spoken spontaneously by congregants, these prayers are rooted in daily life. By means of these prayers, the people themselves come before God and thereby their world is sanctified.

One of the most important liturgical changes in recent decades has been at this point in the service, and the reason for the change has been to increase the sense of participation by the people themselves. The longstanding custom was for this prayer to be offered by the pastor. In Lutheran and Episcopal Churches, the text was prescribed in the worship book and was the same week after week. In other Protestant churches, the pastor ordinarily offered this prayer, in his or her own words. Some pastors prayed extemporaneously and others wrote out their texts. Whichever method they used, however, each week the prayer was different. Many times these prayers—which often were called the pastoral prayer—were in touch with the grace of God, events in the world, and the pastoral needs of the congregation. They were delivered with reverence and brought the congregation into the presence of God. Unfortunately, these prayers could also be devoid of these qualities; and this part of the service would be empty. Whether weak or strong, however, this prayer became the pastor's offering rather than the people's.

In all kinds of churches the people now participate directly in this part of the service. In many congregations they are invited to speak out their joys and concerns, which then are gathered into prayer by the prayer leader. In other congregations, congregants are invited to the front to stand with the pastor during the prayers, thus physically indicating their solidarity with the words that are being spoken. In many congregations a more formal pattern is used which includes invitations to pray on specific themes, followed by silence for personal prayers, and concluded with a brief prayer by the leader. In most congregations these prayers are spoken, but some use musical responses. Whatever the pattern, the intention is to open up this part of worship to the congregants themselves.

Most Protestant congregations still conduct services of the Word without the eucharist on most Sundays of the year. In such liturgies the prayers of the people are the culmination of the service. Even in these liturgies, however, thankful praise for Jesus Christ can be the concluding celebration. Every time the liturgy is celebrated, a paragraph remembering Jesus Christ can be included at this point in the service. Specific references to bread and wine and explicitly eucharistic topics would not be used in these prayers, but Jesus would be remembered, his teachings would be called to mind, and the renewal of his presence would be invoked.

An Alternative Form for the Service of the Word

The service of the Word described in this chapter is a logical sequence of singing, reading, preaching, and praying. In many churches these elements are arranged in a straightforward pattern that moves in a rationalized way from beginning to end. Everything is done "decently and in order," to borrow Paul's phrase (1 Corinthians 14:40). Many worshipers, especially those with Protestant backgrounds, are accustomed to a different system of connecting the several parts of worship. This pattern begins with a song service that intersperses hymns and spiritual songs with brief prayers, and then moves to the offering, reading the scripture text and delivering the sermon, and concluding with the invitation to Christian discipleship. This traditional order of worship can also serve as an alternative form for the service of the Word in preparation for the celebration of the Lord's supper. In some places and with certain communities, it is to be preferred to the patterns usually reported in the published liturgies. For many worshipers this traditional form conveys the feelings of informality, immediacy, and emotional intensity that are important to worship and which they may not experience in the more formal pattern assumed throughout this book.

If such a service of the Word is to be used as the beginning of the eucharistic celebration, leaders of the service, and especially the preacher, need to understand that this modified form of popular Protestant worship is to prepare the people to meet Christ at the communion table. The song service and prayer could remain much the same as they have traditionally been. For reasons that will become evident in the next chapter, the offering would be moved to the second half of the service. The sermon would need to include gathering at the table as an intended outcome along with the confession of faith in preparation for baptism and church membership. The participatory spirit of the popular Protestant service invites the prayers of the people to be done in a free style following the sermon. Congregants could be encouraged to participate vocally.

Then would come the movement toward the communion service, which could be conducted in ways that are consistent with the informal service of the Word that has just been described. The criterion for eucharistic services of the Word is that they prepare people to praise God as they gather in Jesus' name around the table of remembrance.

The Recovery of the Bible in the Church

When the liturgy of the Word of God is strong, one of the most important needs of the churches today will be ministered to. As individuals and collectively as the church, Christians need a foundation for belief and ethical decision making. In every generation Christians face the danger of being "tossed to and fro and blown about by every wind of doctrine." What we need is a source of authority for "speaking the truth in love" and growing up every way into Christ (Ephesians 4:14–15). Throughout all of the history of the churches, the Bible has been this foundation. Because this collection of sacred writings is accepted as a faithful communication from God, trustworthy and understandable, Christians study its contents, expound its teachings, and live in ways that are faithful to what they discover in their interaction with scripture.

One of the impacts of modern scientific and historical thought is that many Christians approach the Bible differently from ways that were common prior to the early 1900s. For much of Christian history biblical authority was based on three assumptions: that God is the immediate author of the Bible, that the Bible's current form is essentially identical with its original form, and that it is internally consistent. Today many Christians base their understanding of the Bible's authority on different assumptions that can be suggested by an analogy. The Bible is like a stained-glass window, with glass of varying colors and thicknesses. The same sun shines through all of the glass, but the character of the transmitted light depends upon the glass through which it passes. Similarly, the word of God shines through all of the writers of scripture, but this word is affected by the qualities of each writer. The conclusion is that the Bible, like other ancient books, shows evidences of development and varieties of conviction that are similar to what scholars find in other ancient literature. Thus, it is much more difficult now to use the Bible as the unambiguous and persuasive basis for faith and life.

The use of the Bible in worship, as described in this chapter, provides a way to move past this impediment. In worship the Bible's primary function is to evoke the recognition that God is present and that God's will is to be reckoned with. Furthermore, the Bible helps worshipers grasp how people long ago understood the divine will and its implications in human life. Then comes the sermon in which a thoughtful leader of the church connects these historical understandings with contemporary circumstances. These connections are partly the result of intuition, partly of logical correspondences between the ancient world and the modern. This combination of ritual reading and homiletical proclamation appeals both to the mind and heart of worshipers. It re-establishes their primary connection to God and thus energizes the secondary processes of thinking about the faith and developing strategies for life.

In order for the liturgy of the Word to function effectively, pastors need to give renewed attention to their labors as students and expositors of scripture, and they need to read and preach with ritual and rhetorical power. Intelligent, devout zeal is the personal quality that should mark leaders of the service of the Word of God.

Encouraging the Conversation

If I were to ask you which part of the Sunday service means the most to you, what would you answer? Are you one of the great host of people whose answer is the sermon? Then it is probably the case that for you the "word" is the root metaphor for worship. If you answered the prayers, "word" may still be the organizing principle of your theology of worship.

If, however, you answer music, then you are moving away from "word" to some other metaphor. Even more is this the case if you said that the Lord's supper is the most important part of the service for you. Here words diminish in importance and another form of religious experience is the basis of your theology of worship.

Now that you've had time to think about it, which is the metaphor? Is it "word?" Or is it sacrament?

Some other questions to encourage the conversation:

1. How important is the spoken word in contemporary culture? What impact does the entertainment industry of our time have upon worship?

2. In your church, who decides which scripture to read and how much to read? What is the relationship between these scriptures and the sermon? How does the practice in your church compare with the lectionary method described in this chapter?

7

Service
of the Table

Just as the service of the Word consists of four segments, so the service of the Table has four actions: offertory, thanksgiving prayer, the breaking of bread, and communion. Three of these—bringing gifts, breaking bread, and eating together—are actions in which physical participation, with all the people fully involved, is more important than the words spoken. These three actions are the focus of this chapter. Embedded in these things done is something said, *the great thanksgiving prayer*, which is a complex formula by which the meanings implicit in the actions are made explicit by the congregation's solemn proclamation to God. This major prayer of the liturgy will be the topic of the chapter following.

The Offering

Reduced to its basic form, the offering is the simple action of setting the table for the eucharistic meal. Congregants place upon the table the bread and wine. This preparation of the table can be accomplished in a strictly utilitarian manner, doing nothing more than setting the table with whatever is needed to conduct the meal ceremonies. The table could be set with as little ceremony as is used to unlock the doors of the church or turn up the thermostat before the service starts; and in some churches, the table is prepared beforehand in just this way. Churches that use trays of individual cups are most likely to set the table in this manner. The physical act of bringing the filled trays forward in a ceremonial way may seem too complicated for public worship. In most liturgies, however, the preparation of the table is part of the public action of worship, performed with the deliberate care that indicates that the meaning is greater than meets the eye. Those who prepare the table invest themselves

114

in their action. Even when they do nothing more than place the bread and wine of communion upon the table, congregants present "heart and mind, possessions" to God in thanksgiving for all that God has given them.

This offering of self is even clearer when the offering takes on the more complex form that is normal in most liturgies. Ordinarily the liturgical offertory consists of three parts: the prayers of the people, money given to the church, and the bread and communion wine to be used in the eucharist. These three things are the elements that the people use to present themselves to God.

The prayers of the people are the bridge between the service of the Word and the service of the Table. They represent the people's response to the word that has been proclaimed, and they prepare for the meal of thanksgiving by bringing to God the daily life of the congregants and their church. The range of this life in the world is indicated by a list of concerns and causes for prayers at this point in the liturgy published in the *Book of Worship* of the United Church of Christ (*BW* 1986, 122f.):

> The church universal
> the nations and all in authority
> justice and peace in all the world
> the health of those who suffer
> the needs of families
> single people, and the lonely
> reconciliation with adversaries
> the local community and all other communities
> all who are oppressed or in prison.

Life itself, in all of its variety, is thus brought to God and offered in words before the throne of grace.

The second part of the offering consists of *gifts brought by the people*. In our time the gifts usually are money, but sometimes the people bring different kinds of commodities as their gifts, such as canned goods to be distributed to people in need. In most churches the collecting and bringing forward of money is the most conspicuous part of the offertory. Ordinarily a scriptural invitation or exhortation to give is stated and then deacons or stewards move through the congregation gathering the gifts. They bring these offerings forward, usually with the congregation standing and singing a brief hymn. A prayer over this offering may also be proclaimed.

It is interesting to note, however, that the several worship books describe this part of the service in significantly different ways. The instruction in *The Book of Alternative Services* of The Anglican Church of Canada says: "During the offertory a hymn, psalm, or anthem may be sung. Representatives of the people may present the gifts of bread and wine for the eucharist (with money and other gifts for the needs and responsibilities of the Church) to the deacon or celebrant before the altar" (*BAS* 1985, 240). In contrast the instruction provided in the *Book of Worship* of the United Church of Christ speaks first of the tithes and offerings and then suggests that the people "may express their dedication and thanksgiving to God through music, prayers, dance, and other acts." Even later, as the conclusion to the instruction, it says that "the communion elements may be brought to the table with the other gifts" (*BW* 1986, 43). The *Lutheran Book of Worship* speaks in ambiguous language, first stating that "the OFFERING is received as the Lord's table is prepared." It then refers to the presentation of the gifts, without stating what these gifts are. Following an offertory verse sung by the congregation and a unison offertory prayer, the instruction continues: "The ministers make ready the bread and wine" (*LBW* 1978, 88). Money gifts are not mentioned but they can be assumed, for in services "when there is no Communion," the instruction still says that "the OFFERING is received and may be presented at the altar" (*LBW* 1978, 96).

This variety in the liturgical instructions about money gifts reveals ambivalence within the churches concerning the theological and liturgical functions of money. Because money is needed for the support of the church and its ministries in the world, it has to be acquired by the church. Many church people, however, including many pastors, are embarrassed to ask for money, and this embarrassment is expressed by the way that money is underplayed in liturgical instructions. There are also theological problems with money as the form of the offering. Churches resist the idea that people can earn their salvation by their good works or that they can buy their way into God's good favor. When the offering has little intrinsic value (which is the case when the offering consists of prayers or the bread and wine), the danger of works righteousness is minimal. When the offering has intrinsic worth (as offerings of money do), then the danger of works righteousness increases. Another factor in the ambivalence is that money works well as symbol for the self-giving of the congregants. In this regard, cash is for most people a fuller sign of their lives than a little bread and wine brought from home. Yet, the more important symbolism in the eucharist is that which comes from the other direction—from God to the worshipers. Here the bread and wine, which present Christ's own life to the worshipers, is a much more explicit symbol than money could ever be.

In weekday celebrations of the eucharist and in eucharists at special occasions such as weddings, the offering of money is much less prominent than in the Sunday liturgies. The intercessions of the people will be offered, and the bread and wine will be placed upon the table, but offerings of money usually are not expected. However graphic money may be as a sign of the life of the worshipers, it fades from the liturgical offertory whenever the program and mission needs of the congregation are no longer dependent upon voluntary cash contributions.

The offertory also includes *the bread and wine to be used in this celebration of the eucharist*. In principle, they too express the life of the people and the congregation. Often, however, this sign function is obscured by the source of the elements and the way that the loaf and cup are brought to the table. Whereas the money offerings come from the people, the eucharistic bread and wine ordinarily are purchased commercially much as any other supplies, and thus they have little connection with anyone's life. A stronger practice is for congregants to bring the bread and wine, baking the bread, if possible. The ceremonial function of the eucharistic elements is increased if they are placed on a small table near the entrance to the worship room. As people pass by, they make some association with this particular bread and wine to be used in that eucharist. In some churches, the bread is in the form of small wafers and people expecting to receive bread during communion transfer a wafer from the storage container to the paten that will be carried forward during the offertory. During the offertory, these elements are brought through the congregation to the communion table, thus increasing even more the people's sense of identification with them.

The bringing of gifts to the table is primarily action, but it is common practice for the congregation to sing as the gifts are brought forward and for one of the leaders to offer a prayer. The verse most familiar to Protestants is Thomas Ken's hymn stanza sung to the tune OLD HUNDREDTH:

> Praise God from who all blessings flow;
> praise him all creatures here below;
> praise him above ye heavenly hosts;
> praise Father, Son, and Holy Ghost.

The strength of this text is that it states clearly the source of these gifts, namely the Triune God, thus undercutting the tendency for worshipers to think of themselves more highly than they ought to think. The primary liturgical limitation of this Doxology is that it does not point forward to the use of these gifts at the eucharistic table. It also depends upon exclusively masculine metaphors for God.

The fuller meaning of the offertory is expressed in a Lutheran liturgy as the people sing:

> Let the vineyards be fruitful, Lord,
> and fill to the brim our cup of blessing.
> Gather a harvest from the seeds that were sown,
> that we may be fed with the bread of life.

Gather the hopes and dreams of all;
unite them with the prayers we offer.
Grace our table with your presence,
and give us a foretaste of the feast to come.

A hymn from the American folk Protestant tradition also expresses the two-directional character of the offering:

We place upon your table, Lord,
the food of life, the bread and wine,
as symbols of our daily work,
according to your grand design.

Within these simple things there lie
the height and depth of human life:
our pain and tears, our thoughts and toils,
our hopes and fears, our joy and strife.

Accept them, Lord; they come from you;
we take them humbly from your hand.
These gifts of yours for higher use
we offer up as you command. (*Chalice Hymnal* #417)

It is common practice for a brief offertory prayer to be offered at this point in the liturgy. The texts provided in the *Lutheran Book of Worship* express in exact language the ideas about the offering that this chapter presents:

We offer with joy and thanksgiving what you have first given us—our selves, our time, and our possessions, signs of your gracious love. Receive them for the sake of him who offered himself for us, Jesus Christ our Lord. Amen. (*LBW* 1978, 108)

One of the strengths of this prayer is that it gives a hint of the content of the eucharistic prayer that will follow, but does not encroach upon the great prayer of thanksgiving.

The Roman Catholic Order for the Mass is distinctive in the way that it extends the prayer at the offering, thus stating the intention that later is said more fully in the eucharistic prayer. Even in this liturgy, however, the offertory prayers are distinct from the eucharistic prayer. The offertory prayers bless God for the bread and wine, stating that each element expresses God's goodness and that each has been given by earth or vine and made by human hands. After prayers over bread and wine the presiding minister continues:

Lord God, we ask you to receive us and be pleased with the sacrifice we offer you with humble and contrite hearts.

After ceremonies that express penitence, the congregation prays:

May the Lord accept the sacrifice at your hands for the praise and glory of his name, for our good, and the good of all his Church. (*Mass* 1975, 670)

This bold formulary states openly an idea that is hidden in most other offertory liturgies. These other liturgies use phrases such as bring an offering and present gifts. They are less likely to use the phrase offer gifts, and avoid language that calls the gifts a sacrifice made to God. These other liturgies do use more open language, including sacrifice, in the eucharistic prayer itself, but discussion of these ideas will be reserved for the next chapter, which analyzes the eucharistic prayer in detail.

Some churches conduct the offering in ways that dramatize its function as sign of the people's lives. Instead of having a few people collect the gifts and bring them forward, these congregations encourage the people to come forward with their gifts and place them in baskets at the communion table. When the space around the table is large enough, congregants are invited to stay close by so that their very location in the church intensifies the signification of coming forward with gifts. When the active character of bringing gifts is so strong, the need for explanatory words is lessened. Congregants can be invited to bring their thank offerings, and then their bodily involvement in the liturgy communicates in an elemental manner the meaning of what they do.

The Breaking of the Bread

After the table is prepared and the great thanksgiving prayer is offered (see chapter 8), the bread is broken for distribution in the eucharistic meal. In some churches the fraction, which is the term often used for the breaking of bread, is done this very way. Following the eucharistic prayer, the presiding minister takes up the single loaf of bread over which the prayer has been offered and breaks it. This loaf then is broken into even smaller pieces for worshipers to eat. In most churches, however, the fraction continues as a dramatic ceremony with a wafer large enough for the people to see even though the communion bread consists of small wafers given to the congregations individually. In some liturgies the fraction has ceased being a separate section of the liturgy and, under the title of "the manual acts," has been incorporated into the eucharistic prayer itself.

At its core, the breaking of the loaf, like the preparation of the table, is a utilitarian action. The fraction prepares the bread for distribution so that each congregant may partake. From very early times, however, this ceremony of hospitality has been given theological interpretations. Paul was first in the line with his teaching that *the church is one body even though it is made up of many members.* The proof he gives is that the congregation eats from one communion bread (1Corinthians 10:16–17). The form of his statement implies that a single loaf would have been used by the Corinthian congregations. The theological force of his statement, however, is that Jesus Christ is the bread, the one loaf, which worshipers eat and which makes them one. The clarity of his illustration is increased if the actual bread used in a celebration of the eucharist consists of a single loaf.

A second meaning has developed in the eucharistic faith of the churches: *that the fraction is a connection with Christ's sacrificial giving of himself for the world.* This meaning is stated in the instructions for "Breaking Bread and Pouring Wine" found in the *Book of Worship* of the United Church of Christ: "The bread is broken and the wine is poured as visible and audible reminders of the sacrificial self-giving of Jesus Christ. The actions call to mind the cost as well as the joy of Christian discipleship" (*BW* 1986, 72).

Quite early in the life of the churches, the use of a single loaf disappeared. Congregations quickly grew too large for all of the people to eat from one loaf. It may also have been the case, as Gregory Dix suggests (Dix 1945, 132), that the eucharistic bread and wine were taken from the offerings in kind brought by the people. In our time, most congregations are too large for one loaf to suffice, and the distribution to so many people is much easier when the bread comes as individual wafers. Even so, it is common practice for the presiding minister to break a larger wafer or a small loaf during the fraction, thus preserving the idea of one loaf even though the communion bread comes as individual pieces.

Although the fraction, like the offering, could be a wordless dramatic ceremony, the custom is for a brief text to be spoken or sung as the action is done. In some liturgies the text used is the narrative of the institution of the eucharist from 1 Corinthians or one of the Gospels. Ordinarily the liturgies following this practice do not include the words of institution within the text of the eucharistic prayer itself. In any case, this part of the service calls for a deliberate and full ceremony of breaking the bread and holding it up for all to see. The attention of all the people is thereby focused upon Christ's self-offering and his own words of interpretation. Even though people, and especially the children, may not understand the theology of salvation or of Christ's presence with the church in its sacramental life, they grasp something of its import during this dramatic part of the service.

Another text is an adaptation of Paul's language from 1 Corinthians 10. Again, the *Book of Worship* gives a good example. While the bread is being broken, the pastor says: "Through the broken bread we participate in the Body of Christ." After the pouring of the wine and lifting up of the cup, the pastor says: "Through the cup of blessing we participate in the new life Christ gives" (*BW* 1986, 72, 73). This simple combination of gesture and text is theologically strong and devotionally appealing. It quickly sets the stage for the communion meal that follows.

Similar to this pattern is a series of seasonal responsories provided by The Anglican Church of Canada. As an example, the following is provided for the Easter Season:

Celebrant: Lord, we died with you on the cross.

All: **Now we are raised to new life.**

Celebrant: We were buried in your tomb.

All: **Now we share in your resurrection.**

Celebrant: Live in us, that we may live in you. (*BAS* 1985, 213)

A more highly developed pattern for the fraction, found in the current Roman Catholic order for the Mass, offers a deliberate approach to communion. At the conclusion of the great thanksgiving prayer, the extending of the peace of Christ and the breaking of the bread are connected together in a powerful fashion. The presiding minister begins with a prayer asking the Lord Jesus Christ to "grant us the peace and unity of your kingdom." The people then offer signs of peace to one another. The breaking of bread follows during which the people sing or say:

Lamb of God, you take away the sins of the world:
　　have mercy on us.
Lamb of God, you take away the sins of the world:
　　have mercy upon us.
Lamb of God, you take away the sins of the world:
　　grant us peace.

Then the leader's bread is broken for all to see and a small portion is mixed in with the wine in the chalice. The priest says while doing so: "May this mingling of the body and blood of our Lord Jesus Christ bring eternal life to us who receive it."

In addition to "Lamb of God," other musical texts are appropriate to the fraction. The Episcopal *Book of Common Prayer* presents:

Alleluia. Christ our Passover is sacrificed for us;
Therefore let us keep the feast. Alleluia.

Another is the text by Theodore Dubois:

　　Christ, we do all adore thee,
　　and we do praise thee forever,
　　for on the holy cross hast thou
　　the world from sin redeemed.
　　Christ we do all adore thee,
　　and we do praise thee forever.

Thus a simple ceremonial action that started out as little more than getting ready to serve the bread has become a significant transition in the eucharist. It moves from the theologically objective thankful praise of God for redemption through Jesus Christ to the experientially subjective worship of Jesus Christ, suffering savior and source of life. Whatever the ceremonial actions and accompanying words, the fraction prepares for the communion which follows. "All things are ready; come to the feast."

The Communion

In peace and joy the people of God eat and drink at the banquet table. Here the ritual drama reaches its climax, *for Christ our Passover is sacrificed—for us—and therefore we keep the feast*. In this sharing of bread and wine, the people of each Christian assembly enjoy communion with one another, with Christians of every time and place, and with the living God who comes to us in Jesus Christ.

During the first decades of the church's life, Christians celebrated the eucharist by eating a full meal, beginning with special ceremonies with bread and ending with similar ceremonies with wine. They followed customs that were long-established within the Jewish community and were similar to those that Jesus and his disciples followed in their travels. These customs were similar to the annual celebration of the Passover meal, but they were adapted for use on other, more ordinary, occasions. During the period of time described in the New Testament the meal came under pressure, as Paul makes clear in 1 Corinthians 10 and 11. Instead of assembling as people whose faith overcame all social divisions, they were severely divided according to the social stratification of their life in the world. Their meal around the table thus was reinforcing the very conditions that Christ had overcome. It is no wonder that banqueting in the church came under a cloud. By the end of the church's first generation the full meal had disappeared, leaving the ritualized ceremonies with the loaf and the cup. Ever since, the eucharistic feast has consisted of the highly stylized participation in these two elements.

Even if the significant tensions reported by Paul had not developed, the full meal would surely have disappeared. Banquets can only be managed now and then, but Christian worship at the eucharistic table was much more frequent, at first daily and then weekly. Furthermore, the Jewish practice of religious meals took place in private homes and gatherings, whereas Christian worship developed according to the models of public assemblies, such as the temple with its communion meals and the synagogue with its public study of scripture. These assemblies soon became too expansive to be contained in houses, even those of the wealthy.

The meal may also have disappeared for reasons inherent in ritual itself. The eucharist takes a natural human activity—eating and drinking together—and uses it to express a highly specific set of ideas. If the full meal were to remain in place, the attention could easily focus upon the regular food and its consumption rather than upon the special activities with bread and wine. The pleasure of being together and the delights of the table could easily become the dominant features of the assembly rather than the remembrance of Jesus Christ and the union of worshipers with their God who meets them in bread and wine. In order to intensify the symbolic message of the eucharist, the details of eating and drinking needed to be abridged.

Yet not too much, for there must be real eating and drinking if the symbol is to be strong enough to convey the religious meaning. Many worshipers in churches today encounter this problem of the diminution of the meal itself. The challenge to belief is not to believe that the bread becomes the body of Christ but that the tiny wafers are actually bread! Furthermore, the modes of distribution often undercut participation in the meal. Eating and drinking have been so slight that there can scarcely be the sense of receiving food and drink. In addition, this part of the eucharist often is conducted in ways that emphasize individual relations with Christ rather than the communal relations to Christ and to one another.

In order for communion actually to be communion, four aspects of the celebration need attention. First, *the liturgy itself can state clearly that we are in fact eating and drinking, and that in so doing we share the church's family meal.* The basic texts used in the eucharist are sparing in their language. In the Words of Institution Jesus mentions eating the bread and drinking from the cup, and this language therefore appears in all communion services. In most of the published liturgies, however, little else is said about eating and drinking. Two exceptions are liturgies provided by the United Church of Christ and the Episcopal Church. The *Book of Worship* provides these sentences as one of the options to be used when giving the bread and cup: "Eat this, for it is the body of Christ, broken for you;" and "drink this, for it is the blood of Christ, shed for you" (*BW* 1986, 73, 74). The *Book of Common Prayer* provides a formulary for optional use: After giving this invitation to the people, "The Gifts of God for the People of God," the celebrant may add: "Take them in remembrance that Christ died for you, and feed on him in your hearts by faith, with thanksgiving" (*BCP* 1979, 364, 365).

The language of eating and drinking is clearly stated in a few of the hymns and songs sung at communion. "This is the hour of banquet and of song," says Horatius Bonar. "This is the heavenly table spread for me." A contemporary text by Omer Westendorf provides this refrain:

You satisfy the hungry heart with gift of finest wheat.
Come, give to us, O saving Lord, the bread of life to eat.

An older hymn by Josiah Conder is even more explicit:

Bread of heaven, on thee we feed,
for thy Flesh is meat indeed;
ever may our souls be fed
with this true and living Bread.

The second aspect of communion that needs attention is *the character of the bread and wine that are used in the celebration. They should seem like the real thing, like bread and wine; and their proportions should be suitable to the occasion.* Greater variation has been present in eucharistic bread than in communion wine. In Roman Catholic, Lutheran, and Episcopal churches the communion bread has usually consisted of small, very thin, uniformly shaped wafers. The presiding minister has used a larger wafer of similar composition. Many of the other Protestant churches use a different kind of wafer, a smaller chip that still suggests its derivation. In an earlier time these churches used communion bread that was baked in a flat white sheet which was scored so that it could be broken into tiny segments. Both forms of the communion bread, however, reduce the breadlikeness of the bread so much that it is hard for these wafers to carry their symbolic message. One response has been for churches to use bread of larger dimensions. At least, this larger bread is used by the presiding minister; and in many settings it can also be used as the communion bread for distribution to the congregation.

The presence or absence of leaven in the bread has been a topic of considerable debate. It is likely that in the ancient church the bread used at the eucharist was leavened. In the eastern churches, the bread has always been leavened. In western churches, unleavened bread came to be used during the Middle Ages. The sixteenth-century reformers continued the practice. In order to recover a bread that seems more like bread, many worshiping assemblies are again using leavened bread in the eucharist. Because of the practical difficulties of quickly distributing small pieces of bread to large congregations, however, the use of unleavened wafers continues to be common.

The realism of the wine is more easily sustained. Even when small quantities are used in a service, wine is recognizably what it is. The people may wonder what they are eating when they receive the wafer, but they know what they are getting when the cup touches their lips. The major complication concerning communion wine is the debate over its alcoholic content. The New Testament does not use the word wine in reference to the last supper. Jesus refers to the cup; and the phrase "fruit of the vine" (Matthew 26:29; Mark 14:25; and Luke 22:18) appears in the Gospel accounts, and in no other place in scripture. Some interpreters have concluded from this absence of the word *wine* that Jesus used unfermented grape juice; and people influenced by the American temperance movement of the nineteenth and twentieth centuries have been convinced that this presumed example of Jesus was intended to be binding upon the church throughout the ages. In these churches the cup at the eucharist contains unfermented grape juice. This line of thought is undercut by the fact that under natural conditions grape juice stays unfermented only a short time following harvest. Only during the past century have people been able to preserve grape juice so that it stays unfermented throughout most of the year. Prior to the modern era the only fruit of the vine available much of the year was fermented wine.

At the beginning of the twentieth century, as public consciousness of the principles of bacteria and hygiene became widespread, many of the people who objected to the use of fermented wine also became apprehensive over the use of the common cup. Thus the practice became widespread of providing the fruit of the vine in individual glasses. Well into the new century, however, these same churches continued to use one loaf, or a small number of loaves that had to be broken for distribution. The traditional custom was for this unleavened bread to be baked by members of the church. This bread that look like pie crust was gradually replaced by large flat crackers, usually matzos. As a result of these developments, the more Catholic churches maintained the single cup but used individual wafers while the more Protestant churches maintained the one loaf but replaced the one cup with individual glasses. Both patterns weakened the symbolic power of the eucharist. Because the one loaf features so prominently in Paul's teaching (1 Corinthians 10:17), the loss of the common loaf is perhaps more to be regretted than the loss of the one cup.

The third aspect of the service needing attention is *the way that the individuals who have come to worship are helped to become a congregation.* If congregants are to be a community gathered for the eucharistic banquet, then the service needs to foster their communion with one another and with God. Eucharistic celebrations, however, often encourage individual relations to God rather than a communal sense of union with the Divine.

One way of binding people more closely is to invite them to greet one another with the peace of Christ. This ceremony can be found at different places in eucharistic liturgies. The United Methodist order calls upon worshipers to "offer one another signs of reconciliation and love" between the confession of sins and the offering, and the Episcopal liturgy provides the same placement. The Presbyterian liturgy also connects the peace with the confession of sin, but these two acts come early in the service, prior to the reading of scripture.

The scriptural foundation for this placement is Matthew 5:23ff., where Jesus tells his hearers that before taking their gift to the altar they should make peace with a brother or sister who has something against them.

The liturgy in the *Lutheran Book of Worship* provides for the peace either before the offering or between the Lord's Prayer (at the conclusion of the eucharistic prayer) and prior to the distribution. This latter placement is developed fully in the Roman Catholic communion rite, which intertwines the sign of peace and the breaking of the bread. Immediately following the Lord's Prayer, the presiding minister prays to Jesus Christ to grant the congregation the peace and unity of Christ's kingdom. Then the priest and people greet one another with appropriate signs of peace. As the bread is broken, the congregation sings or says the devotional text "Lamb of God, have mercy upon us, and grant us peace."

Then comes the distribution to the people. The prayers used during this part of the service refer to forgiveness and healing, implying that the gifts are directly connected to the peace of life in Christ's kingdom. This communal action at the most solemn part of the ritual makes possible an intense awareness of connection with one another. And the incorporation of the fraction in this act dramatizes the Pauline assertion that we are united into one because we all share in the one bread, which is Jesus Christ given for the life of the world.

Even though the congregation comes to God as one body, there comes a time when their individuality must also be expressed. In most services this personal moment with God happens during the administration of the elements. In some churches communicants go forward, stand in line, and one by one receive the elements. In other churches, they stay in their seats and partake of the elements passed from row to row. In both cases the people may move into deep communion with God. If the emphasis upon community has been cared for, then this time of personal appropriation of communion brings the religious dimensions of the service to their fullness.

The fourth aspect of the communion rite that needs attention is *the ceremonial mode, the combination of pastoral style, musical expression, and movements of worshipers.* Even when the text invites people to participate in the family meal of the people of God, one or more aspects of the ceremonial mode can inhibit that participation. The liturgy itself may send one message while the conducting of the liturgy sends another. Those who preside must do so with warmth and solemnity, with relaxed earnestness. Their spirit quickly permeates the liturgy and the entire assembly. Therefore leaders need to cultivate the ability to represent the inviting hospitality of Christ who prepares the banquet.

The music is also important, whether it be congregational song, instrumental music, or the words of the liturgy sung by cantor and priest. Music brings out more clearly the rhythm and texture of the service, and it highlights the emotional character of what is being said and done. Music helps people participate or inhibits their readiness to do their part.

The actions of the people also are a factor. If they stay seated in their pews, it is difficult for the intensity of their participation to change from whatever level it reaches in other parts of the service. If they move around, however, the possibility of greater intensity comes into play. They can kneel at their place, or stand. They can go forward to the chancel steps or onward to the table itself. They can receive standing or kneeling, and by breaking off bread with their own hands or receiving it on the tongue from the hand of the communion minister. All of these matters affect the sense of communion that is present in the service.

As this chapter draws to a close, three more points need to be made. The first is that the community gathered at any communion table consists of those who have come together on this one occasion, and a much wider congregation. All other Christians in every time and place are included in each congregation. So too are the saints and martyrs who in their glorified state continue to be present with a congregation and its members. Most of all, God is present in the Word, in the bread and wine that become for worshipers the body and blood of Jesus Christ, and in the Holy Spirit who lives within the church and within each of its people. This larger company is affirmed in the hymn fragment that occurs in the midst of most eucharistic prayers. The people proclaim:

Holy, holy, holy Lord, God of power and might.
Heaven and earth are full of your glory.
Blessed is he [Jesus] who comes in the name of the Lord.

A second point is that the bread and wine connect worshipers to earth and heaven—the bread and wine which have been placed upon the table as our offering of life to God. Yet by these same gifts Christ's body and blood are conveyed to us. The world we know by physical senses and the world we know by the eyes of faith are united into one.

The third point brings these others to their conclusion. The church is often called the body of Christ. So too the communion bread, and so is Christ's earthly body now glorified and seated at God's right hand. The effect of the eucharist is to draw these separate meanings of Christ's body into one, so that through the communion of the Lord's supper, the church becomes what it already is, Christ's own self given for the life of the world.

Encouraging the Conversation

This chapter gives a strong emphasis to the offering as the first part of the service of the Table. In workshops and classes that I lead, people often respond with surprise at two points. First, they have not been accustomed to using offering to include the bread and wine, and the prayers, as well as financial gifts. Second, when they have focused directly upon money, they have felt uneasy about making it so integral to the eucharist. As one man (a banker by occupation) put it one time: "I like to keep tainted money separated from the more spiritual parts of the service." As you think about your experiences with offerings in worship, are you surprised in either of these ways? How do you interpret the meaning of the money offering in worship?

This chapter also discusses the way that the meal is served, indicating that practices vary widely across the churches of the world.

- How is the meal distributed in your church?
- Why is it done that way?
- What are the religious values and the impact upon the congregation that seem to grow out of that mode of administration?

8

The Great Thanksgiving Prayer

The great thanksgiving prayer is a tightly constructed, theologically precise set of words by which the churches present themselves and their worship to the holy God. What is implicit elsewhere in the liturgy now becomes explicit. In this prayer the theology of the Lord's supper as a whole is put forth in a solemn address spoken to God but phrased in plain speech that all can understand. As prayer, this set of words *expresses meaning*. Furthermore, through the faith-full saying of these words, *this meaning becomes real* to all who participate in faith. The purpose of this chapter is to work our way into this prayer so that we can understand it with heart and mind.

This prayer has been given several titles. The earliest may well have been *the eucharist*, the thanksgiving. Something of this spirit was captured in the phrase *the great thanksgiving*, which began to be used in *An Experimental Liturgy*, published in 1958 (G. Cope, J. G. Davies, and D. A. Tytler), and which later has come into prominence in liturgical publications. *Anaphora* is another name that has long been used for this prayer, coming from a Greek word that means *offering*. Another title is *canon*, which is derived from a Greek word meaning *rule* or *measuring rod*. Originally it was used as a heading for the prayer to indicate that the following text was fixed. (See articles "Anaphora" and "Canon" in *A New Dictionary of Liturgy and Worship*.) Still another name given to this prayer is consecration. This word emphasizes the offering that the church is presenting to God and asks that God accept and bless these gifts. The most generic of these terms is *eucharistic prayer*, and this is the title that is most used in this chapter.

Cautions to Be Observed

In this emphasis upon the eucharistic prayer we necessarily will focus upon written texts. As we do so, however, three cautions need

129

to be voiced. First, *worship is much more than the texts in prescribed worship books*, just as music is far more than scores on the printed page. Worship is an event in which words and actions come to life in the voices and bodies of worshipers. Yet words are part of the event. Sometimes they are the script that is closely followed, or the text may be a stimulus for the creation of new words. Whether as script or stimulus, these words provide part of the action.

One reason for studying the words of prayer is that they help us understand the intentions of the ritual. Sometimes this explanation is easily grasped. The words spoken in the ritual, the interpretations given to the ritual itself, and what actually takes place may be fully consistent with one another. At other times, and these may be the more frequent, the meaning stated in the formal text and the meaning observed in the actual doing of a ritual may not agree with each other. Noticing this discrepancy, the careful observer will explore more deeply both the text and the action in order to discern the true meaning of what is taking place. (Among current writers who emphasize the limited importance of the texts are James F. White in *Protestant Worship* and Lawrence Hoffman in *Beyond the Text*. Suggestions for a method of observation are based on the proposals of Victor Turner 1967.)

Second, *the similarities of experience that we express in the language of worship are hard to sustain when we move to other levels of theological language.* Although Christians may differ from one another, and sometimes passionately, they usually find that the powerful language of hymns, sermons, and prayers is generally truth-telling even when that language comes from traditions other than their own. Soon, however, this primary liturgical language gives rise to two further types of theological language. If prayers are the first order of theological language, then the second order is the explanation that arises as believers begin to describe and interpret their experience. This language of explanation converts the poetry of worship to prose. Here too, people in various traditions find a significant degree of common understanding. The third order of theological language consists of technical definitions and systematic expositions. This more developed form of speech is the location of much that separates Christians from one another. We can sing hymns that speak of the heavenly banquet that Christ provides. With some readiness we can also tell one another that the communion service is when we feel closest to God. Here, as in the hymns, we can join with people in a wide range of church traditions. When we discuss how we are joined with God— whether by being raised to heaven by the power of the Holy Spirit or by eating and drinking Christ who comes to us in a bloodless way— we move into third order language; and the extent of agreement diminishes.

One of the positive developments of our time is that the long impasse over the third level of theological language may finally be breaking down. Certainly the wide acclaim given to *Baptism, Eucharist and Ministry* is strong evidence that the churches are finding ways of speaking that can be understood and appreciated across the ecclesial and theological boundaries that so long have kept them separated from one another.

The third hesitation that should be observed is that *the form and language of eucharistic praying is a living reality and therefore changes even when the communities using these prayers seem completely stable.* The fact that eucharistic faith, practice, and prayer change will be especially apparent in the next section of this chapter, which traces the early history of the prayer, and in the closing section, which points toward further experimentation with the form and language of the prayers at the communion table. Even in the middle sections of this chapter, however, the living and changing character of eucharistic life can be inferred.

Early Patterns of the Prayer

Since midway through the twentieth century, a significant body of research has been devoted to the eucharistic prayers of the churches. An earlier period of scholarship had collected these prayers from churches around the world and throughout Christian history, making these texts available for further study. The goals of recent scholarly work have been to develop a history of the evolution of texts and to comprehend the development of the eucharistic theologies stated in these prayers.

One aspect of this recent study of eucharistic praying has been the effort to trace its connections to the ancient Jewish traditions of prayer. It is clear that Christian prayer emerged from the milieu of Hebrew liturgical life expressed in the psalter and in other ancient sources. The prayers in the synagogue service, often called blessings or benedictions, were framed by the phrase "You are praised, O God...." This strong reference to God is consistent with the principle of Jewish prayer that focuses not on the human condition but on God, God's actions, and God's expectations. (See essays by Jakob J. Petuchowski and Baruch Graubard in *The Lord's Prayer and Jewish Liturgy,* in Petuchowski and Brocke 1978, 45-72.) Echoes of this prayer form are found in Daniel 2:20 and 1 Chronicles 29:10b: "Blessed are you, O LORD, the God of our ancestor Israel, forever and ever." The prayer continues by referring to God's majesty, power, and might. The first paragraph concludes, "And now, our God, we give thanks to you and praise your glorious name" (29:13). Three prayers from the synagogue are especially interesting because they affirm "the three cardinal doctrines of biblical religion: Creation, Revelation, and Redemption" (Petuchowski and Brocke 1978, 49).

Jewish practice depended upon a tradition of oral prayer in which form and contents were firmly established around the world, but in which the exact phrasing was left to local development. Thus, in the various Jewish communities where churches came into being, the inherited tradition was already diversified. When Christian assemblies modified these local prayers, in keeping with their belief in Christ Jesus, this variety increased even more.

Scholars have not yet reached consensus concerning which of the ancient eucharistic prayers known to us today are earliest and most authentic. William Crockett sums up the earliest prayers, which retained their close connection to Jewish forms, as consisting of a paragraph that combined the blessing of God with thanksgiving for creation and redemption. A second paragraph consisted of intercessions, beginning with the request that God remember the church and leading to the petition that the kingdom come (Crockett 1989). Crockett's description draws upon an idea proposed by Geoffrey Cuming and other historians of the eucharist. They suggest that the earliest eucharistic prayers were brief, consisting of fewer than twenty lines of text, blessing God for creation and redemption, and concluding with a doxology or the Sanctus (Holy, holy, holy Lord...). Cuming proposes that this brief prayer was then followed by other liturgical statements and actions that were part of the eucharistic celebration but, strictly speaking, not part of the eucharistic prayer itself. These additional elements, which later were folded into the eucharistic prayer, included the words of institution read "as a warrant for the celebration of the eucharist," a short prayer of offering, and a prayer for the Holy Spirit (Cuming 1984, 168-72).

The next stage in the development of the eucharistic prayer becomes evident in the third century and two patterns can be seen. One of them, which is illustrated by the prayer of Hippolytus, has three parts: thanksgiving for creation and redemption, the reciting of the biblical words of institution and a remembering of Jesus, and a prayer for the Holy Spirit along with a Doxology of praise (Crockett 1989, 42). The second pattern is illustrated by the liturgy of the Apostles Addai and Mari, which came to life in the churches of eastern Syria and continues as the foundation of worship in the Malabar Church of our time. Crockett identifies these elements: thanksgiving for creation and redemption, intercessions, the prayer for the Holy Spirit, and a Doxology.

A third pattern from this same period is associated with Alexandria and the early history of the liturgy of St. Mark used in Egypt. This pattern was simple, consisting of thanksgiving for creation, which included a prayer offering the church's "reasonable sacrifice," intercessions, and a Doxology. This pattern may in fact be the oldest available to us, still expressing its connections with Jewish practice, and not yet exhibiting some of the elements that later were to become standard elements of the eucharistic prayer.

The developments described above took place in Egypt and Asia, lands that were the eastern portion of the world and church in Roman times. From the fourth to the sixth centuries, the regional patterns of the eucharistic prayer continued to develop. By the end of this period, they had become stabilized in forms that have continued to be used by eastern churches until now.

A similar process of development took place in northern Africa, southern Europe, Spain, and France. In this more westerly portion of early Christianity, the church maintained organizational unity, and one of the results was that the early regional variations in worship diminished and the liturgies became similar. In theology, church government, and liturgy, the practices of the Church of Rome became dominant across western provinces. Whereas in the eastern liturgies, the eucharistic prayers were unified and coherent compositions, in the Western church one complex prayer emerged, consisting of a series of brief prayers. Although this series of prayers has been remarkably stable for more than a thousand years, its early history is still not well understood.

During the sixteenth-century Reformation in Europe, much attention was given to the eucharistic prayer that had been inherited from the Roman Catholic Church. Each of the first-generation Reformation churches recast the Mass and its prayers, determined to purge them of error and make them liturgies of the people. All of these churches rejected the traditional form of the Catholic canon and also the major themes of Catholic eucharistic theology. Yet each of these churches continued the practice of using only one pattern as the prayer in celebrations of the Lord's supper. Thus stability of eucharistic praying continued in these newer churches just as it had been maintained in the older churches of east and west.

Late in the 1500s and on into the early 1600s, a significant departure from this pattern of stable prayer was pioneered by some of the churches that were created as a result of the Reformation. A new practice of extemporaneous prayer came into being not only in church life in general but also at the communion table. The foundation of this practice was the Reformed tradition of Zwingli, Calvin, and others who called for major reforms in the pattern and theology of public prayer. Already in the continental Reformation of the sixteenth century, ministers were allowed a limited amount of freedom for extemporaneous prayer. By the end of the century, this limited freedom was expanded by the Puritan parties in England. Some Puritans concluded that the published prayers were neither scripturally nor pastorally adequate. Others concluded (and this point of view came to dominate) that the problem was that the very idea of reading prayers violated the nature of prayer. Christians, they believed, were to pray as the Spirit leads and therefore only free prayer could be allowed. (For discussions of the development of extemporaneous prayer see Davies 1970, 255-93; and Davies 1990.)

In the Puritan churches of New England this emphasis upon extemporaneous prayer was developed even further, becoming the spring that fed an ever-widening liturgical stream of American Protestantism. Churches within the Reformed tradition, including Presbyterian, Congregationalist, and Disciples of Christ, offered extemporaneous prayer both in services of the Word and at the communion table. Methodist churches, both Black and White, practiced extemporaneous prayer in services of the Word but continued the use of prescribed prayer for the eucharist.

The Pattern of Contemporary Prayers

Although there are many eucharistic prayers in use today, with significant variations in outline and contents, it still is possible to discuss them together. Despite variations in detail, most prayers follow an outline that begins with a dialogue between presiding minister and congregants, followed by the thankful praise of God, remembrance of Jesus Christ, invocation of the Holy Spirit, intercessions, and conclusion. This logical sequence of ideas shapes the following exposition of the eucharistic prayer.

Dialogue

Nearly all eucharistic prayers, including the most ancient texts known to us, begin with a brief dialogue between the presiding minister and other worshipers. Although the wording varies, this exchange ordinarily consists of three couplets. The first is a simple greeting: "The Lord be with you; and also with you." The second couplet focuses attention upon the transcendent realm where God dwells in majesty: "Lift up your hearts; we lift them to the Lord." The third couplet invites the church to praise God: "Let us give thanks to the Lord our God; it is right to give our thanks and praise."

This dialogue at the beginning of the prayer establishes the fact that *the congregation offers these words to God* even though one person does most of the speaking. There have been times and places when the congregation's role was nearly forgotten. Not only have the people not spoken their lines, but most people have scarcely recognized that the congregation is the company of actors performing the liturgy. The dialogue, however, is clear. The celebrant says "let us give thanks," and the people respond: it is right that *we* give *our* thankful praise. The implication is that the entire prayer is really the church's corporate address to its God.

This implication is confirmed later by other parts of the prayer where the people again speak in their own voice. From ancient times the people have concluded the first section of the prayer by singing or saying a brief text that begins "Holy, holy, holy Lord, God of power and might." In recent liturgies the people have also been invited to proclaim: "Christ has died. Christ is risen. Christ will come again." The prayer concludes with the people joining in singing or saying the Lord's Prayer. In a few liturgies a more significant part of the prayer is spoken by the people. One example is Eucharistic Prayer C in the *Book of Common Prayer*, which is in a responsive format, thus providing a full participation by the congregation. Patterns recommended for use in the Christian Church (Disciples of Christ) also include a significant portion of the text for the congregants to say. (See *Thankful Praise* 1987 and Watkins 1991.)

Even though the eucharistic prayer as a whole belongs to the people, one person does most of the speaking. Such has been the practice in virtually all churches throughout Christian history. In the early church, when the prayer was oral rather than written, it was necessary for one person to do the speaking, although unison responses could be learned by congregations. The dramatic character of the service called for a single voice to proclaim these important lines, with the congregation giving its consent. Thus, the monological form of a congregational prayer text was justifiable on pragmatic grounds.

Other, more theological, grounds are also widespread among churches. Some believe that the church is divided into orders of ministry and that responsibilities within the church are assigned to these orders. Some writers explicitly state that the church is hierarchical in its structure and that each level within its life has its distinct authority, power, and liturgical role. According to this doctrine of church and worship the people's proper liturgy is to bring the gifts, and the liturgy of ordained ministers is to offer the major prayer.

An even more complex theological foundation for distributing responsibility is the doctrine that only ordained clergy are authorized by the church and empowered by God to voice the prayer. Only the ordained, according to this doctrine, are able to speak the words by which God brings about the transformation of elements (and people) that the eucharist accomplishes. According to this theological understanding, someone not ordained only says the words, whereas those authoritatively ordained consecrate the bread and wine and bring about the union of believers with the risen Christ.

The churches cannot move quickly toward agreement concerning the theology of leadership at the table. The normal practice, whatever the theology, is for major portions of this prayer to be voiced by the pastor on behalf of the whole congregation. At the same time, at least in Catholic and historic Protestant churches, the congregation is provided a voice, thus making clear that in principle the liturgy is the work of the people.

The most notable departure from the practice described above is in some Baptist churches and in Churches of Christ and Christian churches (including the Disciples of Christ) that have developed from the Stone-Campbell movement in nineteenth-century America. In these two families of churches it is common practice for persons other than the pastor to preside over the celebrations of the Lord's supper. The Christian Church (Disciples of Christ) is an example. At the beginning of their history, Disciples moved to the practice of every-Sunday communion. They also were committed to extemporaneous prayer at the communion table. In most of their congregations, the ongoing religious leadership was provided by mature members of the congregation elected to be elders of the church. These people were at first considered to be the corporate ministry of the congregation, and thus it was common for them to be ordained. Very early, however, that understanding waned, and elders are now understood to be laity rather than clergy. As the doctrine of the eldership changed, a movement away from ordaining these persons also took place. In most congregations, however, the elders continue to voice the communion prayer on behalf of the congregation. In additional to elders, Disciples congregations ordinarily are served by one or more pastors who have been prepared educationally and ordained to the ministry of Word and Sacrament. In most congregations the pastor or another member of the ordained staff participates in leading the Lord's supper. The pastor's role has not included offering the eucharistic prayers, which the elders continue to speak, but the pastor's central role in the service conveys the impression that he or she is presiding over the service. In a few congregations, and the number may be increasing, an ordained minister now participates with the elders in speaking the communion prayers.

Thankful Praise

The first section of the eucharistic prayer consists of thanksgiving to God for life itself and for the new life given in Jesus Christ. More than any other passage of scripture, the first chapter of Ephesians expresses the mood of this prayer. "Blessed be the God and Father of our Lord Jesus Christ, who has blessed us in Christ with every spiritual blessing..." (1:3). This sentence mirrors the phrase from Jewish liturgies that framed the prayers called *blessings* or *benedictions*. Then, the writer of the epistle recounts the actions of God that elicit gratitude: choosing and adopting us to be God's children, redeeming us from our trespasses by the blood of Christ, revealing the mystery of the divine will, giving us the hope of an eternal inheritance, and sealing this promise with the Holy Spirit. All of this leads to the praise of God's glory (Ephesians 1:3–14). The epistle continues by expanding upon the themes presented in the first paragraph. The language that is almost prayer now becomes sermonic meditation. This main section of the epistle reaches its climax with a declaration of praise: "To [God] be glory in the church and in Christ Jesus to all generations, forever and ever" (Ephesians 3:21).

The tone of this Ephesian passage is important, especially since it contrasts so sharply with that which has been common in eucharistic liturgies. Ephesians expresses confident joy, based on God's character and actions, rather than the self-deprecating anxiety that for many people has defined their experience of eucharistic worship. Because worshipers are estranged from God, from one another, and from self, penitence is the proper stance for all to take as they come into the presence of the Holy One. The relationship with God, however, is determined neither by our sin nor by our remorse. Although we are dead because of our sins, the Ephesian preacher reminds the congregation, God "who is rich in mercy" and who loves us with "a great love," makes us alive in Christ Jesus. "For by grace you have been saved through faith, and this is not your own doing; it is the gift of God" (2:8).

The two themes of biblical religion that predominate in the Ephesian passage are revelation and redemption. Virtually absent is the doctrine of creation, which is the other theme central in biblical religion. In fact, creation has been eclipsed by redemption in much of the history of eucharistic worship. The new life given in Christ has been proclaimed so loudly that natural life, given in our birth and continued in every interchange with nature and the human community, nearly disappears from consciousness and from our speech. The earlier prayers of Israel, however, keep God's work in creation very much in the forefront. Psalm 104, for example, praises God who is "clothed with honor and majesty" and "wrapped in light as with a garment" (104:1b–2a). The psalm continues with a dramatic description of the earth and its inhabitants, and of the intimate intertwining of God and nature. The climax to this hymn of praise comes with two closely related declarations: "May the glory of the LORD endure forever" and "I will sing to the LORD as long as I live" (Psalm 104:31a, 33a). This tradition of creation-prompted blessing continued in Christian assemblies, and therefore was the framework within which worshipers expressed the ideas that were explicit to the Christian community. Thus eucharistic worship implicitly praised God for creation even while explicitly praising God for revelation and redemption through Jesus Christ.

One of the characteristics of contemporary eucharistic theology is the interest in strengthening thanksgiving for creation. In part, the reason for this development is the recognition that many contemporary Christians experience the natural world as something to be consumed and exploited rather than as the material for communion with God. Another reason is the recognition that many contemporary Christians find a theology that starts with creation to be more compatible with their experience than a theology that starts with redemption. Whereas at an earlier time thanksgiving for salvation led to thanksgiving for creation, the sequence today is reversed.

We can be grateful that creation is becoming a more prominent theme in eucharistic prayers. An especially graceful example is a text prepared by Roman Catholics but now widely studied in other church and scholarly circles. It is published in the Presbyterian *Book of Common Worship*:

> Blessed are you, strong and faithful God.
> All your works, the height and the depth,
> echo the silent music of your praise.
>
> In the beginning your Word summoned light,
> night withdrew, and creation dawned.
> As ages passed unseen,
> waters gathered on the face of the earth
> and life appeared.
>
> When the times at last had ripened
> and the earth grown full in abundance,
> you created in your image man and woman,
> the stewards of all creation (*BCW* 1993, 142).

It is clear that many Christians in churches today value brevity in prayers. The readiness to listen to extemporaneous prayers of an hour's length disappeared long ago. The traditional eucharistic prayers in older books also are experienced as being too long even though they take only a few minutes to proclaim. The pressure upon composers, editors, and pastors is for prayers to be succinct and strong.

Here we meet a serious conflict. How can short prayers express the fullness of praise for creation, revelation, and redemption? Each of these biblical doctrines is complex; each is experienced in a wide variety of ways. Even long eucharistic prayers could not contain the fullness of the Christian experience that the eucharist dramatizes. Much less can short prayers proclaim the glories of God's love in giving life and renewing that same life in Jesus Christ.

One way to overcome this conflict is for a series of these eucharistic prayers to be offered during the course of the church year. The principle of seasonal variation has long been established in the variable prefaces that some liturgies insert in the first section of the eucharistic prayer. Each of them is a brief paragraph that praises God for some aspect of the story of redemption. If a small part of thankful praise can change from season to season, then it should be possible for the entire section to change over the course of time. Indeed, the United Methodist and Presbyterian worship books have done something very much like this by developing prayers for the seasons of the church year and other major religious festivals.

Another way to include the wide range of variations upon the central themes is to develop these prayers locally, and perhaps offer them extemporaneously. Local development opens the door for including many aspects of the experienced reality of creation, revelation, and redemption. Even though some current worship books provide instructions for extemporaneous eucharistic prayers, most churches expect prayers at the table to be careful in their theology and emotionally strong in their form. These two characteristics are difficult to include in extemporaneous prayers, until the leaders of prayer have developed depth of piety and a strong sense of language. Therefore, it seems likely that pastors and their congregations will continue to draw upon the published prayers for the Lord's supper.

Holy, Holy, Holy

Thankful praise closes with a strong congregational acclamation. Since early times this climactic portion of the prayer has consisted of two scriptural acclamations. The first (called the *Sanctus*, the Latin word for *holy*) is taken from Isaiah's vision in the temple (see Isaiah 6:3): "Holy, holy, holy is the LORD of hosts; the whole earth is full of his glory." The second acclamation (called the *Benedictus*, the Latin word for *blessed*) comes from Psalm 118:26 and was used by the crowds in their enthusiastic reception of Jesus on Palm Sunday: "Blessed is the one who comes in the name of the LORD." On Palm Sunday and in the eucharistic liturgy, "the one who comes" refers to Jesus. This section of the eucharistic prayer is similar in spirit to the great doxologies in the book of Revelation in which the crowds around the throne cry, "You are worthy, our Lord and God" (Revelation 4:11a) and, "Worthy is the Lamb that was slaughtered" (Revelation 5:12a).

These hymns in Revelation are sung by the residents of heaven, a complex company of angels and archangels, other heavenly creatures, the martyrs, and all others who have died in Christ. In keeping with this biblical precedent, the eucharistic liturgies have prefaced these acclamations with a declaration that the people around the table are joining their voices with this whole company of heaven:

Therefore we praise you
joining our voices with the heavenly choirs
and with all the faithful of every time and place
who forever sing to the glory of your name. (*BCW* 1993, 126)

Thus the eucharist becomes the golden staircase that connects
heaven and earth. It is a way for people today to live in the presence
of past generations and to affirm that each worshiper, after death,
will continue in the company of those who praise God.

The climactic and exultant character of this acclamation calls for
it to be sung rather than said. Repeatedly, the texts in Revelation
state that the residents of heaven sing their praise of God and of the
Lamb. (See Revelation 4:8, 10; 5:9; 7:12.) The Sanctus and Benedictus
have been set to music many times for singing by congregations.
Other texts could also be used, including verses from hymns that
congregations already are accustomed to singing. The final stanzas
of two well-known hymns illustrate this possibility:

Holy, holy, holy! Lord God Almighty!
All thy works shall praise thy name,
in earth and sky and sea.
Holy, holy, holy! Merciful and mighty,
God in three persons, blessed Trinity.
(usually sung to NICEA)

Glory to God and praise and love
be ever, ever given
by saints below and saints above,
the church in earth and heaven.
(usually sung to AZMON)

Isaac Watts' paraphrase of "A Song of the Lamb" is another possibility. It can be sung in common meter tunes (including NUN DANKET ALL
UND BRINGET EHR).

Come, let us join our cheerful songs
with angels round the throne;
ten thousand thousand are their tongues,
but all their joys are one.

Stanzas two and three begin "Worthy the Lamb that died," and "Jesus
is worthy to receive / honor and power divine." The hymn concludes
[in the original the third line reads "of him"]:

The whole creation joins in one
to bless the sacred Name
of God who sits upon the throne,
and to adore the Lamb.

Remembrance of Jesus Christ

The portions of the prayer described above—dialogue, thankful praise for creation and redemption in Christ, and a doxological chorus—concentrate attention upon the core of the gospel that is celebrated at the communion table. As was stated earlier in the chapter, prayers of this type may well have been the eucharistic prayers in the first generations of the church's life even though these mini-anaphoras do not contain some of the elements that now are standard components of the prayers. Most Christians had come from Jewish backgrounds and thus understood this prayer form. Even though the contents of these brief prayers were compressed, the meaning hinted at rather than expounded, these prayers communicated a rich theology of the eucharistic connection to Jesus Christ.

The churches found it necessary, however, to expand these hints into full statements. One way they did this was by inserting new material into the prayers they already used. An even more important development was to add materials after the congregation's doxology, thus creating a second half to the prayer. By creating this second half, the churches began the never-ending process of developing eucharistic theology. They moved from first-order theological language (prayers and hymns) to second-order theological language (the more expanded and exact interpretation of their experience). It should be no surprise that as the prayer moved from praise to explanation, doctrinal variety and disagreement among the churches increased.

While doctrinal development is necessary and differences of understanding and conviction are inevitable, separation and the breaking of eucharistic fellowship are neither necessary nor inevitable. The fact that the churches have for so long been divided by the sacrament of unity in Christ is reason for confession of sin, and the evidences of our coming together again are reasons for hopeful joy.

The second half of the eucharistic prayer details the role that Jesus plays in the reconciliation that God establishes with humankind. On the night before his betrayal, as Jesus and the disciples broke bread together, he gave a new meaning to the traditional ceremonies that accompanied the meal. "Do this," he told them, "to remember me." As these friends ate together, the historical, symbolic, and religious themes of the Passover season were at their annual high point. The next day, as the passover lambs were slaughtered, Jesus died on the cross. On the third day, and for forty days thereafter, his earlier declaration was fulfilled when he appeared to them as risen from the dead. All of these experiences of Jesus, along with the memories of his ministry during the previous months, were interpreted by the ceremonies with bread and wine. The God who had delivered their ancestors from slavery and returned them to their promised land had come to them in Jesus Christ, and by Jesus' death and resurrection had brought salvation.

In the communion prayer the most sharply focused way of remembering Jesus is the recitation of the narrative of that Last Supper and the repeating of Jesus' own words of interpretation. From the time of Hippolytus onward, eucharistic prayers have incorporated the words of institution as part of their prayer addressed to God. Most of these prayers have also recited, either before or after the institution, a brief summary of Jesus' saving work. All of this is presented to God as a fulfilling of Jesus' command that the church remember him, as an act of thanksgiving to God, and as the basis for asking God to remember them.

The function of the words of institution in the liturgy has varied. Some traditions have used these words from Jesus as a formula of consecration. When a properly authorized minister of the church speaks them during the liturgy, these churches maintain, the bread and wine become what Jesus says they are: "my body given for you; my blood of the covenant poured out for you." In contrast, other traditions have described these words as the warrant for doing the eucharist. Rather than being prayer addressed to God, according to this second view, these words are declared to the congregation, reminding them of Jesus' command that they do this sacrament to remember him and the redemption that came about because of his death upon the cross.

Perhaps these two ideas are closer together than the above paragraph would indicate. The liturgical function of the words of institution includes both references. They are addressed both to the people and to God. The people are encouraged to draw near to God in trusting love. Yet an entreaty moves upward to the throne of grace, asking that God's promise of forgiveness be renewed because of Jesus' giving of himself in an atoning act that is forever alive and effective.

This portion of the communion prayer is often referred to as the *anamnesis*, the Greek word that is usually translated *remembrance*. Interpreters expound *anamnesis* in a dynamic way by stating that it means more than recalling. Liturgical remembrance is a vigorous engagement of spirit with the people and events that are being remembered, and the strong anticipation of being joined with the past and with God at the end of the age still to come. This is one of the places that many modern liturgies invite the congregation to speak a portion of the prayer:

We remember his death,
We proclaim his resurrection,
We await his coming in glory.

It is inevitable that the liturgical remembrance of Jesus Christ express theological ideas about atonement. Even Jesus' own words include references to the covenant that God makes with those who participate. Clearly, Jesus' death has some impact upon the relationship between believers and God. Words like *sacrifice* and *forgiveness* come quickly into the conversation. These theological ideas are forcefully stated in one eucharistic prayer that has shaped generations of worshipers. It gives thanks to God who "of thy tender mercy, didst give thine only Son Jesus Christ to suffer death upon the Cross for our redemption." This same prayer continues by affirming that on the cross Jesus made "a full, perfect, and sufficient sacrifice, oblation, and satisfaction for the sins of the whole world" (*BCP* 1928, 80).

Very different is the parallel passage in a liturgy published by that same church half a century later. This new text offers thanks for Jesus whom God has sent "to be the Savior and Redeemer of the world." The prayer continues: "In him, you have delivered us from evil, and made us worthy to stand before you. In him, you have brought us out of error into truth, out of sin into righteousness, out of death into life" (*BCP* 1979, 368). Both in doctrine and tone these two prayers are very different from each other, but each one expresses a theological understanding of the atonement. Such will always be the case in the eucharistic prayer. Most Christians will agree that Jesus is redeemer, and also that in the Lord's supper we and that redemption come together. As we move beyond this agreement to fuller statements of how this union occurs we will forever find new ways of stating our central experience of salvation in Jesus Christ.

Prayer for the Holy Spirit

At this point in the prevailing pattern of eucharistic prayers, the character of the prayer changes. Until now everything, including the words of institution, has developed the phrase in the opening dialogue of giving God "our thanks and praise." Now, the prayer becomes petition. God is asked to do something for which the words of institution have prepared the way. This part of the eucharistic prayer has two names, both of which mean to call: *epiclesis* (derived from Greek) and *invocation* (from Latin).

The language varies in the many liturgies, but the ideas are parallel. The epiclesis asks that God send the Holy Spirit so that by the bread and wine of the eucharist the crucified and risen Christ and the worshipers will be joined together. Historically, most prayers include some reference to change of the bread and wine, but the language is guarded because the theological ramifications are so complex.

This petition again deals with the center of Christian faith, the salvation wrought by Jesus Christ. Devout Christians debate the theo-

logical interpretations of how the eucharist connects people of today
with an ancient event and how it projects them into their eternal life
with God. Some traditions hold the conviction that the eucharist is
effective because the bread and wine are transformed into Christ's
own body and blood. Others hold that what changes is not the way
that the material of the eucharist is experienced, but rather the way
that time is experienced. In some traditions the major focus is upon
the elements themselves and their changing from bread and wine
into flesh and blood. In other traditions the focus is upon the people
who receive the elements in faith; the people are transformed so that
bread and wine are for them something quite different from what
they are for other people. Another way of contrasting doctrines of
the Lord's supper is to speak of Christ's presence in this sacrament.
Some say that he is bodily present, although in a mode that our senses
cannot discern. Others say that he is spiritually present, but in a mode
that is unique.

Because the epiclesis is a prayer rather than a theological statement, it is necessarily condensed and carefully nuanced. The following example, which I have written, connects the prayer for the Holy
Spirit with a brief recital of God's redemptive work in Jesus Christ:

The recital:
All of this we remember here at the table
as we come to you with our own selves,
a living sacrifice to you.
Especially do we recall our Savior Jesus Christ,
fully one with you,
fully one with us,
who offered his own life as a sign
of the covenant you make with humankind.

The epiclesis:
By your Word and Holy Spirit
bless these gifts of bread and wine
and your church here gathered,
that Jesus' own words may be fulfilled:
My body given for you.
My blood of the covenant poured out for you.

Another example of the epiclesis, prepared by the United Methodist Church, has been described by John H. McKenna (Roman Catholic) as the most complete resumé of elements traditionally associated
with the epiclesis" (Senn 1987, 182).

Pour out your Holy Spirit on us gathered here,
and on these gifts of bread and wine.

Make them be for us the body and blood of Christ,
that we may be for the world the body of Christ,
redeemed by his blood.
By your Spirit make us one with Christ,
one with each other,
and one in ministry to all the world,
until Christ comes in final victory
and we feast at his heavenly banquet. (*UMH* 1989, 10)

One of the noteworthy aspects of this prayer is that it pushes forward to the completion of human life at the end of the age. This emphasis upon the redemption of creation and the coming of God's Holy Commonwealth is very much a part of the long history of eucharistic piety and doctrine.

Supplications

The prayer just quoted illustrates the tendency of eucharistic prayers to come quickly to a close following the epiclesis. The benefits of communion are summed up in a few phrases referring to life in this world and in the world to come. In liturgies that have already provided for intercessions dealing with a broad range of issues, there would seem to be little need to include those same concerns here.

Yet, there is a reason of the heart to offer our supplications to God as the communion prayers come to a close. Jesus now sits at God's side, offering intercessions for all the world and for Christians everywhere. Thus, the prayers of the people gathered at the communion table can be joined with those of Jesus Christ. Those who pray are confident not because of their own merit or eloquence but because they are united with Jesus by baptism and thus joined with him in his everlasting prayer for all creation.

At this point some eucharistic prayers include references to the offering that has taken place earlier in the service. The classic language comes from the *Book of Common Prayer*. "And here we offer and present unto you, O Lord, our selves, our souls and bodies, to be a reasonable, holy and living sacrifice unto thee." The prayer continues by "humbly beseeching" that worshipers will receive Christ's body and blood and that their sins will be forgiven.

Conclusion

Eucharistic prayers are unified and sequential, moving to a climax that consists of praise. In most traditions, the concluding lines speak to the triune God whose redeeming work has been proclaimed in the prayer now coming to a close. The final portion of the prayer sounds the grace note of the church's thankful praise. Together the people of God pray the words that Jesus gave his disciples:

>Our Father in heaven,
>hallowed be your name....

Exploring New Forms

The development of new forms for the eucharistic prayer continues. Five factors can be mentioned as the driving force for this continuing work. First, it now is clear that the redeeming grace of God that is summarized in this prayer is far richer than any one can ever express. The second driving force is a growing interest in the recovery of local and individual responsibility for the communion prayer. Although the possibilities of using such prayers in public worship are still restricted, many people are finding opportunities to create forms that are especially adapted to local circumstances. Third, churches around the world are committed to acculturation, which means the clothing of Christian faith, worship, and life in the various cultures of humankind. Noteworthy in this respect are eucharistic prayers in East Africa that adapt traditional African prayer forms and use them to proclaim the church's thankful praise to God (Shorter 1973a, 114-116; 1973b). Fourth, the churches that for so long have been separated from one another, especially at the communion table, are now living their way into new forms of unity. As part of this effort they are contributing to one another out of the fullness of their various eucharistic traditions. New prayer texts are inspired by these encounters.

The fifth reason for new prayer texts is the radical change occurring in the world in which the churches offer their thankful praise. This prayer is an *anaphora*, an offering up to God of life in the world. The shape of that world and the character of the events that take place within it affect the minds and hearts of believers. The reconciliation earnestly desired has to be shaped to the particular distress of history at the time the church prays. While the specific details of life in the world will be more fully stated in the prayers of the people earlier in the liturgy, this same life can infuse the eucharistic prayer with color and intensity. Old prayers hardly seem to do in new times.

A powerful example of a text adapted to new conditions is a Mexican eucharistic prayer that is locally specific in its thanks for creation:

>With joy we praise you
>for the high mountains and their trees,
>for the rushing waters of Usumacinta and Grijalva
>which give energy and fruitfulness.... (Link 1984, 47-51)

The prayer remembers the history of oppression in Egypt and its parallels in Mexican history. The epiclesis asks that God send the

Spirit of Jesus that all who eat and drink at this table "may be united in the work of preparation for the Feast of the Free People" for which Jesus laid down his life. The prayer links worshipers and "the company of the day-laborers with a thousand cares," and with "all who are persecuted for justice…and all those others who have sacrificed themselves in the endeavour to turn our native land into a tiny part of the Kingdom" of God's Son.

The fact that new prayers are being developed and the fact that the circumstances surrounding eucharistic worship often are so unique lead a growing number of people to develop their own prayers for the communion service. In response to this trend, various liturgical commissions have developed guidelines for people to use. One of the first was developed by the Consultation on Church Union (published in 1978) and stated that these prayers should "include these themes which reflect aspects of the eucharistic prayer commonly expressed by the Church from ancient times" (COCU 1978, 32). Three themes were then listed:

(1) Thanks for God's creation and redemption of the world in Christ;
(2) Thanks for the gift of this sacrament expressed in a way that recalls Christ's words of institution;
(3) Thanks for the gift of the Holy Spirit whose presence is invoked (*BCP* 1979, 402-05).

Lists of themes for extemporaneous eucharistic prayers are also published by the United Church of Christ and the Episcopal Church. In the *Book of Common Prayer*, the expectation is that the first half of the prayer will be extemporaneous, including thanks for God's work in creation and revelation and remembrance of the particular occasion when the service is being conducted. Then it gives two versions of the second half of the prayer, expecting one or the other of these will be used with the extemporaneous first half.

The outline presented in *Book of Worship* (BW 1986, 72) is the most complete:

- Give thanks for God's goodness to us shown in the creation of the world and in the events of history.
- Remember people of faith through whom God has spoken to the human family as witnessed in scripture.
- Give thanks for the birth, life, death, and resurrection of Jesus Christ.
- Remind us that our participation in Holy Communion is a sacrifice of praise that includes the offering of our lives to God.

- Briefly proclaim faith in Christ who has died, is raised, and will return at the close of history.
- Give thanks for the gift of the Holy Spirit whose presence is invoked.

A few of these experimental and extemporaneous prayers will mature in their contents and form so that they will be used by worshiping communities over some period of time. Most, however, will be useful among the people and on the occasions for which they were prepared, but cannot long endure. The more specific the language, the less likely that a text can be adequate for use "always and everywhere," to use a classic eucharistic phrase.

The theological challenge in writing eucharistic prayers is self-evident. When the "jot and tittle" mentality dominates, only those prayers can be used that survive exacting theological scrutiny. First drafts rarely pass, and locally developed texts tend to be too idiosyncratic in their phrasing to fulfill theological expectations. Even when the theological filter is of a large mesh, new prayers often do not pass through because of the novelty of language. To sum up the salvific center of the Christian faith in a prominent and public prayer is a difficult task. Most efforts achieve partial success only.

Another difficulty in developing new prayers is more literary than theological. Beauty of phrasing and sincerity of heart must be distinguished from each other. God hears the simplest prayer in whatever language it is uttered. Yet spoken prayer is more than the muttering of religious intentions; it is the speaking forth of words that are consistent with the one who is the God of beauty as much as of goodness, wisdom, and justice. Speaking of the difficulties of liturgical translation, Alexander Schmemann once said that what usually is lost is the poetry, and "having lost the poetry, we have lost everything." The question of literary beauty is part of the ongoing debate about the terse, colloquial style of much modern liturgy, including the work of the Roman Catholic International Commission on English in the Liturgy. This same battle used to be fought when new translations of the Bible came along. Is the new translation beautiful enough to be read in public worship?

As time has moved on and the churchgoing ears have become accustomed to hearing the contemporary idiom in worship, most people have been converted. We want the English, or other languages of our time, to be used in worship. Yet most people also want that language to be graceful, sharp, and penetrating. Perhaps people use the word beautiful less than formerly. Instead they are likely to ask for speech that is strong, eloquent, and expressive.

Whatever descriptive words are used, writing such prayers is difficult to do. Even a brilliant first draft usually benefits from trial use and revision. Many locally developed or otherwise experimental texts reach the public ear before that process of revision and maturation has reached its conclusion. Thus the prayers, regardless of their theological merit, fall short in usage. Despite these difficulties, the creating of new eucharistic prayers is good for those who select the words and good for the congregations whose worshiping life is the context in which these words come to life. Thus the work of finding the words with which to proclaim the great thanksgiving continues until that time when we join the heavenly chorus.

Encouraging the Conversation

In this chapter I describe the eucharistic prayers as summaries of the Christian faith, highlighting creation, revelation, and redemption. One way for you to understand and evaluate your experience at the Lord's table is to examine representative prayers from your tradition. For some of you these prayers will come directly out of the published books that are the regular source of prayers for sacramental occasions. Others of you, however, worship in congregations where the communion prayers are ordinarily spoken extemporaneously. You too can gather up prayers. You can makes notes on the main themes of communion prayers that you hear people offer at the table. If some worship leaders write out the texts they say, you could use those notes. Still another way of getting texts is to record that part of services and use the transcription of prayers as your case material.

With these prayers in hand, it is possible to study them and the worshiping practice in which such prayers are used. Some suggestions:

- Develop an outline of communion prayers used in your church.
- Compare this outline with the one presented in this chapter and evaluate your experienced practice and the practice of other churches.
- Summarize the doctrinal content of the prayers suggested in this chapter. In the light of this chapter, what do you say about these prayers?
- If you were to develop a communion prayer for general use in your church tradition, what would that prayer be?

III

OTHER SERVICES

Although the Sunday service is the primary act of worship in a congregation, this major event is surrounded by other liturgies. Some are services of praise, preaching, and prayer that can be offered at any time or place that Christians gather. Some are occasional services prompted by events in the life cycle of individuals or communities—baptism and the renewal of baptismal vows, marriage, thanksgiving for the birth or adoption of children, and death rites. These occasional liturgies are also part of the churches' *thankful praise of God*, for the foundation of all that we ask or think in public assemblies is God's gracious offering of life through Jesus Christ.

Baptism, discussed in Chapters 9 and 10, is a time of rejoicing before God because in this rite sins are forgiven, estrangement is overcome, and hope for the future is provided. Weddings, in Chapter 11, are times to give God thanks for the gifts of life and love, as well as for the promise of happiness for life. Funerals, also in Chapter 11, praise God for the mystery and power of life, for the person memorialized, and for the promise of life in union with God.

For all of these services the encouragement offered in Colossians continues to be the norm for Christian worship: "And whatever you do, in word or deed, do everything in the name of the Lord Jesus, giving thanks to God the Father through him" (3:17). The challenge facing all of us who carry responsibility for worship is to prepare and lead these services so that this thankful praise of God is central.

9

Recovering the One Baptism

This interpretation of the outer circle of Christian worship begins with baptism because it is the second most important liturgy in the life of the churches. The history of baptism and closely related rites is complex, with pastoral, theological, and political issues connected together in a complicated pattern. Because Christian identity, life in the church, and standing in society are included in baptism, the various ideas and practices are held with great intensity. Regrettably, churches have battled one another fiercely over the meaning and form of baptism, with the result that its character as an act of praise has been obscured by polemics.

One of the happiest aspects of the current renewal of worship is that the controversial mentality is being replaced by a new mood. Even the debates over infant and adult baptism and between sacramental and obediential interpretations of baptism have become more theological and less political in nature. The fact that contemporary Western culture is increasingly indifferent to, and often hostile toward, the gospel and churchly life has shifted the battle for Christians. Now we are struggling with the "principalities" and "powers" (Ephesians 6:10–12, RSV) rather than with other branches of the one Church of Jesus Christ.

The Continuing History of Baptism

Christian baptism is founded on Jesus' baptism in the Jordan River by his cousin John. Although he came from a family with hereditary duties in the temple, John moved away from the central shrine, preaching a message of reform. He called upon his people to repent of their sins and reclaim the heritage handed down by Moses and the prophets. The sign of their repentance and reclaiming of this heritage was a ritual cleansing in the River Jordan. The Greek verb *baptizo* connotes being overwhelmed by the water, but we do not know how these baptisms occurred: whether by dipping or some other dramatic application of water. The Gospel accounts emphasize that large numbers of people responded, drawn especially from groups marginalized in the political and economic systems of the time, but including a few from the religious and military elites. Jesus was drawn to this renewal movement and presented himself for baptism, "to fulfill all righteousness" (Matthew 3:15).

Soon thereafter Jesus began preaching in his own right, and included baptism in his version of the movement. Quickly Jesus' branch of the movement became more popular than John's, but John responded to the reports by recalling his earlier pronouncement that Jesus must increase and John must decrease (John 3:25–30). In this same account the explanation is given for John's continuing practice of baptism that "water was abundant there" (3:23). A little later this same Gospel reports that Jesus was making and baptizing more disciples than was John, but then adds "although it was not Jesus himself but his disciples who baptized" (John 4:2). At that point, Jesus and his band left the Jordan and moved into the hill country, where we can presume that water was less abundant. Whether because of the absence of water or for other reasons, Jesus seems no longer to have emphasized baptism in his program for the renewal of his people.

The reclaiming of the Jewish vision of God's purpose, with its watery rite of renewal, carried the dual promise of power and great danger. Even before Jesus came to him, John himself spoke of the coming one who would baptize with the Spirit and with fire. When Jesus was coming out of the water, he experienced the opening of heaven, the descent of the Spirit as a dove, and a voice declaring him to be God's Son. Later in his ministry, Luke reports that Jesus made this further declaration: "I came to bring fire to the earth, and how I wish it were already kindled! I have a baptism with which to be baptized, and what stress I am under until it is completed!" (Luke 12:49–50). Mark reports another use of the word *baptize*. In response to the request by James and John that they be permitted to sit at his right and left in glory, Jesus responds by speaking of the cup that he must drink and the baptism with which he must be baptized. He asks them if they are able to participate in these experiences, to which they respond affirmatively. Jesus then states that he cannot grant them their request to sit beside him in glory. He affirms, however, that they would drink from the same cup as he would drink from and be baptized with the same baptism (Mark 10:35–40). On the Mount of Olives, Jesus prays fervently that this cup, which means his suffering and death, would pass from him (Luke 22:39–46). Thus, baptism has been understood to refer to his suffering and death.

One way to summarize the emergence of baptism in the life of the early church is to say that it became the way that Jesus' followers could be incorporated into Christ's suffering and death. This theme is especially prominent in Paul's discussion of baptism in Romans 6. Those who are baptized into Christ Jesus are baptized into his death, and they also rise to new life with him. This passage says little about the ritual itself, either the text or the ceremony, but it does say much about union with Christ.

The emphasis upon the Holy Spirit was also moved into early Christian practice. On the Day of Pentecost following the Passion of Christ, the Holy Spirit, appearing in tongues as of fire, came upon the disciples with power. Impelled by the Spirit, they burst into the streets of Jerusalem, proclaiming the resurrection. Speaking on behalf of the others, Peter instructed the people: "repent, and be baptized every one of you in the name of Jesus Christ so that your sins may be forgiven; and you will receive the gift of the Holy Spirit." He continued his instruction in a way that would make sense to Jewish hearers, affirming that the generations were bound up together. "For the promise is for you, for your children, and for all who are far away, everyone whom the Lord our God calls to him" (Acts 2:38–39).

From this first reference to Christian baptism in Acts we can infer much of what developed later in the history of this rite. Although the preaching was to Jews, they came from all over the Roman world. Thus the universalizing tendencies of the Christian message of God's commonwealth were already implicit. The preaching was addressed to people who were old enough to understand the message, evaluate their own lives, and make clear decisions about their religious affiliation. Yet, the renewal of the covenant was to include their descendants throughout the generations. Thus, on this first day of gospel preaching the potentially conflicting foundations for baptism were presented: conversion and commitment; covenant and initiation. In these earliest days of the Christian community, baptism was conducted "into the name of Jesus Christ" for the forgiveness of sins and was followed by a strong sense of spiritual power. Those baptized became members of a joy-filled community of praise. Other episodes described in the book of Acts continue these themes (see Acts 2:43–47; 3:7–10; 16:30–34). Later, the theological contents of the rite seem to have been increased. Baptism was often described with the metaphor of new birth; and also of being washed clean of one's sins. The liturgical form of baptism was also in transition, for at a later date, as Matthew records, baptism was "in the name of the Father and of the Son and of the Holy Spirit" (Matthew 28:19).

During the generations following the New Testament era, and perhaps beginning during the apostolic generation, three issues became increasingly important: the place of baptism in the politics of church and empire, the changing definitions of salvation, and the participation of children in the covenanted community. The first of these issues pushed toward a stringent understanding of church membership and intensified the adult character of baptism. The second pushed irresistibly toward the baptism of infants and their incorporation into the church a a very early age. As a result of both pressures, the status of children became a matter of concern.

Early in the church's life baptism became a matter closely connected to political identity. During New Testament times, baptism into the name of Jesus marked the separation of one group of Jews from the main body of Judaism. It became a way of distinguishing between Roman citizens who lived safely within the disciplines and constraints of organized communities and those who moved outside normal limits of citizenship in secular society. The relations between church and synagogue, between church and empire, and between churches of various ethnic identities became increasingly hostile, with violence often the result. Therefore over a long period of time questions about the validity of baptism and the requirements of membership in the churches became volatile. Many people lost their lives in the battles over the political implications of baptism.

One of the most important of these struggles was based in North Africa and is called the Donatist controversy, borrowing the name of a one-time leader of the church in Carthage. His segment of the church emphasized a rigorous understanding of the gospel and insisted upon clear separation between the church and secular government. Other leaders of the African church, including Cyprian and Augustine, affirmed a doctrine of the Christian life that included greater openness to participation in Roman culture. These two segments of the church split into two parts. Later, when there was a movement to recover unity, the validity of baptisms performed by the splintering group became a highly controversial topic. It was within this framework that the conclusion was reached: the validity of baptism depends not upon the ecclesial status of the one doing the baptizing, but upon the efficacy within the rite itself and upon God's blessing that action with the Holy Spirit.

From the earliest sermon by Peter, baptism and the forgiveness of sins were connected. It can be inferred that this forgiveness of sins is part of the process of being saved from sin and its consequences. The New Testament, however, is reticent in making explicit statements to this effect. Only in 1 Peter is the language straightforward. After referring to Noah's being saved through water, the writer continues: "And baptism, which this prefigured, now saves you—not as a removal of dirt from the body, but as an appeal to God for a good conscience, through the resurrection of Jesus Christ" (1 Peter 3:21). Throughout the New Testament sin is described primarily in terms of individual disobedience to the law and thus to God, or in terms of rejecting Christ.

There are only the slightest hints of a foundational sin that extends from generation to generation and automatically embraces all new people even before they are old enough to violate the law. A reasoned approach to adults, calling upon them to repent and be baptized, was consistent with this way of understanding the unredeemed condition. Gradually the doctrine of sin was extended to incorporate hereditary sin, a doctrine that has some foundation in earlier Jewish piety. This state of sinfulness took hold of everyone, even before they were able to act on their own. An adult baptism was too late for people who were sinners from infancy onward. Thus, the practice of incorporating children by baptism into the redeemed community became a normal part of church practice, certainly by the fifth century.

Normal practice came to be the baptism of infants soon after birth. In the Eastern churches the rite continued to be the full classic form, conducted in parish churches by the pastor of the congregation. In Western churches, baptism was conducted in the parish churches by the priest in charge; but the post-baptismal laying on of hands with prayer for the Holy Spirit was reserved for the bishop of the diocese and ordinarily was administered at a later date. In Eastern churches infants were given the eucharistic elements at the conclusion of the baptismal rite, which meant that technically they were in full communion with the church despite their tender age. In Western churches infant communion was ordinarily not practiced, but first communion took place in early childhood, usually prior to confirmation by the bishop. Thus, in these churches, too, children technically were communicants despite their young age. Once in place, this pattern of baptizing infants and then phasing then into the church on a gradual basis became the standard way of doing things in the Western church.

During the sixteenth-century Reformation, baptismal questions came to the fore once again. Again issues were theological and political, dealing both with participation in the Commonwealth of Heaven and in the Empire of Earth. The reformers rediscovered the doctrine of salvation by grace through faith, and they tended to preach it in a way that made sense of adult baptism. Yet, they were convinced of the solidarity of society, the necessity that all people in the realm be united in faith and ecclesial identity. This side of their convictions, inherited from earlier ages, kept infant baptism very much in the forefront of their attention. This tendency was strongly reinforced by the rebellions against the secular order by zealots, some of whom believed in adult baptism only. The result was that most of the new Protestant churches retained their traditional practices of infant baptism.

The exceptions to this tendency were Anabaptists and later the Baptist churches. Both groups called for a stricter application of biblical examples and norms. Both emphasized an ecclesiology that separated the church from the world rather than accommodating itself to the world. In these churches infant baptism made little sense. This emphasis upon believer's baptism was brought to the United States and has become widespread in Anabaptist and Baptist churches, in churches of the Stone-Campbell movement, and in charismatic and evangelical churches. Thus, today in North America the greater number of Christians continue to practice infant baptism, but the number of Christians who baptize only people able to speak for themselves is moving toward a nearly equal proportion.

One new development came in the historic churches of the Reformation. They had scruples against confirmation by bishops, and they were committed to a church whose members understood and lived according to the gospel. These convictions led the reformers to transform the liturgical act of confirmation, making it into an extended process of instruction and nurture. Furthermore, they rearranged the sequence of first communion and confirmation. In the new Protestant order, baptized children were not received at the holy table until after they had completed the pedagogical and liturgical processes of confirmation, now done under the leadership of the local pastor. Thus the mature pattern in Lutheran, Reformed, and Anglican churches was infant baptism that conferred a preparatory membership in the church; a process of instruction followed by affirmation of baptismal vows; and then full membership in the church with admission to the eucharist. In churches of the Baptist, Disciples, and Pentecostal families, however, baptism was always administered to people able to speak for themselves; and it was followed by immediate and full admission to the table.

Even though scholars and pastors have been involved in the modern discussions of liturgical questions related to the Lord's supper since the mid-nineteenth century, relatively little attention had been given to baptism and closely related services. It is true that the Faith and Order Commission of the World Council of Churches was conducting its long-standing study of baptism (under the title *One Lord, One Baptism*), trying to broaden the discussion from the narrow polemical form it usually took. Even so, the ancient and unproductive debates over infant and believer's baptism still flared up. Most scholars, pastors, and publishers continued their work as though their own traditional practices of baptism would remain in place.

In the decade of the 1970s, however, these calm waters became tempest-tossed. Protestants and Catholics alike gave renewed attention to the basic theological foundations of Christian baptism. As they did so they realized that normal pastoral practice was often—

perhaps we could even say usually—out of step with basic belief. Formal theology insisted that baptism, even of infants, was full and complete. Yet the common practice was to deny baptized children access to the eucharist for several years, and usually then only after a second liturgical rite, confirmation, had been conducted. Thus the issue became the relationship of baptism to later initiatory rites and to full life in the church. The political meaning of baptism once again became important. What is the relationship between membership in the community of faith and membership in the civil community? These problems were especially prominent in churches that traditionally baptized in infancy, confirmed them in late childhood, and then admitted them to communion. This Western synthesis of initiatory rites became unglued, as one scholar stated the matter.

In somewhat different ways, churches that ordinarily baptized people old enough to speak for themselves also faced serious questions about baptism, membership in the church, and citizenship in the larger society. Despite the assumption that church children need to be converted, the tendency is to initiate them routinely as they enter into late childhood or early adolescence. Is this practice consistent with believer's baptism? Whenever baptism occurs in these churches, the ecclesial standing of these children is ambiguous. Are they members of the church to some degree, and thus eligible to partake of its life? including the Lord's supper? Or are these unbaptized children of believers no different from pagans? Even in churches that practice believer's baptism, members (and churches themselves) become accommodated to culture. If distinguishing between world and church is an important objective, then is believer's baptism any more effective than infant baptism?

In all of the churches, regardless of the age and mode of baptism, another question pushes itself forward. Does baptism in water bring with it the experience of the power of baptism? The accounts in the New Testament are clear that when people were baptized, the experience was transforming. Lives were radically changed and they exhibited a psychic energy and courage that were amazing to the people who watched. The power of the new life in Christ continues to be promised to people who enter into covenantal relationship with their crucified and risen Lord. Yet large numbers of people in the churches believe but do not experience that spiritual energy. Why not? What conclusions should churches draw?

A New Consensus

The result was that a new liturgical discussion unfolded around baptism that compressed into a few years what had taken several decades with respect to eucharistic discussion. During this same period of time, the Commission on Worship of the Consultation on Church Union was moving from its consideration of eucharistic worship to a consideration of baptism and related initiatory rites.

The members of the Commission carried dual responsibility. On the one hand they had to be faithful to the traditions of their respective churches. On the other hand they had to move toward common ground that was broad and firm enough that all of their churches could stand on it together. Consequently, these scholars found themselves restating classical understandings of baptism and reshaping the full range of baptismal practice in keeping with these restatements. They also focused upon the relationship between baptism and life in the modern world.

At that time the COCU Commission on Worship was the most fruitful gathering place in North America for liturgical scholars responsible for the new wave of official reform and publication. Meetings were held twice yearly, and they brought together representatives of the nine (sometimes ten) participating churches and of other churches interested in liturgical reform. Noteworthy among the observer-participants were delegates of the Inter-Lutheran Commission on Worship and the Roman Catholic Church. Thus, the discussions in COCU meetings shaped not only the materials published by the Consultation but even more important the trial liturgies of the several participating churches. (In later years this consultative relationship has been broadened and continued in English-speaking North America by the Consultation on Common Texts and internationally by the English Language Liturgical Consultation.)

Although there is considerable variation in the detail of the resulting baptismal liturgies, the unity that characterizes them is even more impressive. We can speak with greater accuracy than has previously been possible of the "one baptism." This one baptism can be described under five headings.

First, *the liturgical standard for baptism is the full set of actions that the Western churches have tended to split into separate rites and ceremonies.* Churches that baptize infants have had a three-step process: baptism soon after birth, affirmation of baptismal vows and prayer for the gift of the Holy Spirit, and reception into the church. Churches that practice believer's baptism have tended toward a two-step process: confession of the Christian faith, then baptism (with reception into the church implied). In both patterns admission to communion has ordinarily followed. In the new liturgies, however, the liturgical norm is for all of these actions to be arranged in their classical order, with the strong implication that they all be done on one occasion. The COCU liturgy includes these parts: liturgy of the Word, presentation of the candidates, prayer over the water, the baptismal affirmations, the administration of the water, and post-baptismal ceremonies. Other liturgies follow a similar pattern, with the Presbyterian outline especially clear: presentation, profession of faith, thanksgiving over the water, the baptism, the laying on of hands, and welcome (*BCW* 1993, 402).

Drafters of these liturgies have assumed that pastors would draw from this unified service those sections that might be needed on any one occasion. For example, "the Baptismal Covenant I" published in *The United Methodist Hymnal* (*UMH* 1989, 33), lists five sections (Holy Baptism, Confirmation, Reaffirmation of Faith, Reception into the United Methodist Church, and Reception into a Local Congregation) and then gives this rubric: "This service may be used for any of the above acts, or any combination of these that might be called for on a given occasion" (33).

This new liturgical standard also calls for using water generously. Of course, churches that have ordinarily baptized by immersion are already following this injunction, but many of the churches have used water minimally for many generations. Water is now being poured in noticeable ways during the liturgy, and it is applied more generously than has been the practice. In some churches, immersion even of infants is being practiced as a more ordinary form of applying the water of Christian baptism.

Second, *the baptism of people able to speak for themselves is the theological norm for the new rites.* An especially forceful statement of this idea is given by Roman Catholic scholar Aidan Kavanagh in a book entitled *The Shape of Baptism: The Rite of Christian Initiation* (Kavanagh 1978, especially 108f.). From early in the church's life, baptism has been administered at different points in the life cycle. The earliest examples, including that of Jesus himself, are of adults who are making a conscious choice to reclaim or to enter into a particular faith tradition. Conversions described in The Acts of the Apostles refer to households who were baptized along with the one whose conversion is described. Thus, from the very beginning the social contract was as prominent as the individual faith commitment of one person.

Even so, believer's baptism clearly is the common practice, the normal pattern. Only later does infant baptism become increasingly common. It became a normal part of the church's practice when two conditions were in place—the doctrine of original sin and the growing connection between the church and the civil jurisdictions of society. Even in these earlier centuries, there was also a fairly common practice of delaying baptism until late in one's life so that its forgiving properties could cover a more substantial body of the sins of a lifetime. There came a time in most of the Western churches that the most common practice was infant baptism, even though adult conversion continued to take place. The gradual shift that occurs is that the most common practice gradually takes on theological prominence and becomes the basis for interpreting all else.

What now is occurring is that adult baptism is once again seen as theologically primary for all aspects of baptismal practice. Even though infant baptism continues to be administered, and may even be the more common practice throughout the church, the full rite as administered to believers is now regarded as the basic form; infant baptism is now interpreted as a variant of the norm rather than as the norm itself.

Third, *other rites and ceremonies for early childhood are being given greater prominence, at least in the new worship books.*The instinct of families that birth is a moment of transcendence is trustworthy. It is appropriate to offer thanks to God for the new child and for the preservation of the mother's life. It also is appropriate for the community of faith to gather around the family to share with them the responsibilities of rearing the new child in the love of God and neighbor and in the values of life that are consistent with that love. Even when parents have resisted the doctrines of sin and salvation inherent in infant baptism, they have tended to hold to the rite because of its strength concerning thanksgiving and solidarity.

Fortunately, other services can be celebrated to convey these qualities that are central to the state of infancy. One of the strongest examples of these rites was published by the Episcopal Church under the title "A Thanksgiving for the Birth or Adoption of a Child" (*BCP* 1979, 439-45). The rite is simple and direct, and focuses upon the natural instincts of families rather than upon the theological convictions concerning sin and salvation. It can be conducted any place and any time. The outline includes: statement of the purpose of the gathering, an act of thanksgiving using psalms and a prayer, and other prayers. The one prayer offered as standard for the rite is explicitly Christian, although not salvific:

> O God, you have taught us through your blessed Son that whoever receives a little child in the name of Christ receives Christ himself: We give you thanks for the blessing you have bestowed upon this family in giving them a child. Confirm their joy by a lively sense of your presence with them, and give them calm strength and patient wisdom as they seek to bring this child to love all that is true and noble, just and pure, lovable and gracious, excellent and admirable, following the example of our Lord and Savior, Jesus Christ (*BCP* 1979, 443).

A similar type of service, widely practiced by Baptists and Disciples, is somewhat more ecclesial than this simple rite of thanksgiving at the birth or adoption of a child. It is a service in the presence of the congregation and includes the elements discussed just above, but adds vows for family and congregation to take. Often infants are given their names at this same rite.

Fourth, *the decisive character of baptism for the scheme of redemption is being reclaimed*. The ecumenical consensus statement *Baptism, Eucharist and Ministry* (*BEM* 1982, 2f.), for example, presents five themes in its summary of the meaning of baptism: participation in Christ's death and resurrection; conversion, pardoning, and cleansing; the gift of the Holy Spirit; incorporation into the body of Christ; and the sign of the Kingdom. Baptism, in other words, once again is understood as central to the process by which God in Christ reconciles the world to God's self. This emphasis upon the role of baptism in God's saving work leads to another conclusion. If one is baptized, then admission to the eucharist necessarily follows. Or, to put the point in reverse form, once a person is baptized, nothing can be permitted to stand between this new Christian and full participation in the church's life. Baptism cuts across denominational lines. No matter under whose auspices one is baptized, membership is in the church universal. Baptism is done only once. As interpreted in contemporary literature, this claim means that no church has the right to redo baptism when it has already been done. The reason is that God through the Holy Spirit is the primary actor in baptism, and for the church to presume to redo God's action is highly presumptuous.

Because baptism is understood in so decisive a way, then this sacrament becomes the foundation for other important ecclesial acts. The three that have been most important in recent ecumenical activities are the mutual recognition of members, the mutual recognition of churches, and the mutual recognition of ministries. Churches still have difficulty acting on the implications of these claims, but they continue to move forward and toward one another. Once the claim is made that there is one baptism, in which God is primary actor, then the next steps follow inexorably. The problem and the opportunity are both illustrated in the Consultation on Church Union. Conversations began with the tacit acceptance of one another as in some sense truly Christian and of one another's churches as in some sense true parts of the one church of Christ. Participants in COCU discussions, therefore, had to define this tacit agreement, which led to the mutual recognition of baptism. But if by baptism Christians are all members of the one church, then these separate historical communities all must partake in some sense of the real church, and the ministries that guide them must be in some sense true ministries.

It is easier, however, to agree to these ideas in the abstract than to realize them in the actual ecclesial practices of the churches. Throughout much of their modern history, many churches have insisted upon the theological necessity of certain elements of form in their ecclesial practice. Two examples are especially important because they are so closely parallel. Some churches have insisted that faithfulness to apostolic teaching and example requires that full immersion be the form of Christian baptism. Other churches have insisted that the apostolic witness of the church requires that ordination include the laying on of hands by a bishop who stands in the unbroken line of bishops beginning with the apostles and continuing until now. In contemporary ecumenical discussions many people in these two traditions have acknowledged that the apostolic core of baptism and of ordination is present in the rites of churches that do not possess these necessary signs of immersion and of apostolic succession. Even so, the realization of full mutuality is very difficult to achieve despite the earnestness of theological affirmations.

The fifth characteristic of the current consensus is that *even though baptism is done only once, baptismal vows can and need to be made repeatedly*. Certainly baptism is a time when something decisive happens to people. By the Holy Spirit God acts to forgive sins and redeem a life. The person baptized also acts, obeying the divine command and embracing the Christian life. Yet, forgiveness and the practice of the Christian life continue to mature. From time to time, new moments of decision and crisis occur when the renunciations of sin are necessary and the promises to Christ need to be made anew. One time is when a person baptized in infancy makes the Christian profession in his or her own right. Another is when a more mature recognition of the Christian faith takes place. Another is when a person repents after a period of lessened participation and comes back into the church's life. At such times the one baptism is not redone, but the vows of loyalty to Christ can be remade, signs of reconciliation offered, and the renewing of the relationship to God through Christ can be celebrated. An extended discussion of several types of reaffirmation, with suggested liturgical texts, is provided in *Holy Baptism and Services for the Renewal of Baptism* (*Holy Baptism* 1985).

The Continuing Discussion

The consensus described above is strong and widespread, and the liturgies in the generation of worship books from the 1970s onward are shaped by these ideas—and in the next chapter will be discussed in greater detail. Despite this consensus, or perhaps because of it, theological, liturgical, and pastoral discussions continue. Five of these topics are especially important.

First, *some people express a fundamental indifference to baptism, and as a result they treat matters related to baptism in a cavalier fashion*. I have encountered, for example, this defense of infant baptism: "Although the theology supporting adult baptism is stronger than the theology supporting infant baptism, my church practices infant baptism. I like my church and therefore will practice infant baptism even though there is little theological support for that practice. It is possible for me to do this because baptism doesn't amount to anything anyway." For these students, and many other people like them, baptism is a pleasant ceremony after birth with little more significance than the baby shower before birth. Other students suggest a different way of trivializing the rite. They stand in the American evangelical tradition that emphasizes adult conversion as an inner spiritual experience. Baptism follows this experience, but these people strongly resist the idea that God is at work in the water rite itself. Therefore baptism is made part of the discipline of getting into the church, but has no salvific efficacy in itself.

Attitudes such as these may be the result of formal teaching about baptism in some churches. The greater likelihood is that people develop such attitudes because their churches have neglected their teaching responsibilities and their liturgical practices concerning baptism. If the rite has been handled as though it were a trivial matter, then participants in these churches are likely to grow up with similar attitudes. The appropriate response in churches is to give greater attention to teaching about baptism and to the ways that they administer this sacrament. When the people of the churches experience baptism as an act of decisive importance, they are likely to develop a strong sense of baptism and its effects in their lives.

Second, *pastoral practice has trouble keeping up with theological and liturgical reform.* Some would state the problem in another way— that theological and liturgical reform is unrealistic and out of touch with the real life of churches. Although I prefer the first of the statements, both forms make the claim that pastoral practice and the revised rites are not yet adequately synchronized. Again citing comments by students, I hear some negative reaction to the baptismal liturgies published in *The United Methodist Hymnal.* The reason given is that it is too hard to pick one's way through the full text and isolate the parts that one wants to use. For some people making this comment, the problem is strictly one of rubrical awkwardness. In other cases, however, the problem is deeper. The services in their new form make it harder to separate the aesthetic ceremonies from the theological claims about sin and forgiveness, nature and grace. People who want to do something traditional and beautiful to babies for the sake of the families find that the new rites require them to do far more. They are not sure how to respond to this theological deepening of the baptismal waters. Taking baptism seriously is a serious undertaking.

Another example of the disjunction between theory and practice can be seen in discussions about evangelism. The question can be asked: how great a change in life is necessary as one comes to baptism? Some churches have established as their norm one of the versions of the adult catechumenate, which presupposes a slow process of conversion and major changes in life before baptism can be administered. The instruction and nurture of the catechumenate can radicalize converts and the church into which they enter. (Although the modern "adult catechumenate" is associated with the Roman Catholic Rite for the Christian Initiation of Adults, it also has Protestant versions, including two that are published in *The Book of Occasional Services* (1979, 112-25) and *Baptism and Belonging* (1991, 109-22). Other evangelists, pastors, congregations, and many casual attenders are not sure that they want to make such a radical commitment. Baptism, they believe, should come early in the process of conversion, with major changes in life coming only gradually thereafter. Culture Christianity dies hard.

These first two topics are relatively superficial problems with the new baptismal rites. They are matters requiring attention even though they do not cut to the quick of sacramental theology and practice. Topics three and four, however, are more likely to draw blood, and to them I now turn.

The third issue for continuing discussion is *the relationship between baptism and eucharist*. The traditional practice is firmly established and is supported with several theological rationales. Briefly stated, the uniform tradition is that baptism necessarily precedes participation in the eucharist. The first sacrament is often referred to as the sacrament of birth, and the second as the sacrament of growth. Some use a political metaphor, stating that baptism is the rite of naturalization and eucharist the rite of full citizenship. Clearly, these lines of explanation mandate that baptism come first. When baptism is routinely administered during infancy, then there is little occasion to question this traditional pattern of relationship. Churches that baptize people old enough to speak for themselves, however, have a different experience. Church families routinely face the parental and pastoral challenge of nurturing their own children during the years prior to their confession of faith and baptism. The question is whether or not these children may be received at the table along with older members of their family. Here the household argument so long used to support infant baptism also is invoked. In the Hebraic tradition of religiously shaped meals, children are always included along with other members of the covenanted family. We have no record, nor any biblical instruction, limiting the Lord's supper to those who are baptized (and confirmed). What grounds, therefore, do we have to deny these little ones in church families the enjoyment of the family table?

This line of argument can be carried one step further. If either of the sacraments is the one that invites people into relations with the living and loving God, then it is the one that offers hospitality at the table. If either of the sacraments represents the drawing of the line based on decisions for or against the gracious God, then it is baptism, especially when administered to mature people. The conclusion some draw is that eucharist is the sacrament associated with birth and the nurturing of faith in its earliest years, and that baptism comes at the time when people are ready to claim the faith and the Christian life as the careful act of mature people.

  ·   This question is most urgent among Disciples. Their normal Sunday service includes the celebration of the Lord's supper, with the communion elements passed to the congregants sitting in the pews. Disciples also practice believer's baptism, which means that the children of their own families are not baptized until pre-adolescent years and thus according to the older tradition are not eligible to receive communion. Most Disciples congregations, however, receive people from other churches by simple transfer of membership even when they had been baptized as infants. Thus the baptized small children of these families are eligible to partake while the Disciples children sitting next to them in the pew are not. While this situation may be explainable to the more technically minded, neither the logic nor the appropriateness of this tradition makes sense to parents or their children. Many congregations have failed to discuss this problem and have left parents unprepared for making decisions. Even when congregations guide parents, the final decision is always made by those in the pews. One of the encouraging developments among Disciples is that recognized leaders, some with wide experience in ecumenical discussion, are now taking up this topic. The most easily accessible are published statements by Michael Kinnamon (*Baptism and Belonging* 1991, 125-30) and Colbert C. Cartwright (Cartwright 1992, 77-83). Although both writers believe that the unbaptized children of the church are appropriate guests at the table, neither is ready to turn decisions over to parents or to move in ways that ignore the longer ecclesial traditions. Cartwright offers a promising proposal. Children would be enrolled as members of the covenant. They and their parents would be helped to understand, in ways suitable to their ages, what this meal means. These children would not routinely receive communion, but on stated occasions, a service designed with them especially in mind would be conducted at which they would be communicants.

  The fourth issue now under discussion is *the form of the confession of faith that is required for baptism*. Put in its barest form the question is this: does the validity of baptism require the use of the formula "I baptize you (or you are baptized) in the name of the Father, and of the Son, and of the Holy Spirit?" Or may a church use another set of words that also affirm the traditional Christian faith in the triune God? It is generally acknowledged that the earliest Christian baptisms were "into the name of Jesus." (See, for example, Acts 2:38.) During the first century, however, the move to the trinitarian formula took place (see Matthew 28:19), and that practice has been virtually universal ever since. The use of water and the trinitarian name of God have become the basic and essential elements of the baptismal liturgy. The universality of these two elements has been part of the basis on which churches have claimed that there is one baptism even though the form of baptizing has varied so widely.

For many people what is at stake in this discussion is Christian identity itself. Is the initiatory rite used by the church its own or God's? Who has the power and right to change it? These people conclude that only by retaining the classical formula and practice can continuity with the churches of all times and places be maintained. (This argument is presented more fully in my essay "Tradition, Authority, and the Baptismal Formula" in *Baptism and Belonging* 1991, 140-46.)

Resistance to this formula is prompted primarily by the fact that it requires the use of a patriarchal metaphor, for God at this highly significant point in the life of Christians and of the church. Many who offer this objection stand at the center of the church's theological tradition but argue that the God described as Father, Son, and Holy Spirit transcends this metaphor, and that this metaphor has been given such importance that it now approaches idolatrous standing. Their conclusion is that other ways of confessing the trinitarian faith must be developed for the baptismal rite. The fullest treatment of this topic has been offered by Ruth Duck in her book *Gender and the Name of God* (1991). She states that the baptismal formula "epitomizes the contradiction between the church's offer of new life through Jesus Christ and its use of language reflecting patriarchal social systems" (Duck 1991, 4). Duck's proposal for solving this problem is that churches return to an ancient practice of using three questions to which baptizees and sponsors respond. This confession of faith in the triune God affirms classical Christian belief, but in language that moves beyond the limitations in the traditional formula. People are asked to confess their faith in "God, the Source, the fountain of life," in "Christ, the offspring of God embodied in Jesus of Nazareth and in the church," and in "the liberating Spirit of God, the wellspring of new life" (Duck 1991, 185). Another resolution to this challenge, which I discuss in the next chapter, is to say nothing during the act of baptizing, depending upon the other parts of the liturgy, to express the trinitarian faith into which these people are being baptized.

Conclusion

What is taking place in this continuing discussion of baptism is a testing of the old claim that praying shapes believing. The assumption behind this formula, so important to the theological and liturgical traditions, is that the church's praise and petition express the most basic truth claims of the church. These primary statements of faith, vividly expressed in hymns, prayers, and sacramental rites, provide the material used by systematic theologians who condense them into the formulas of technical theology. The "Father, Son, Holy Spirit" language has been a foundational element in worship and in technical theology. Now, however, the people of God in their prayerful rites and ceremonies are no longer content with the technical language that has been bequeathed them. Thus they are casting about for new ways of responding to the one true God who is revealed in Jesus Christ and continues with us as Holy Spirit.

The discussion will continue because our experience of God changes and our understanding of the Christian faith keeps reaching out for new language. Much is at stake in this discussion, and therefore we must move carefully and responsibly. The next decades of work promise to be exciting.

Encouraging the Conversation

1. One of the best ways to get into this discussion is to spend a few minutes remembering your baptism. When did it happen, and where? Can you remember it yourself, or are you recounting what your parents and others tell you about it? Are you "reconstructing" your own account of what probably happened, drawing upon your later observations of others being baptized? What does your baptism mean to you now? As you reflect upon your own experience, what generalizations do you draw about baptism in general and the practice of your own church in particular?

2. What is the normal practice of baptism in your church?

- At what age does it take place?
- How is the water applied?
- What is the theology of baptism as expressed in the text of the service?

3. Are you aware of any changes in baptismal practice and teaching in your church during the past few years? And if so, what are these changes?

4. Think about the challenges mentioned in the latter part of this chapter. How would you counsel people in your church concerning any one of these topics?

10

By Water
and the Spirit

The form of the baptismal liturgy that this chapter presents is the full service of baptism and confirmation adapted for use in the regular Sunday liturgy of the congregation. Although baptism may be celebrated in abridged form under special circumstances or in fuller form on occasions like the Easter Vigil, the normal rite is a fully developed sequence of introduction, promises, prayers, and reception into the church, with the washing in water as the centerpiece. It has been common practice to divide this complete rite into its parts, and to celebrate them at different times; but the meaning of baptism is most clearly revealed and completely accomplished in the pattern that this chapter presents. When celebrated in the normal Sunday gathering of the church, the baptismal rite is spliced into the service of the Word on the one side and the service of the Table on the other, providing focus for the word and energy for the eucharistic meal.

This chapter also assumes that the liturgy is being celebrated in the church where the congregation gathers for its principal liturgies of word and sacrament, rather than in a separated chapel or in running water out-of-doors. The location and character of the baptistry are important to the fullness of celebration. Three factors, often conflicting with one another, influence the location. Traditionally baptism has been understood as the port of entry into the community of faith, with the architectural result that the baptistry is near the principal entrance to the main worship room. Baptism is also understood to be a sacrament in which the full worshiping congregation participates. Thus the font or pool needs to be located so that worshipers can see, hear, and speak their parts. When adult immersion is to be practiced, the pool needs to be located so that plumbing can be provided, the weight of the water supported, and dressing facilities be

170

vided, the weight of the water supported, and dressing facilities be conveniently available. Many newer buildings and successful renovations have provided solutions to the location of the baptistry so that these three needs are met.

Many churches, however, will necessarily continue to baptize in locations that fall short on one or more of the criteria mentioned above. Often the problems can be addressed by an imaginative use of processions. The baptismal group can come to the front of the congregation for the initial portions of the rite, with the full congregation able to participate. Then the pastor and baptismal group can process to the font or pool. The congregation can turn or move around in order to watch the baptism itself. When baptism is by immersion, the liturgy needs to be planned so that all participants are present with the congregation for the complete baptismal liturgy. Time must be provided for people to dress for baptism and to change clothes afterwards.

The baptismal liturgies in recently published service books are very much alike in structure and contents, although the sequence of parts varies slightly, and each tradition develops its own variation of classic baptismal language. The Presbyterian outline is a good example of this consensus in form (*BCW* 1993, 402). It consists of six elements that form the outline for the following exposition.

Presentation
Profession of Faith
Thanksgiving over the Water
The Baptism
The Laying On of Hands
Welcome

In all of the newer liturgies for baptism, the text of the service and the guides for celebration make clear the assumption that the theological and liturgical core of the rite is the same regardless of the age and condition of the people being baptized. There are, however, variations that adapt the service to the particular circumstances of each celebration, and they will be noted as the chapter develops. Some aspects of the baptismal liturgy are also present in other ceremonies such as the liturgy of Thanksgiving for the Birth or Adoption of a Child, and references to these other liturgies will be made where appropriate.

Presentation

The liturgies for Christian baptism begin with an act of hospitality and validation. The persons to be baptized, along with a select group of family, friends, and representatives of the congregation assemble at a place designated for this purpose. They present themselves to the person, ordinarily one of the pastors, who is presiding at this celebration.

The leader begins by stating the purpose of baptism, drawing upon passages of scripture such as Matthew 28:18–20; Ephesians 4:4–6; and Romans 6:3–4. At this point, the Presbyterian liturgy offers these words, stating the meaning of baptism:

> Obeying the word of our Lord Jesus,
> and confident of his promises,
> we baptize those whom God has called.
>
> In baptism God claims us,
> and seals us to show that we belong to God.
> God frees us from sin and death,
> uniting us with Jesus Christ in his death and resurrection.
> By water and the Holy Spirit,
> we are made members of the church, the body of Christ,
> and joined to Christ's ministry of love, peace, and justice.
>
> Let us remember with joy our own baptism,
> as we celebrate this sacrament (*BCW* 1993, 404).

This introduction to the rite establishes the context of meaning within which the rest of the liturgy takes place.

The fact that candidates are accompanied by others already members of the community of faith is partly a sign of hospitality and solidarity. The church is glad to open its life to new people now coming to baptism. Often these sponsors have spent time with candidates during their inquiry into the faith and have nurtured them in the meaning and forms of the Christian life. Now they stand with the people whom they have helped come to Christ. When the candidates are very young the sponsors' responsibility points more to the future than to the past. They affirm that they are themselves members of the Christian community and that they will do all within their power to bring these little ones into the life that their baptism promises.

The presentation also indicates that the people coming to baptism do so voluntarily and with clear intentions. The question put to them is clear: "Do you desire to be baptized?" And the answer is equally firm. "I do." This voluntariness is especially important because we live at a time when secular values and life patterns are diverging from the values and patterns of life that are honored by the church. In this regard, churches today are very much like churches in the first Christian generation. Becoming a Christian promises to separate a person from the dominating culture; and therefore should be entered into advisedly and with clear conscience. Nominal conversions, under cultural or political duress, are not wanted.

When the people being baptized are very young, and the question is posed to the parents and sponsors, the force of voluntariness is somewhat different. Obviously the very young are not deciding to become Christians. For them, baptism without confirmation functions as the means by which they are incorporated into the religious reality that is important to the parents. That reality includes two dimensions—the horizontal or social dimension of life within the Christian community and the vertical or soteriological dimension of union with Christ. At a later stage in their lives, these children will participate in the confirmation aspect of the baptismal rite, and thereby make their own decision concerning the Christian way of life. They too will be among the people presented to the church in this portion of the liturgy.

The use of *confirmation* as the title of the latter part of the baptismal rite needs comment. This word has been used since the third century to describe the gestures and prayers associated with the gift of the Holy Spirit in baptism. In churches of the West, these elements came to be separated from the rest of the rite. Because they were done by the bishop rather than the pastor of the congregation, and to people able to answer for themselves rather than to infants, they seemed to be more important than baptism itself. Recent service books tend not to use the term *confirmation* for this part of the baptismal liturgy, but this title has strength that alternative titles don't possess. In the confirmation aspect of baptism, these former infants now express their own decision to be Christians, thus confirming the actions taken on their behalf at an earlier time. The church renews its acceptance of these people into its life. Most important—and this is the primary meaning of the word *confirm*—the church prays that by the renewed gift of the Holy Spirit God will empower this person for the Christian life.

On many occasions some of the people presented in the first section of the baptismal liturgy are persons coming for the confirmation portion of the rite. Even though they had been baptized before they could decide for Christ and the Christian life, they now come by their own decision, thus making the former act their own.

The parents bringing their young children are asked if they desire that their children be baptized. Here they give their consent, thereby renewing their own commitments to Christ and indicating their intention that this new member of their family be joined with them in the Christian way of life. They declare that the religious life is at least as important to them as are other aspects of the social system into which they incorporate their child. Infants learn the family's language, patterns of relating with one another, dietary habits, and deeper cultural motifs. In most families these same infants are taken to church and brought into the patterns of religious experience and ethical conviction characterized by that church. One reason for bringing their children for baptism is that the parents thereby intensify the importance of the religious nurture of children and make it part of their deliberate and determined pattern of activity.

A similar act of conscious commitment is part of services of thanksgiving and blessing that some churches use to welcome children. Even when baptism does not follow, the church can welcome infants into its family life, and parents can declare their intention that these children be reared in the Christian faith. The blessing of God can be invoked.

Profession of Faith

The seriousness of baptism becomes more explicit in the second portion of the rite, which consists of the change of loyalties from one controlling center to another. This portion of the liturgy could be looked upon as the public form of the interior experience of repentance. Here, in the presence of the church, candidates for baptism swear off of one set of allegiances and swear on to another set.

The traditional language of the renunciations uses highly personal language to refer to the center of loyalty that candidates are rejecting:

> Dost thou renounce the devil and all his works, the vain pomp and glory of the world, with all covetous desires of the same, and the sinful desires of the flesh, so that thou wilt not follow, nor be led by them? (*BCP* 1928, 277)

Even in the more recent version, the language continues to show this force:

> Do you renounce Satan and all the spiritual forces of wickedness that rebel against God? Do you renounce the evil powers of this world which corrupt and destroy the creatures of God? (BCP 1979, 302)

Here the evil one is given a name and other evil forces are spoken of as though they were capable of deliberately committing evil. If anything, the new language is more direct and more powerful than the older.

The renouncing of one set of allegiances is followed by claiming a new set. The Presbyterian order provides a graceful transition. Immediately after the final renunciation, candidates are asked: "Do you turn to Jesus Christ and accept him as your Lord and Savior?" to which they respond "I do." Then the liturgy continues with the candidates, sponsors, and congregation "affirming the faith in the words of the Apostles' Creed" (*BCW* 1993, 407).

It must be noted that the faith confessed is *the* faith, meaning the Christian faith rather than the beliefs of the people being baptized. The assumption, of course, is that the candidates for baptism share the church's faith. Yet the basis for baptism is not the faith of a person, or even that of a congregation; rather, it is the Christian faith that sustains the entire church of Christ of every time and place. The universality of the faith confessed is indicated in two ways. The first is the fact that the faith is recited by the congregation as a whole rather than by the candidates individually or as a group. The second is the use of the ancient summary of that faith known as the Apostles Creed. From the origins of this declaration, early in the church's life, it has expressed the church's faith in the triune God. In form, the Apostles Creed is a cross between poetry and prose. It says things in the language of antiquity, and its continued use connects the church of every time with the church across time. Most baptismal liturgies around the world use this creed, although in slightly varying forms. Some call for the leader to ask three questions and the respondents to answer with the three sections of the creed. Some liturgies call for unison affirmation. Some liturgies adapt the language slightly, while still retaining the general character of the creed.

Despite the antiquity and universality of the Apostles' Creed, many Christians find this formulation difficult to use and are exploring other ways of confessing faith in the triune God. Although the old creed grows out of biblical material, it was shaped by the thought and the controversies of an ancient period of time. The archaic character of this formulation is for many people a barrier that keeps them from confessing the Christian faith. The problem is intensified since the Apostle's Creed depends upon one metaphor to describe the God who is herein confessed: the Father-Son relationship of Jesus to the God of the Ancestors. Although this metaphor has been adopted as a technical formula in theological documents, it continues to be a metaphor that is only partly truthful in what it says about the God whom Christians worship and confess. This metaphor, furthermore, creates special difficulties because it is so easily associated with a social system that gives precedence to men and holds women in subordinate relationships.

Consequently, theologians and liturgical leaders are exploring other ways of confessing the Christian faith in baptism. The two essential elements are "baptism in water and the confession of the blessed Trinity" (Holeton 1988, 71). David Holeton suggests that a threefold interrogation of adults and "an assertive form of the baptismal interrogation" for infants provides a way of retaining the trinitarian confession but with modified language. The first element could be "Do you believe in God, creator of heaven and earth?" The second element states the relationship between this God and Jesus

Christ who is now confessed: "Do you believe in the child [Son] of God, Jesus Christ?" The third clause could then confess the Holy Spirit, stating the relationship of Spirit to Jesus Christ and God, something not now done in the baptismal creeds. Although all of the specific formulas being suggested require careful evaluation, liturgical scholars such as Holeton and Ruth Duck are pointing toward a new way of confessing the trinitarian faith in the context of the baptismal liturgy.

The faith required at baptism is the Christian faith of the whole church, yet the occasion focuses specifically upon one or more persons who now are being incorporated into this community's faith. The unison affirmation makes clear that the particularities of individual belief are enfolded into the universality of the church's faith, but the person or persons being baptized need to be clearly in the center of things. In some churches, especially those that baptize only believers, the individuality of commitment is manifested when each one being baptized makes his or her own confession of faith. The power of this experience is diminished if there is no opportunity for the candidate to claim the faith individually. The order for baptism published by the Consultation on Church Union provides a pattern that includes both. A candidate can respond to three questions about belief in God, Christ, and Holy Spirit. Then candidates and congregation join in unison recitation of the Apostles Creed.

Thanksgiving over the Water

The principal prayer of the baptismal liturgy is closely parallel in form and function to the major prayer at the communion table. Each prayer praises God with special reference to the physical elements that are central to the ritual being performed. Each prayer asks God to do the creating and redeeming work that the liturgy describes and celebrates. The church's conviction is that in and through the liturgy the action talked about comes into being. The parallel between the eucharistic and baptismal prayers is signaled in the liturgy of the Anglican Church of Canada, which begins the blessing of the water with a dialogue similar to the one that begins the eucharistic prayer:

> The Lord be with you.
> **And also with you.**
> Let us give thanks to the Lord our God.
> **It is right to give our thanks and praise.** (*BAS* 1985, 156)

After naming God, most of these prayers move immediately into a pattern drawn from traditional Jewish prayer forms. The prayers give thanks to God for what God has done and promises to continue doing, and in this way the people offering these prayers proclaim God's greatness and consecrate the people and the baptismal water to their intended uses. The most common pattern recites three of God's actions described in the Old Testament. First, God's Spirit moved over the waters and created all that is, and through water God continues to sustain life. Second, God destroyed evil in the waters of the flood and with the ark established a new beginning for humankind. Third, when God's people were slaves in Egypt, God led them to freedom through the sea. At this point in the prayer, the United Methodist liturgy provides an acclamation for the people, thus highlighting the praise-filled character of this prayer:

> Sing to the Lord, all the earth.
> Tell of God's mercy each day. (*UMH* 1989, 36)

The next section of the prayer recites New Testament references to God's work through water. The one theme that appears in nearly all of the prayers is Jesus' baptism by John in the Jordan. The tendency is then to move directly to the "baptism of his death and resurrection," with the result that this portion of the prayer focuses less upon water as natural element used by God and more upon water as symbol that conveys a spiritual meaning. In contrast to these other prayers, the "Prayer of Baptism" of the United Church of Christ provides a much fuller recitation of New Testament uses of water:

> In the fullness of time you sent Jesus Christ
> who was nurtured in the water of Mary's womb.
> Jesus was baptized by John in the water of the Jordan,
> became living water to a woman at the Samaritan well,
> washed the feet of the disciples,
> and sent them forth to baptize all the nations
> by water and the Holy Spirit. (*BW* 1986, 141)

When the United Methodist prayer completes this second section of the blessing, another acclamation by the congregation is provided:

> Declare his [Jesus'] works to the nations,
> his glory among all the people.

At this point the prayers make an important move. After recounting God's use of water in creation and redemption, the prayer turns to this occasion and to this water. One liturgy makes the transition this way:

> Calling upon your name, O God, we come to this water. By the power of your Holy Spirit, make it a cleansing flood that washes away sin and gives new life to those who today confess the name of Christ. (COCU 1973, 32)

The remembrance describes how God has worked in the past and provides the basis for the request that follows—that God use this water to accomplish similar purposes with these people who now come to it.

These purposes are stated in varying degrees of detail. One Lutheran liturgy is an example of the more concise prayers:

> Pour out your Holy Spirit, so those who are here baptized may be given new life. Wash away the sin of all those who are cleansed by this water and bring them forth as inheritors of your glorious kingdom. (*LBW* 1978, 122)

A more extended listing of the benefits of baptism is presented in the Presbyterian prayer:

> Send your Spirit to move over this water
> that it may be a fountain of deliverance and rebirth.
> Wash away the sins of all who are cleansed by it.
> Raise them to new life, and graft them to the body of Christ.
> Pour out your Holy Spirit upon them,
> that they may have power to do your will,
> and continue forever in the risen life of Christ....
> (*BCW* 1993, 411)

Across the full range of these prayers—Roman Catholic, Lutheran, Episcopalian, Methodist, Presbyterian, and United Church of Christ—the language is direct and expectant. These texts ask God to forgive sin, transform lives, add them to the church, and make them ready for the world to come. Implicit in this liturgy are the new humanity and redeemed creation that Paul describes so eloquently in Romans 6—8. This conviction that a new reality is first experienced in worship relativizes the longstanding debate between catholic and evangelical. The traditional catholic view has been that the sacrament of baptism is a powerful event in which God forgives original and actual sin and enters a person into the covenant of grace. Baptism is thus essential in the ordinary process of salvation. The evangelical view, especially as it emerged in nineteenth-century America, relocates the locus of activity from the liturgical act of baptism to the interior experience of conversion. Baptism is a sign of what has already been done by the operation of the Holy Spirit and an act of obedience by the one who has been converted. These baptismal prayers are consistent with the catholic tradition in their claiming that something actually happens at baptism, but they move beyond the juridical and political characteristics that have tended to dominate classical theologies of forgiveness and incorporation into the church. Like evangelical theologies of baptism, these prayers assume that lives are changed and that they are charged with the power of the Holy Spirit.

The prayers conclude with a doxological formula that expresses vigorously what has been implicit throughout the service. In its own right baptism is eucharistic, an act of thankful praise offered to God both by the church and by those who are presented for baptism. One liturgy ends with this powerful text from the apostolic church:

> Amen! Praise and glory and wisdom,
> thanksgiving and honour, power and might,
> be to our God for ever and ever.
> Amen! (*NZPB* 1989, 386)

The Baptism

To this point the liturgy has consisted primarily of words, but now dramatic action takes over. The "strong name of the Trinity" has been confessed, and immediately, dramatically, the people coming to God through this faith are overwhelmed by water. I choose the word *overwhelm*, following the lead of I. Howard Marshall (1973, 130-40), to suggest the force of the Greek word *baptizo*, which the New Testament uses in reference to water, fire, and Holy Spirit. Marshall's intention is to find one English word that can be used with all of these elements by which or into which people are baptized. The word must equally well convey the overpowering of the person by water, fire, or Holy Spirit. Initial word studies of the *baptizo* group of words lead to translations such as *dip*, *immerse*, or *plunge*, all of which make sense when used with water, but make less sense when used with Spirit and fire. Marshall concludes that *overwhelm*, while less specific concerning how water, fire, or spirit are applied, clearly conveys the impact of the event.

We don't know how John, Jesus, Peter, Paul, and other early Christians applied water in baptism. There are references in post-New Testament documents, such as The Apostolic Tradition of Hippolytus, to being overwhelmed with water three times, indicating the confession of the threefold name of God. Yet earlier when baptism was into the name of Jesus rather than in the name of the Father, Son, and Holy Spirit, a triple application of water seems unlikely. What we can be sure of is that our twentieth-century ceremonies are not good guides to ancient practice. John the Baptist and Jesus developed their modes of administration according to models available to them in their world and not according to any of the invented styles of the modern world. We cannot assume that water was applied in their time according to any of the modes of baptizing used in churches today.

Two tendencies are present in liturgical practice: the effort to condense the sign to barest essentials and the contrasting effort to expand the sign to exuberant excess. The form of bread and wine used in the eucharist illustrates the one tendency. No longer a full meal, the Lord's supper in most churches consists of the tiniest swallow of wine and the receiving of a suggestion of bread. Yet most worshipers seem able to use this food stripped of all fullness as the means of feasting upon Christ who offers himself anew at the communion table. The contrasting tendency was blurted out by Peter when Jesus tried to wash his feet at the Last Supper. When Peter objected, Jesus responded by saying that "unless I wash you, you have no share with me." Peter cried out, "Lord, not my feet only but also my hands and my head" (John 13:6–12). Through most of the church's history, the minimalist use of water has been the liturgical tendency, and even today sprinkling and pouring continue this way of using water. Whether in the eucharist or baptism, the simplification and stylization of the sign allows worshipers to concentrate upon Christ's action that the sign conveys.

The sign, however, can be done in such a minimalist manner that its capacity to signify is compromised. So it is with the wafers and pellets used in the Lord's supper, which can hardly convey the "bread from heaven" that can satisfy our hunger forever (John 6:35–40). And so it is with some uses of water in baptism. How can a moistening of the brow be experienced as the washing away of our sins or as union with Christ in his death and resurrection? In response to the weakness of the sign in baptism, churches are restoring water to the rite—pouring water over head and shoulders instead of sprinkling, and with ever-increasing frequency using some form of plunging or immersing. Roman Catholic churches, for example, are building baptistries for adult immersion even though the pouring of water on the heads of infants will continue to be the more common practice.

A few churches, such as Baptists and Disciples, insist that the form of application is an essential part of the action. For them immersion is as important to the sign of baptism as eating and drinking are to the sign of the Lord's supper.

The action with water is usually accompanied by a brief declaration stated by the minister presiding over the service. Traditionally this statement is, "*Name*, I baptize you in the name of the Father, and of the Son, and of the Holy Spirit." In some churches the statement is put in the passive form: "*Name*, you are baptized...." In either form these few words state in a highly compressed formula the central Christian affirmation that has already been confessed more fully in the earlier parts of the liturgy. The first reference to the use in the baptismal liturgy of the formula based on Matthew 28:19 is in the sermons of John Chrysostom in the fourth century. Leonel Mitchell notes this fact and indicates that the probable reason was "to shorten the service by permitting the candidates to respond to the creedal questions all together before the baptism instead of individually as they stood in the water" (Mitchell 1985, 109). Clearly the combining of formula and action with water is not essential to the rite. What is important is that the doctrinal foundation of the action be affirmed in the earlier sections of the liturgy.

Although it is common practice that these words accompany the overwhelming with water, there are times when it is difficult to do so. The immersing of several people in a river, for example, calls for total concentration upon the action. The necessary words will have already been proclaimed by congregation and candidates. Now is the time to let all human words be swallowed up in the roaring of the water. Indeed, the pressure to speak during the action of baptism may increase in proportion to the diminishment of the sign—the less water, the greater the need to say something! If waters are poured out abundantly, their own sound is eloquence enough at this point of the service.

It is better to have no speaking during the act of baptizing than to bring in experimental lines or texts, especially those that paraphrase the classical formula, such as "...in the name of the Creator, Sustainer, and Redeemer." If the Holy Trinity of classical Christian faith has been confessed in the earlier portion of the rite, then the doctrinal framework for the action has been established. To bring in language that is considered by some to be a tampering with the heart of the Christian faith, and to do this at the most solemn moment in the baptismal liturgy, should be avoided.

The generous and public use of water has implications about how people dress and other matters of decorum. Adult baptisms by immersion in outdoor streams and pools call for informal and practical garb such as jeans and shirts of opaque material. The same service inside the church, in the presence of the congregation, invites the use of specially prepared robes and other garments. If water is poured onto the head and shoulders of a young person or adult, then they need to wear clothes that water does not damage, and towels need to be close at hand. With infants, nudity during immersion does not offend public sensitivities. When infants or small children are baptized by pouring or sprinkling water on them, the water is not likely to get on their clothes and they may be dressed in garments of finer fabric.

The Laying On of Hands

At this point in the baptismal liturgy three polarities affect the service. The first is the focus upon salvation and empowerment. Each theme is part of the baptismal tradition. In this action of God and the church, sins are forgiven and power is given to lead the life of faith and grace. The second polarity is the action, with one pole being the application of water and the other pole being the laying on of hands and anointing. The third polarity is the minister of the liturgy, with the pastor of the congregation being one officer of this service in some churches and the bishop of a larger region being the minister of the rite in some other churches. The liturgies of the several churches move between these poles in different ways depending upon their theologies of baptism and confirmation, the stage of the ecumenical discussion when their rites were published, and factors internal to the decision-making processes of the churches.

Until recently, the common practice in Protestant churches would have been to emphasize action with water and to have no further action related to the reception of the Holy Spirit. Even as recent a publication as the *The Worshipbook* published by Presbyterians moves directly from baptism with water to an intercessory prayer , without a second action, that all of the church may "live in your Spirit and so love one another" (*The Worshipbook* 1970, 46). In more recently published liturgies two patterns can be seen. Some include a separate action related to the Spirit and include it in the liturgy on a par with the use of water. These liturgies convey the impression that this second action is a necessary part of any baptism. Others present the action related to the Holy Spirit so that it can be inferred that it is a separate, and in some liturgies less important, stage in the liturgy of reception and empowerment.

Examples of the close linking of the two actions can be found in publications of the Christian Church (Disciples of Christ) and The United Methodist Church. In the United Methodist rite, the following direction and text follow immediately upon the baptism with water: "Immediately after the administration of the water, the pastor, and others if desired, place hands on the head of each candidate, as the pastor says to each:

"The Holy Spirit work within you,
that being born through water and the Spirit,
you may be a faithful disciple of Jesus Christ."
(*UMH* 1989, 37)

One set of texts recommended to Disciples follows their traditional patterns but adds a new feature. The element that will be unfamiliar to most Disciples is the following instruction and text: "The candidate is immersed. Then, immediately after the baptized has recovered stable footing, the pastor places his or her hands on the head of the new Christian and says:

"Dying, Christ destroyed your death;
Rising, Christ restored your life.

Receive the gift of the Holy Spirit!"
(*Baptism and Belonging* 1991, 30)

A close, but slightly ambiguous, connection is offered in the Episcopal *Book of Common Prayer*. A brief prayer and a set of actions are prescribed, but the directions indicate that either one may precede the other immediately following the baptism with water. The prayer thanks God for the forgiveness and new life that God has bestowed through baptism and then asks: "Sustain them, O Lord, in your Holy Spirit." The action prescribed is this: "Then the Bishop or Priest places a hand on the person's head, marking on the forehead the sign of the cross [using Chrism if desired] and saying to each one: N., you are sealed by the Holy Spirit in Baptism and marked as Christ's own forever" (*BCP* 1979, 308). Commenting on these elements in the 1979 rite, one Episcopal scholar states that some people believe the anointing and signing "to be explanatory ceremonies—like the giving of a lighted candle—which illuminate the meaning of what is done in baptism. Others see them as a separate sacramental act by which the Holy Spirit comes to dwell in the newly baptized." He then concludes that this rite in the Prayer Book is one "which all Christians should be able to regard as containing all things necessary for the celebration of the sacrament of Christian initiation" (Mitchell 1985, 113).

A less exact connection between baptism with water and successive actions is indicated in the directions in the rite published by the Consultation on Church Union (1973). The first rubric uses the directive *shall*: "The minister shall immerse each candidate in water, or pour water on the candidate's head…" The second rubric uses the permissive *may*: "The minister may place a hand on the head of each person, making on the forehead the sign of the Cross (using oil prepared for this purpose, if desired)…" (COCU 1973, 33). In the commentary on this liturgy, the COCU editors note: "In the ancient Greek-speaking churches, the laying on of the hand was originally concurrent with immersion—the hand of the minister pushing the candidate into the water. In the West, the gifts of the Holy Spirit came to be associated with the laying on of hands immediately after the act of water baptism" (20). The effect of this COCU treatment is to provide a way for the two actions to be conducted, and to encourage them. Clearly, however, the action with water is necessary whereas the laying on of hands, anointing, and asking for the Holy Spirit are desirable but not essential to the rite.

Welcome

In some liturgies, the anointing and blessing of the newly baptized blend easily into the receiving of these people into the life of the congregation and especially to its fellowship around the communion table. The Presbyterian order, however, separates them. The actions related to the gift of the Holy Spirit remain linked to the baptism with water. Then, under a separate heading, a formal act of receiving them into the "holy catholic church" takes place. The congregation itself is charged with the responsibility to care for these who have been baptized. The congregation responds:

> With joy and thanksgiving,
> we welcome you into Christ's church
> to share with us his ministry
> for we are all one in Christ.

Then the congregation may "extend signs of God's peace, greeting those who have been baptized" (*BCW* 1993, 414).

Most rites receive the newly baptized into the church universal with only implicit references to the congregation or denomination. For example, one liturgy gives this welcoming statement: "*N.*, we recognize you as a member of the one holy catholic and apostolic Church, and we receive you into the fellowship of this Communion..." (*BCP* 1979, 310). "This Communion" refers to the Episcopal Church and its worldwide family of churches, often referred to as the Anglican Communion.

In contrast, one liturgy is explicit:

> As members together with you
> in the body of Christ
> and in this congregation
> of The United Methodist Church... (*UMH* 1989, 43).

The liturgies include further signs of welcome, such as offering the peace of Christ and sharing the eucharistic meal. All is done with great joy, for Christian baptism is energized by God's redeeming love, received in trusting obedience, and experienced as a life overflowing in grace. Therefore people today, like the newly baptized described in scripture, come "up out of the water" and go on their way rejoicing (Acts 8:39).

Renewal of Baptism

Although many churches believe that baptism is to be done only once, most churches agree that the baptismal covenant can be affirmed repeatedly. The resistance toward rebaptism is based on the doctrine that God is the primary actor in baptism, and that what God does is forgive, reconcile, and incorporate the baptized into the body of Christ. Thus baptism is in part a naturalization ceremony by which God moves a person from the domain of death into the commonwealth of eternal life. These actions, it is believed are done only once; and to repeat them is a dishonoring of God. Furthermore, to repeat baptism indicates that the sacramental actions of the church doing the earlier baptism are not respected. On either count, to repeat baptism is a grievous action. Other churches proclaim a doctrine of baptism that permits baptism to be repeated. Salvation is understood to be a continuing process of maturation in the Christian life, with God active at every step along the way. The cleansing that baptism expresses, so these churches would say, needs to be repeated throughout one's life; and at critical turning points a forceful renewal of the foundation of one's Christian life is appropriate. These renewals of baptism are appropriate when the first baptism was done within one's own church; and therefore no affront toward other churches is implied by repeating baptism. The larger block of opinion, however, remains on the side that says baptism ought not be repeated.

The central action with water is the focal point of this discussion, because most churches do support the practice of renewing the baptismal vows and the later actions focusing upon the Holy Spirit and life in the church. These affirmations and reaffirmations are especially suitable under four sets of circumstances. The most common is the time when people who were baptized as infants affirm for themselves the vows that were made at the time of their baptism some years earlier. A second time is when persons experience a renewal of their life of faith. Often, this comes after an extended period of separation and perhaps alienation from the church. A third time is when one moves from one church to another. This could be a transfer from one congregation to another within the same family of churches, or it could be the movement from one communion of churches to another. In the latter case, the renewal of vows implies that one is leaving the discipline and care of one church and entering into a different set of covenant relations. The fourth time for reaffirmation is when a congregation renews its baptismal vows.

A strong set of texts is offered in the UCC *Book of Worship* for the confirmation and affirmation of baptism. The leader addresses the congregation:

> Friends in Christ, we all are received into the church
> through the sacrament of baptism.
> *This person has/These people have* found nurture and support
> in the midst of the family of Christ.
> Through prayer and study
> *she/he/they has/have* been led by the Holy Spirit
> to affirm *her/his/their* baptism
>
> and to claim in our presence
> *her/his/their* covenantal relationship with Christ
> and the members of the church.

using the gifts which the Holy Spirit bestows.

The liturgy continues with sentences from scripture and the profession of faith in quite a full form. Then with the leading of the pastor the candidates offer this prayer:

O God, my God, known to me in Jesus Christ,
I give myself to you as your own,
to love and serve you faithfully
all the days of my life. Amen.

The operative prayer of this service is spoken by the congregation:

Almighty God, who in baptism
received these your servants into the church,
forgave their sins, and promised them eternal life,
increase in them the gifts of your Holy Spirit.
Grant love for others, joy in serving you,
peace in disagreement, patience in suffering,
kindness toward all people, goodness in evil times,
faithfulness in temptation, gentleness in the face of
     opposition,
self-control in all things.
Thereby strengthen them for their ministry in the world;
through Jesus Christ our Savior. Amen.

The candidates are invited to kneel, and the pastor and other representatives of the church may lay hands on them. Four prayer texts are available in the liturgy. Two ask that God bless and strengthen each person, but with no mention of the Holy Spirit. The other two invoke "your Holy Spirit" to come upon each person (*BW* 1986, 145ff.).

In some liturgies candidates are anointed with oil. Another common practice is to include water in the rites of renewal, although in ways that do not imply that baptism is occurring once again. Leaders of the service, for example, could walk through the aisles with a bowl of water, and with moistened fingers scatter drops of water toward the congregation, calling out, "Remember your baptism and be thankful."

This discussion of Christian baptism needs to conclude, as it began, by affirming that this sacrament is dominated by the thankful praise of people who experience God's redeeming love shown forth in Jesus Christ. Despite the remembrance of humanity's sin, and of our own participation in that sin, despite the harshness of the story of salvation, baptism is even more a story of God's love and abundant grace. It is the assertion that death is swallowed up in victory dant grace. It is the assertion that death is swallowed up in victory not only for Jesus Christ but for all who call upon his name. Therefore the exclamation in the congregational renewal of baptism is the continuing theme for all Christians: "Remember your baptism and be thankful."

Encouraging the Conversation

What does it mean to be a Christian in the world we now live in? What values must be affirmed, what values rejected? These questions are ever more important as we think about renewing baptismal practice. One way to think through these matters is for you to try drafting a service of Christian baptism. How would you answer these questions in the text of the liturgy?

- What should baptismal candidates reject?
- What beliefs should they affirm, and what positive promises about the life they expect to live should they be asked to make?
- What should the service ask God to do to and for these persons?
- What should be asked for in the prayer over the water?

After you have come up with your answers to these questions, examine the texts from one of the books used as illustrations in this chapter, or compare your answers to the statements and prayers ordinarily used in baptisms in your church tradition. How closely do your ideas coincide with those in your larger church tradition?

What are the theological and practical connections between baptism in water and baptism in the Holy Spirit?

11

Worship
for the Way

This chapter discusses two life-affirming ceremonies that are prominent in the work of pastors. Weddings are festivals that express the exuberance of life, when human couples are linked in public covenants of love and procreation. Funerals are the solemn acknowledgment that persons who have lived out their allotted years now "dwell in the house of the Lord forever." Celebrations at these two events along life's way are part of human cultures everywhere; there is nothing uniquely Christian about getting married or dying. Yet the churches are interested in these turning points of life and through them continue to express the great thanksgiving that characterizes the Christian stance toward life.

Significant changes are taking place in Western cultures, and weddings and funerals are directly affected. People can now be sexually active but avoid giving birth to children. Many in our time find it very difficult to keep long-term promises, especially those as in marriage, which in the Christian tradition have been intended to be lifelong. The longtime ideal of rearing children in a two-parent household is increasingly difficult to realize, so difficult, in fact, that many people believe the ideal itself needs to be restated. Given the suffering of our time, many people question whether one can in good conscience bring children into the world. Traditional wedding ceremonies could give thanks to God because they were celebrated in circumstances that were sufficiently uniform and sufficiently hopeful that gratitude could be assumed. Not so now; and therefore one wonders whether it is possible to assume that weddings are regularly occasions for the thankful praise of God.

Similarly difficult questions arise concerning dying, death, and the ceremonies related to death. In many parts of the earth people still live short lives, brought to an early end by illness, famine, injury, or other violations of the person. Even in areas where a fuller life span is possible, medical technology can now keep bodies from dying long after recognizable human processes have ceased. Our living patterns separate people from one another so completely that many people now die virtually isolated from any community of close family and friends. Under such circumstances it is hard to see funerals as occasions when people affirm the goodness of God and give thanks for that goodness as expressed in the life of the deceased.

In this time of great change, the chief responsibility of the churches and their pastors is to proclaim the name of God. The principal participants in these events properly have their minds on many things that need not concern pastors of churches. Pastors do not come as social consultants or family counselors, but to affirm that God is present in every relationship, every commitment, every beginning, every ending. Following the example of the biblical psalms, we can acknowledge the suffering experienced by people around us and complain because life seems so unfair. Having confessed these feelings to God, we can move past guilt and despair into a new kind of reality-tested hope.

Weddings

Sexual relationships, the procreation of children, and the nurturing of the new generation are universal and will take place whatever the church says. In much of the world and throughout much of the history of the church, responsibility for regulating the relations of the sexes, governing marriage, and overseeing the care of children has been vested in civil rather than religious authorities. Many of the churches, especially within the Reformed tradition, have at one time or another insisted that only the state should care for these matters and that the church's primarily participation is to offer a blessing of the marriage already established. Echoes of this practice in currently used liturgies for marriage are the blessing of the couple, which in some churches only ordained ministers may offer, and rites for ecclesiastical blessing of marriages conducted by civil authority.

Regardless of who conducts weddings, whether civil or ecclesiastical authority, weddings are social occasions surrounded by customs that vary widely from community to community. Often this surrounding cluster of activities takes more energy than does the creating of the legal and religious relationship that is the heart of marriage ceremonies. It is important, therefore, that the ceremonies of the church be organized around the elements of greatest religious and moral import. Ministers can be largely disinterested in the larger cluster of festivity except at the points where they may contradict the central claims that the church makes concerning the meaning and form of marriage between two Christians.

Unfortunately, representatives of the church often have acted as though they were to control all aspects of human life, even those relationships of universal scope. Furthermore, churches have unwittingly been aligned with social systems that have maintained unequal relationships of economic and social power, favoring men and making life difficult for women and children. Even in the religious ceremonies of marriage these oppressive systems have been expressed, as is illustrated by the traditional question, "Who gives this woman to be married to this man?" The newly published wedding rites show a growing sensitivity to these problems. For example, the *Book of Common Prayer* no longer includes this action in the main text of the wedding rite. Instead, a rubric indicates where such an action would take place and refers users of the book to a page entitled "Additional Directions" to suggest texts. The United Methodist service offers a very different way to express the relationship of families with a section called "Response of the Families and People." Similarly the United Church of Christ offers an extended section called "Pledge of Support" with this explanation: "This pledge of support should be used at the discretion of the pastor and in consultation with the people involved. It allows the family and congregation to pledge their support and encouragement to the couple. It is important to consider use of the pledge when there are children from previous relationships" (*BW* 1986, 331). It is hard to imagine a more significant change of understanding!

The church's rites for marriage include two major themes. First, they express the foundation for the church's participation in this event—the conviction that the coming together of a man and woman in lifelong union of body and spirit expresses God's own nature and the way that the divine character overflows in creation. This theology of marriage affirms the goodness of human sexuality and blesses the procreative powers that are made possible by the union of woman and man. It implicitly encourages the renewal of society through the creative power now vested in the life of these two people. The church blesses and enters into the joy that is the central emotion as bride and groom begin their new life with one another.

The second theme foundational for Christian marriage is support for the covenant of steadfast love that is the basis of marriage in the holy commonwealth that Jesus proclaimed. When two people are joined in "holy matrimony" they become a new social unit pledged to one another, to the children who may bless their marriage, and to the larger society in which they live out their life together. Because of human sinfulness this kind of life is difficult to sustain. The church prays that God will help the couple live their

Worship for the Way   191

vows faithfully despite the temptations and challenges that come to them, and the church promises to support them throughout their lives. All of this is done with the fullness of hope that, with God's help, these intentions can be accomplished throughout life. The mood that prevails is thankful praise to God, who gives life and love and who brings people together in the union of body and spirit.

The complex interplay of civil society and ecclesial life is illustrated by the wedding rites that continue to be published and conducted by the churches. Some of the elements go back to Roman practice before the time of Christ, and with slight modifications they continue in the latest revisions of the marriage rite. (A brief history of marriage in the church is found in Martos 1981, 399-451). The outlines of these services vary in the items contained and in their order. In many churches, weddings have been celebrated on their own, outside of the regular gatherings of the congregation for worship, and the new worship books assume the continuation of this practice. They do encourage the idea that weddings are part of the church's liturgical life and provide as the first option a pattern in which the explicitly nuptial elements are woven into a service of the Word and, when appropriate, of the sacrament of holy communion. Some of the books also provide a pattern in which weddings are incorporated into the congregation's regular Sunday act of worship.

The Meaning of Marriage

However the rites may vary in detail, they can be condensed into three actions: stating the meaning of marriage, exchanging the vows, and blessing this new covenantal relationship. The *meaning of Christian marriage* is implicit throughout the rite, but most ceremonies state it precisely in the declaration that begins the rite. This is the "Dearly beloved, we have gathered..." section with which the traditional wedding rite began. The new rites provide several statements of this meaning, with the United Methodist text a succinct summary of the traditional materials:

> Friends, we are gathered together in the sight of God
> to witness and bless the joining together of *Name* and *Name*
>   in Christian marriage.
> The covenant of marriage was established by God,
>   who created us male and female for each other.
> With his presence and power
>   Jesus graced a wedding at Cana of Galilee,
> and in his sacrificial love gave us the example
>   of the love of husband and wife. (*UMH* 1989, 864)

Other liturgies are longer, some of them three and four times this length. In every case, the intent is to provide a brief summary of the church's understanding of marriage for the sake of the immediate participants in this wedding and for others who have come to witness and enjoy the celebration.

The meaning of marriage is also stated in a section of the liturgy in which excerpts from the Bible are read. Earlier rites provided a pastiche drawn from the Bible. More recently, this section of the service is an abridged liturgy of the Word, with one or more readings from the Bible, often chosen by bride and groom, and a brief interpretation of marriage in the light of these readings. Unless this part of the service is tightly condensed, the wedding party is seated. When a wedding is incorporated into the regular Sunday liturgy, the service of the word takes its usual shape, but usually with some adaptation to the fact that the marriage is taking place as part of this liturgy.

Exchanging the Vows

With the *exchanging of the vows* we come to the center of gravity of the marriage rite. From pre-Christian times in the Roman world, and continuing throughout the history of the churches in the Western world, these formal promises between a man and woman, made before witnesses, are what constitute the new legal and moral entity that the wedding establishes. In many cultures, these agreements are made between families more than between the two who are being married, and even in contemporary Western cultures a certain aura of family participation continues. In North America, however, the vows are made by the two who are marrying, and for that reason the practice has developed for these two to participate in developing the vows that they intend to make to one another. One method is for bride and groom to write the vows. What this practice overlooks, however, is that the larger society, and in the case of church weddings the Christian community, has a strong interest in the nature of the bond that is being established and needs to influence the language. Some liturgies provide two or more sets of vows and encourage the two people, and perhaps their immediate families with them, to discuss these several vows. Then in consultation with the pastor who is advising them and will conduct the wedding ceremony they choose the text most appropriate. Within limits provided by the disciplines of the churches and the convictions of the pastors these texts may be revised slightly in order to state more exactly and felicitously the promises that the two desire to make.

The church's convictions are that the marriage be entered into freely by both parties, with lifelong intention, on equal terms, and in God's name. These are the ideas that the vows need to express, all within the context of love for each other. These promises are stated by each of the two to the other, in the same words. Because the vows represent the larger society as much as the two who are marrying, it is appropriate that each one repeat the words as they are spoken by the minister rather than recite them from memory.

Two physical signs are associated with the speaking of these promises. The first is the joining of right hands during this portion of the rite. The self-directed initiative that each one is taking in establishing this marriage is vividly expressed if the one who is to speak the vows takes the other's hand and then releases it after speaking the vows. Then the other person does the same thing. "Their hand is their bond," expressing by physical connections a personal commitment that extends into their public life. A second sign that is normal in weddings is the exchanging of rings. Each gives the other a ring to wear, as a sign of the commitments that are made to each other. Inconspicuously, but definitively, these rings declare to the world that each one lives in a covenanted relationship of love and faithfulness.

Blessing the New Relationship

The *blessing of the marriage* is the part of the service that has always been something the church has been ready to do. Since the regulation of marriage has been a civil function in Western societies, and the conducting of the marriage rite done by civil authorities, the church has seen its unique function to be the invoking of divine favor upon these people and their new relationship. Even when religious leaders conduct the entire service, the blessing of this marriage is distinctive to the work that pastor does. Here is where the name of God is pronounced in the most important way—in the mode of prayer. This longstanding understanding continues to be clear in the Episcopal service, which is entitled "The Celebration and Blessing of a Marriage," and which has rubrics at several places indicating that the nuptial blessing may be pronounced only by a priest or bishop.

The section of the rite that is identified as "The Blessing of the Marriage" consists of a prayer and a blessing. Two texts are provided for the prayer, each of which also uses the words *bless* or *blessing*. These prayers ask God to provide this blessing so that the husband and wife may be able to fulfill the vows they have made. In addition, there is a longer prayer earlier in the rite that intercedes on their behalf. This prayer does not use any form of the word *bless* and could be offered by someone other than a priest or bishop. The blessing itself is stated in these words:

> God the Father, God the Son, God the Holy Spirit, bless, preserve, and keep you; the Lord mercifully with his favor look upon you, and fill you with all spiritual benediction and

grace; that you may faithfully live together in this life, and in the age to come have life everlasting. (*BCP* 1979, 431)

Other rites also give prominence to the blessing. Like the Episcopal pattern, the Presbyterian rite includes a long prayer at the center of the liturgy and a more condensed blessing at the conclusion of the rite. The United Methodist liturgy provides a place for intercessions for the church and world (but does not indicate that husband and wife should be included) and then provides the "Blessing of the Marriage" (*UMH* 1989, 868). The United Church of Christ provides alternative brief texts for blessing the couple or the family in the central part of the liturgy and then provides longer texts for a prayer of thanksgiving and intercession, one of which includes an additional request that God bless them and their home.

It is good that the church continue to emphasize the idea of blessing. When the making and keeping of long-term promises is so difficult, the blessing offers the two people entering into this relationship the assurance that an even stronger covenant with them supports the new covenant they make with one another. God is with them, seeking to support them in the joyful life they live with one another.

The character of this new life together is portrayed by the celebration of the eucharist that can follow at this point. The church's feast of joy intensifies the thankful praise that is implicit throughout the marriage rite and it offers wife and husband the first meal of their new household. Texts for the nuptial eucharist are provided in the worship books coming into use. One way of doing this is to provide a nuptial paragraph to be inserted in the regularly used eucharistic prayer. *The Book of Common Prayer* provides a text for marriage using New Testament themes with references to salvation:

Because in the love of wife and husband, you have given us an image of the heavenly Jerusalem, adorned as a bride for her bridegroom, your Son Jesus Christ our Lord; who loves her and gave himself for her, that he might make the whole creation new. (*BCP* 1979, 381)

A wider range of biblical ideas can be expressed when the entire eucharistic prayer is keyed to the occasion of a marriage, as is illustrated by the Presbyterian text. It begins by praising God for bringing the universe into being and creating "us in your image." It continues: "You made us male and female and gave us the freedom to be joined as husband and wife, united in body and heart." (Even though this prayer uses the Genesis idea of image, it fails to mention that our human identity as male and female is central to our capacity of showing forth the divine nature.) The prayer confesses that we turned against God and affirms that God's love is unfailing. Referring to God's covenant with us, the prayer then uses another marriage reference from scripture: "You made the union of husband and wife a sign of your covenant with your people." In the remembrance of Christ, this prayer recalls still another biblical passage: "By his sacrificial love, Christ sanctified the church to be his holy bride. Even now he is preparing the wedding banquet." Then come the Words of Institution. Following the invocation of the Holy Spirit, this prayer includes a specific reference to the wedding couple:

> Give *N.* and *N.* the spirit of peace,
> that they may become one in heart and mind,
> and rejoice together in your gift of marriage.
> Let their love for each other
> witness to your divine love in the world (*BCW* 1993, 872).

The notable achievement of this prayer is that it intertwines the general history of creation and redemption with the specific story of this marriage that expresses the themes of God's wonderful work. Weddings clearly take on the character of thankful praise.

Much of the detail of weddings is determined by habits and expectations of the larger society. The pastor's primary responsibility is twofold. First, pastors interpret the central ideas that the church holds with respect to the meaning and character of marriage. One way of doing this is to discuss the liturgy itself, carefully discussing the ideas that it presents. The other responsibility is to be sure that the central part of the liturgy clearly expresses the core of Christian belief concerning marriage. The text itself needs to be protected from ideas that confuse the clarity of Christian conviction. The ceremonies at the heart of the service need to be kept simple and expressive, free from the clutter of distracting ceremonies. A certain flexibility should mark the demeanor of pastors as they discuss weddings with the people who come to them. Yet, weddings need to be kept simple and direct so that the meaning of the rite, the central vows, and the church's blessing stand out prominently.

Ours is a time when human communities of trust and intimacy are under great stress, so much so that many people despair of the possibility of finding this kind of loved security. It is therefore all the more important that churches and pastors everywhere continue to affirm the vision of such a life. We need, furthermore, to pray that God's steadfast love will so permeate our families that they too can be filled with love. In the weddings we conduct, and in the support we give these families, we can honor the vision of life together, encourage those who are venturing into such a life, and support them in their love and care for one another.

No matter how well we uphold the ideal, many people will come who have not lived up to the standards that long-governed church practice with respect to sexual activity and marriage. Because of the frailty of human life, these people should be received with a generous spirit. Our interest is not so much in what they have been and how they have expressed their love and sexuality; rather, we are concerned about what they expect to be with God's help and with ours. In counseling and in the marriage rites we have one goal: to help bride and groom, their families, and the wider circle of their friends to affirm the goodness of life and give thanks to God who has made us for each other.

Funerals

The power of religion is most sharply revealed in the way that it helps people deal with death, which is the culmination of the many events in which the "terror of life" is experienced. The value of life is intensified by death, which is the negation of life. How can we live confidently, joyfully, and with gratitude when we know that sooner or later all of this will come crashing down in the grave? How can we love the giver of life who is also its taker? These are the questions asked by all people who are conscious of their beginning and aware of the necessity of their ending.

Christians inherit a faith that answers these questions with a primal trust in God's goodness even though that faith is threatened by the suffering, alienation, and injustice that so often dominate daily life. This faith in the God who gives life and takes it away is supremely expressed in the psalter, the devotional literature of Israel, which Christians pray through the lips of Jesus for whom these poems were the form and language of prayer. A hasty scanning of Matthew's Gospel shows how frequently phrases from the psalter came to the lips of Jesus and to those who sought to interpret the impact of his life upon themselves. At the most critical moments in his brief pilgrimage, Jesus drew upon these testimonies of faith, and at the hour of his death these ancient words formed his prayer: "My God, my God, why have you forsaken me?" (Psalm 22:1; Matthew 27:46; Mark 15:34).

The themes of life and death within the context of faith in God are present in the psalter, all spoken as though they were the immediate experience of specific persons even though every one of them has been universalized beyond anyone's autobiography. Among the most expressive is Psalm 90, which begins with this affirmation of trust:

Lord, you have been our dwelling place
    in all generations.
Before the mountains were brought forth,
        or ever you had formed the earth and the world,
        from everlasting to everlasting you are God. (90:1–2)

The psalm continues by acknowledging that human life is brief and fragmentary when seen through God's eyes—like a watch in the night, or like grass that flourishes for only a day and by evening is gone. This psalm speaks freely of God's wrath and of the troubled character of life. It calls out for compassion from God, for joy and fulfillment. It concludes with the prayer:

> Let the favor of the Lord our God be upon us,
>> and prosper for us the work of our hands—
>> O prosper the work of our hands!

These texts from the Psalms abound with the anguish of life and the sense of having been abandoned even by God. Yet through them all is an even stronger sense of God's goodness, mercy, and faithfulness. Thus they testify to a faith that sustains people through all of the struggles of life in a world where suffering abounds.

This same faith, now infused with the conviction that Jesus Christ reveals the God of steadfast love, is found in passages of the New Testament. One of the most powerful is Paul's great confession of trust in God:

> Who will separate us from the love of Christ? Will hardship, or distress, or persecution, or famine, or nakedness, or peril, or sword? As it is written,
>> "For your sake we are being killed all day long;
>>> we are accounted as sheep to be slaughtered"
>>> [Psalm 44:22].
> No, in all these things we are more than conquerors through him who loved us. For I am convinced that neither death, nor life, nor angels, nor rulers, nor things present, nor things to come, nor powers, nor height, nor depth, nor anything else in all creation, will be able to separate us from the love of God in Christ Jesus our Lord. (Romans 8:35–39)

This faith in God factors into several convictions: that life itself is good despite its tragic character; that a power infuses every person and surrounds every person's life throughout their pilgrimage; that when life ends we are reunited with the God who has been with us from the beginning.

In the New Testament this third conviction is expressed in a variety of ways, foremost among them the affirmation that death could not overcome Jesus but that by the power of God Jesus overcame death. Christ's resurrection is stated in a series of stories about his appearing to the disciples following his crucifixion and burial and culminating with his ascension to heaven forty days later. It then is diffused in various accounts of his continuing life with God—seated at God's right hand in heaven, receiving the adoration of the heavenly creatures, and praying for the people who continue in life.

The corollary is that the people who believe in Jesus are united with him through baptism into a death like his and, following him throughout their lives, will also be united with him into a resurrection like his. This theme often appears in the rites of death, sometimes in prayer and sometimes as a statement to the congregation:

> When we were baptized in Christ Jesus,
> we were baptized into his death.
> We were buried therefore with him by Baptism into death,
> so that as Christ was raised from the dead
> by the glory of the Father,
> we too might live a new life.
> For if we have been united with him in a death like his,
> we shall certainly be united with him
> in a resurrection like his. (*LBW* 1978, 207)

Another way of expressing the conclusion of historical life is to affirm that those who die enter into rest. Again a Lutheran text affirms this faith:

> Almighty God, those who die in the Lord
> still live with you in joy and blessedness.
> We give you heartfelt thanks for the grace
> you have bestowed upon your servants
> who have finished their course in faith
> and now rest from their labors.
> May we, with all who have died in the true faith,
> have perfect fulfillment and joy
> in your eternal and everlasting glory;
> through your Son, Jesus Christ our Lord. (*LBW* 1978, 207)

Another way of stating the continuation of life after death is to affirm that the dead continue to inhabit the world they lived in as living persons. They continue as the ancestors. Although this idea, and the experience of its reality, is remote to many people in Western societies, it long was prominent in Christian culture and continues to be a strong part of the life of many peoples in Africa, Latin America, and Asia. A faint echo of this belief is found in this contemporary prayer:

> O God, your days are without end
> and your mercies cannot be counted.
> Make us aware of the shortness
> and uncertainty of human life,
> and let your Holy Spirit lead us

in holiness and righteousness all the days of our life,
so that, when we shall have served you in our generation,
we may be gathered to our ancestors,
having the testimony of a good conscience,
in the communion of your Church,
in the confidence of a certain faith,
in the comfort of a holy hope,
in favor with you, our God, and in peace with all humanity;
through Jesus Christ our Lord. (*LBW* 1978, 208)

A more highly developed Christian expression of this idea continues in the conviction that Christian saints and martyrs actively share the heavenly realm, joining with Christ in interceding for all who continue their earthly pilgrimage.

Many people today are unsure what to believe with respect to death and the succeeding stages of life. A strong tendency toward skepticism concerning any life beyond death is combined with a strong desire that the tragedy of the human biography that always ends in death will be swallowed up in a victory that overcomes this death. A certain composure in the face of one's inevitable demise as historical presence is one way of bringing these two elements together, but so is the affirming of classic Christian metaphors in ways that people today can claim.

The urgency of these questions is intensified for many people in contemporary North American society because they live in such isolation from extended families and communities of support. We live very much by ourselves, and we die very much the same way. Therefore, the hopes and convictions of the community are largely absent in our times of great need, and we are forced to fall back upon our own resources and upon the more stylized expressions of the faith of the larger community. Again, the Lutheran liturgy (which is a remarkably complex composition despite its brevity) provides texts that illustrate the range of ideas. One prayer is firm in its affirmation of life beyond life, while the alternative is built upon the idea that at death we enter into rest with God who is "the rest of the blessed dead" (*LBW* 1978, 210).

These many theological and personal issues come into sharp focus in the church's rites at the time of death. The service books contain patterns for these rites and offer prayers and readings, usually arranged in the order they will likely be used. Even pastors who value spontaneity and extemporaneity in their other liturgical responsibilities are inclined to stay fairly close to the service book when officiating at funerals. Currently, however, the patterns are in flux and pastors must often adjust these services accordingly. The donation of the body or its organs for medical use or the cremation of the body often alter the traditional sequence of funeral service followed by interment. Pastoral adaptations are helped along and the major intentions of these rites are manifested when the major impulses of these rites are identified. The following paragraphs follow this line of approach rather than the approach used elsewhere in this book, which is to comment on the liturgies in the order that they appear in service books.

Three impulses can be identified in the pastoral care of people near death and after death, and they are provided for in the worship books: ministry when death is near, the care of the body, and the memorial itself.

When Death Is Near

It is common practice that pastors and other spiritual leaders of the congregation pay attention to people who are seriously ill. Today, much of this care is derived from the counseling model; but in an earlier time, and in some churches still, the model used is liturgical. Both ways of caring for people are important, but in the following paragraphs the primary attention is given to the liturgical dimensions of this ministry. It should be remembered that the first priority is to the person who is dying rather than to family, friends, or larger community. The one whose historical life is ebbing is involved in a "once-in-a-lifetime" activity and deserves all the help that the church can give. The purpose of religious rites, to adapt an idea of Susanne Langer's, is to bring to people's attention the signs of God's presence and to help them maintain proper attitudes toward "first and last things" (Langer 1951, 134). Certainly the dying person is facing "last things," meaning *final* as well as *most important.*

Three arduous labors must be undertaken. The dying person must deal with the fact of death in the light of that person's life and faith, finish up the unfinished business with family and others who have been close to the dying one and to say good-bye, and enter into the ritual of transition from life as a historical being to the life that "is hidden with Christ in God" (Colossians 3:3). Pastors are likely to have some sense of how to engage in conversation about life's meaning and the coming union with the Divine. Some are able to read scripture and offer brief prayers for strength, rest, and hope. Many pastors in Protestant traditions, however, are unsure about formal rites that focus upon the transition from this world to the next. We have inherited theologies that concentrate upon the finality of this life as the basis of God's judgment for the hereafter, and as a result we have lost sight of traditions that continue to pray for and offer sacramental nourishment to those making the transition. Thus, the new books are especially helpful when they offer texts for these difficult and important moments. These materials connect the dying person to Christ's death and resurrection. Some are bold enough to ask explicitly that the dying one be moved through death from this existence to the existence that is to come. Examples are these prayers that were proposed for consideration by Presbyterians but were not continued in the *Book of Common Worship*.

> Lord Jesus Christ,
> deliver your servant _____ from all evil,
> and set *him/her* free from every bond;
> that *he/she* may rest with all your saints
> in the joy of your eternal home
> for ever and ever. (*The Funeral* 1986, 12)

Later this same liturgy provides these words:

> "Depart in peace, O *brother/sister*;
> In the name of God the Father who created you;
> In the name of Christ who redeemed you;
> In the name of the Holy Spirit who sanctifies you.
> May you rest in peace, and dwell forever with the Lord.

The UCC *Book of Worship* does offer explicit texts, including this one in a section entitled "Time of Dying":

> Eternal God, you know our needs before we ask,
> and you hear our cries through lips unable to speak.
> Hear with compassion the yearnings of your servant *Name*,
> and the prayers that we would pray had we the words.
> Grant *her/him* the assurance of your embrace,
> the ears of faith to hear your voice,
> and the eyes of hope to see your light.
> Release *him/her* from all fear
> and from the constraints of life's faults
> that *he/she* may breathe his/her last
> in the peace of your words:
> Well done, good and faithful servant;
> enter into the joy of your God.
> We ask this through Jesus Christ our Savior. (*BW* 1986, 362)

The church's ministry as death comes near is also extended to the people who continue this life. They too are addressed by the statements to the dying person and by the prayers addressed to God. The service books also provide texts that are addressed specifically to these people, asking that they be empowered to meet this hour and be made ready for the time when they too die.

Caring for the Body

The second impulse of the church's death rites is to dispose of the body in reverent fashion. Human beings are embodied spirits, or spirited bodies. The two aspects of our lives are inseparable. We know one another's spirit only through bodily contact, and contact with bodies is useful only when the spirited character of these bodies is experienced. Because the powerful experiences of life together come through this exchange of bodily relationships, it is understandable that we maintain a regard for the body even after the spirit ceases to function there. Virtually every human society has its ways of disposing of these early remains in ways that each society understands to be suitable. For Christians the death rites also include a due regard to this matter.

The traditional pattern in North American culture has included the bathing and dressing of the body that it might be seen in the guise of repose. Since the invention of arterial embalming, this public display of the body has been somewhat enlarged. Usually there is a period of time when family and friends may come near the deceased "to pay their respects." In many localities, this viewing of the body has continued through the funeral service. There comes a time, either before the service or after it, when the close family views the body for the last time and the casket is closed. The dominant practice in North America has been for the casketed body to be buried in the ground in a cemetery dedicated to this purpose. These burial grounds are ordinarily maintained in pleasant condition so that when people visit graves they are in places that seem to continue the respect for those who have died.

This impulse is the one where the greatest amount of change is taking place in North American culture. Some people deplore the attention given to the corpse, affirming that too much is spent on the dead and that dead bodies do not deserve the care they receive. Another cause of the change is the interest in disposing of bodies in ways other than earth burial. Some donate parts or all of the body to science. Others choose cremation, which leads to a rapid decay of the physical remains. In both cases, the tendency is to abridge the attention given to the body and to rites that are designated for this purpose.

Increasingly, the materials in the service books provide considerable room for adaptation according to circumstances. Two concerns should be kept present throughout. First, the deceased and those who remain both need for the body to be disposed of in ways that honor the life being remembered and that are deemed suitable by the mourners. Death itself is difficult to deal with; there is no need to violate even more the honor of the one who died or the convictions of those who keep watch.

Memorializing the Life of the Deceased

The third impulse in the church's death rites is to memorialize the life of the one who has died. Part of this task is to fix the central attributes of the deceased in the public memory. Who was this person? How do we want this person to be remembered? These questions are important because every life is a complex tapestry of many colors, textures, and patterns. Furthermore, every life combines elements that are remembered gladly and others that are remembered with pain. When families and the larger communities surrounding a person gather because someone dies, people tell stories and reconstruct orally the record of their lives with the dead person whom they now are remembering. Already in this process they are creating the person's memorial. One task of a pastor preparing for the funeral is to listen to such conversations and to develop an outline of how the person is being remembered. Then in the funeral rite the pastor is able to summarize in his or her own way the portrait that has emerged. Often a particular metaphor or story emerges in this remembering that can be highlighted in the funeral meditation. Each one who has known the deceased well will remember much more than the funeral fixes in memory, but the work of creating the living memorial is still crucial to the way that we honor one another in death as well as in life.

Memorializing includes mending the breach that is caused by this person's death. Simply identifying what the deceased did and how this one entered into relations with others still living begins the process. People can begin to see the holes that need to be filled. When the deceased has been prominent in public life, this aspect of memorialization is very clear. When the person has had little connection with other people, then mending the breach seems less necessary and less possible. Even here, however, there are some systems that are affected by the death, and the funeral and reverent disposal of the body provide a way of closing this seam neatly.

Another aspect of memorializing the deceased is committing this person to God. The church, through its prayers and ceremonies, asks God to remember this person forever. God's faithfulness in the past is recalled and used as the foundation for asking God to be faithful into the future. In effect, the prayers say this: "God, you were good to this person during life; now remember this person and be good to this one in all of the time to come."

All of this is done in a framework of thanksgiving that, for Christians, begins with references to baptism and concludes with references to the Lord's supper. One litany is especially eloquent. It refers to Jesus' consoling of Martha and Mary and his weeping at the grave of Lazarus, using these remembrances as a way of asking for his renewed mercy to the one who has just died. Then the prayer continues by invoking the memory of the deceased's participation in baptism and eucharist, again using these remembrances as the foundation for God's mercy and love to this one now entering into life in the heavenly kingdom (*BCP* 1979, 497).

In the Catholic traditions, carried over into the Anglican and Lutheran traditions, funerals (like weddings) customarily took place within the celebration of the eucharist. These requiem masses have inspired some of the noblest music in the Western musical heritage; and even in our time strong music is being composed for these funerals in the form of eucharistic praise. Although most Protestant funerals do not take place within celebrations of the Lord's supper, recently published materials are providing liturgies for such occasions whenever they arise. As might be expected, the *Book of Common Prayer* provides a Preface for the "Commendation of the Dead." The *Book of Common Worship* offers a complete eucharistic prayer that could be used during a service memorializing the one who has died. In strong language it recites God's creating of all in the divine image and then remembers Jesus who "died our death" but through the resurrection has "conquered death" and given us the hope of eternal life. In the last part of this prayer a reference to the deceased is included:

> Remember our *brother/sister* _____,
> whose baptism is now complete in death.
> Bring *him/her*, and all who have died in the peace of Christ
> into your eternal joy and light. (*BCW* 1993, 932)

Thus even death is incorporated into the church's joyful praise of the living God. The one who has given us life, and who stays with us through every experience that comes, takes us back into the everlasting presence where all pain is gone and only majestic joy remains.

Encouraging the Conversation

1) Weddings and funerals give ritual form to two of the universal activities of humankind. Thus there is nothing exclusively Christian about them; yet the churches have developed their own ceremonies at these times of life. Does it seem reasonable to you that these events should be considered acts of thankful praise?

2) Think of weddings and funerals you have attended. To what degree have they expressed this quality of joyful confidence in God and gratitude for God's gifts?

3) Although Catholics consistently have included weddings and funerals into celebrations of the eucharist, such has been less common among Protestants. What do you think about the gradual increase in the use of the Lord's supper as the setting for these human rites of passage?

IV

LITURGY
AND LIFE

Again, we are changing the focus. In Chapter 12 we consider the worshipers—the congregants who come together to present themselves to God, and the ministers and musicians who prepare for their coming and encourage them in their service of God and one another. In Chapter 13 we consider what happens to individuals and congregations when worship is remade according to the principles laid out in this book.

For remaking worship is what we are doing. We serve a glorious God, and nothing that we do can ever be adequate to express our love for the Holy One who gives us life in Jesus Christ. Thus we always need to revise and reform so that we can come a little closer to what we want to do and say to our God.

As we work at renewing worship, we are likely to find that our congregations are also being renewed—and that the life of the world moves another step toward becoming the Holy Commonwealth of God.

12

Ministers Together

One of the convictions lying back of this book is that the congregation as a whole celebrates the public praise of God, including the sacraments of baptism and Lord's supper. A second is that the chief responsibility of the leaders of any service or liturgy is to assist the congregation in doing its work of praising God. This chapter describes the division of responsibility in the liturgy and suggests strategies for increasing the congregation's participation in worship.

This chapter is needed for several reasons. The first is *in order to encourage the people of the congregation to exercise their full responsibility in the liturgical assembly*. In the actual doing of worship the role of the people is usually diminished while that of the leaders is augmented. Reasons for this reversal come as much from the dynamics of organizations as from the theological history of the church, but, whatever may be the reason, the result is a distortion of the proper functioning of the congregation. The church needs to live its life in the fullest and most complete way possible. A second reason is *to generate leadership within the church that is theologically responsible and organizationally effective*. The question is not whether there shall be leaders; rather, the question is what kind of leaders will the church have.

A third reason for this chapter is *to affirm the two modes of ecclesial life, as gathered community of praise and as scattered people of witness*. As the people of God we are to serve as the sign of God's presence in the world, expressing both the mercy and the justice of God. This kind of life is our full liturgy, our full sacrifice of praise and thanksgiving. In our actions during worship we sharpen the focus of everything else we do in our lives. Unfortunately, this close connection between life in church and in the world is often forgotten, and the worldly aspect of the Christian's life is considered to be of little religious value. When life in the world loses its religious core, then life in the sanctuary soon withers, too. Worship in the sanctuary and service in the world are the alternating current of the Christian life. Together they can be called the priestly work of the people of God.

The Congregation as Royal Priesthood

From ancient times *priest* has been one of the titles given to people whose work is worship. When the word arises now in a Christian context we tend to think of the leaders of worship, especially in Orthodox, Roman Catholic, and Episcopal or Anglican churches. For many people the very use of the term implies sharp distinctions between priests as leaders and the people among whom they do their work. This tendency to distinguish between leaders and the led, it must be noted, extends to other traditions where *priest* is not used as the title for religious professions. In many evangelical churches the distinction between preacher and people often is as great as that between priest and people in churches with a catholic bent.

In biblical Israel the word *priest* was sometimes used in reference to the people as a whole. In Exodus, for example, God addresses the people through Moses. "If you obey my voice and keep my covenant," says God, "you shall be my treasured possession out of all the peoples." Then God says, "You shall be for me a priestly kingdom and a holy nation" (Exodus 19:5–6a). Already in this brief passage, two important ideas are stated. Priesthood and covenant are closely connected. Furthermore, the people are to be considered holy for, as other portions of this narrative make clear, the God who calls them and orders their life is the Holy One.

This priestliness of the entire people provides the framework for understanding the specific nature and function of the small number of people who were separated out of the nation as a whole and assigned special responsibilities in the liturgies of the temple. These occupational priests focused the priestliness of the entire nation, carrying Israel's praises to God and conveying the divine Presence to the people. The priests-by-occupation thus mediated between the priests-as-citizens and their God. At some point in its life, Israel developed the office of high priest. In this office, the holiness of the priesthood as a whole was gathered up. The high priest's major liturgy was conducted at the most solemn point of the relationship between Israel and God—the Day of the Atonement. On this important day, Israel acknowledged its sin and lack of faith and earnestly besought the renewal of its covenanted life with God.

The New Testament writers continue two of the three elements of this threefold priestly system. Both in 1 Peter and Revelation, the church itself is called a priesthood, thus renewing the idea that all of the people are priests. Writing to an unidentified congregation, the author of 1 Peter echoes the language of Exodus: "Come to him, a living stone...and like living stones, let yourselves be built into a spiritual house, to be a *holy priesthood*, to offer spiritual sacrifices acceptable to God through Jesus Christ" (1 Peter 2:4a, 5; italics added). Later in the same chapter the people are referred to as "a chosen race, a royal priesthood, a holy nation, God's own people..." (2:9a). Even in heaven this priestly service of God continues. The writer of Revelation says that Jesus Christ has "freed us from our sins by his blood," and made us to be a kingdom, priests serving his God and Father (Revelation 1:5).

The high priestly element of the Jewish system provides the dominant metaphor of the epistle to the Hebrews. Jesus Christ is the great high priest who definitively and finally has presided over a day of atonement that for all time forgives sin. This metaphor is spun out in considerable detail, with full reference to sanctuary and sacrifice, to atonement and justification. The entire system is presented as a means of assuring anxious Christians that their salvation in Christ is fully as secure as that which had been provided in the Jewish liturgies that had previously been so effective for them. Although the writer of Hebrews does not refer to church members as priests, their proper work has priestly qualities. The text does state that they have direct access to God and implies that they are responsible to care for one another. In one brief passage both of these ideas are intertwined. We have "confidence to enter the sanctuary by the blood of Jesus" (10:19b), and therefore "let us consider how to provoke one another to love and good deeds, not neglecting to meet together, as is the habit of some, but encouraging one another..." (10:24–25a).

The element from the Jewish system that is missing not only in Hebrews but in all of the New Testament is the middle term. No priests-by-occupation are to be found in the churches described in this earliest Christian literature. Perhaps the apostles fulfilled this intermediate function. When practical difficulties developed in the Jerusalem church, Peter stated that it was not right that the twelve should neglect the Word in order to wait on tables. Six of the company were chosen by the people to "wait on tables," leaving the apostles free to devote themselves "to prayer and to serving the word" (Acts 6:2–4). Elsewhere in the first Christian writings, the gift of leadership is frequently described. Clearly, leadership is highly diversified and widely distributed. Everyone served one another and the common good according to their abilities and opportunities. When sacrificial language is used, with priestly functions implied, the references are to the whole body of Christians. "I appeal to you therefore, brothers and sisters, by the mercies of God, to present your bodies as a living sacrifice, holy and acceptable to God, which is your spiritual worship" (Romans 12:1). It could be concluded that during the early decades of the church's life all Christians belonged to the one priesthood and each Christian was a priest.

In part, this fluid character of leadership may have resulted from the fact that the church was still in its nascent period. It was still being born and thus lived in the mode of *communitas,* to use a word borrowed from anthropologist Victor Turner (Turner 1974, especially 44ff.). During such a phase in the life of a group, the bonds of the community are "undifferentiated, equalitarian, direct, nonrational (though not irrational), I-Thou or Essential We relationships" (Turner 1974, 47). During such a time there is little need for and even less interest in organized systems of leadership and group maintenance. Everyone is empowered by the direct experience of the vision that brought them together. No group, however, can long live in such a phase. Inevitably, the immediacy of the vision fades into the distance, but the group's life continues. Now, however, differentiated, rationalized processes become important as links between the participants and as modes of continuity. Persons and processes that had come into prominence during the nascent period now are regularized during the organizational period. Furthermore, previously known models of organizational life tend to be replicated, although with significant mutations.

What is clear in the developments reported in the New Testament is that by the end of the first generation leadership coalesced in the congregations around officers with titles such as *elder* (overseer), *deacon* (servant), and *pastor*. With the firming up of the eucharist, increasingly described in sacrificial imagery, as the center of Christian worship, priestly language for the president of the eucharistic assembly came into use. Thus the ordered system of the church's life filled in the missing middle, creating an occupational priesthood stationed between the people's holy priesthood and Jesus Christ's great high priesthood. Leaders of the church came to be looked upon as priests at the table much as Jewish leaders had been understood to be priests at the altar of sacrifice.

Throughout the history of the church, the priestly people and the occupational priests have participated in the church's life and worship with various degrees of intensity. In general, however, the strong tendency has been for the occupational priests to become dominant and the priestly people to become diminished in their functions. Some doctrines of church, worship, and ministry have defined the occupational priesthood as essential in the process of mediation between the royal priesthood and the great high priest. Other doctrinal systems, however, provide for occupational priests but define the office in ways that preserve the essential priestliness of the whole church and therefore its right to approach God in praise, word, and sacrament even in the absence of occupational priests.

In fact, the church needs both a strong priestly people and strong priestly leaders. By their baptism all of the people of God are set apart for their ministries in church and world. A small portion of these priests by baptism are also called to be priests by ordination, and to them is assigned a more highly concentrated ministry within the churches and on their behalf in the world. The authorizing of these more concentrated labors is recognized by the liturgy of ordination in which the church lays hands upon those who are called and prays that God's Spirit will empower them for their work. Both forms of priestly ministry need to be clarified and encouraged if the churches are to fulfill their proper roles in the world. Because the priesthood conveyed by baptism is more important, but also the priestliness more likely to be under-expressed, the work of the people will be addressed first.

Encouraging the People in Their Ministries

The current renewal of worship is reaffirming and encouraging the ministries of the people of the churches. One of the ways that their priestly ministry is being recovered is *by arranging liturgical space so that it helps the people do their part in the liturgy.* Consultants on worship and church architects are designing worship buildings so that the table for celebrating the eucharist extends into the space occupied by the people of the congregation. Although some church designs place the table in the center of the space, with people gathered all around, it is more common for the room to be arranged so that the congregation is seated on three sides of the table. Many older churches were built with a long nave for the people and the table at one end, far removed and protected from contact by the people. Under the influence of new standards for worship, many of these buildings are being rebuilt to meet current liturgical standards. It now is standard practice in these renovations to move the altars away from the chancel wall and to position them closer to the people; or a new altar-table is located at the front of the chancel or in a commanding location that is close to the people. Furthermore, the pulpit is moving closer to the congregants. Rather than being "high and lifted up," to parody Isaiah's reference to the Lord's throne (Isaiah 6:1), the pulpit is now brought low and close up.

As a result both the table and the pulpit seem to belong to the people and to be close enough that worshipers can understand that their own life-liturgies are related to these centers of liturgical action. Of course, they can see and hear more clearly, and in that sense they are better participants in the liturgy. More important, the people can approach these places where the main action takes place. The appropriateness of their being in the holy places from which they once were prohibited is now made clear. Unfortunately, architectural reform does not in itself bring about liturgical reform. Many pastors and congregations have not yet come to an adequate realization that the people are essential to the action both at the table and at the pulpit.

Thus the second movement to encourage the priesthood of the people is *the democratization of the liturgy*. A larger part of the service is led by members of the congregation than has been the case for a long time. Although this transformation has been discussed in earlier sections of this book, it warrants further attention at this point. The people experience worship as something they do *only if they do it*. The point is surely clear when singing is the mode of activity. No matter how inspiring a soloist or choir, special music is very different from congregational song. In order for the congregation to sing the praises of God, the voices of the people must be involved. Only then do they participate in a full, bodily way. The function of special musicians is to help the congregation fulfill its musical role by training the people, supporting them in their singing, and intensifying the song when the people's lack of artistry and training keep them back.

There still is a strong tendency for the leadership of the people to be overshadowed by the power and all-pervasiveness of ministers and musicians. Even when they believe in the liturgical ministries of the people, they find it easier to do things themselves rather than to develop a group of people who are skilled in public leadership. Fortunately, congregations and pastors are giving the people their proper work—in singing the praises of God, in reading and responding to scripture, in offering the prayers, in bringing the offertory gifts, and in administering communion. In some traditions the people are now assigned speaking parts in the eucharistic prayer, which has long been a monologue by the pastor.

Leaders of the current liturgical movement also encourage the *cultural accommodation of the liturgy*, and in this way they provide a third expression of the fact that worship is tied very closely to the regular life of the faithful members. For, when the people's own patterns of thought and speech, music and ceremony, and social relationships are expressed in the patterns of the liturgy, then it is clear that the gifts being brought to God do include their own lives. The need for this cultural accommodation is especially important in countries evangelized through the modern missionary movement. Many missionaries brought a Christianity so intertwined with their own culture that it was hard to separate them. As people began the effort to distinguish between the Christian faith and Western culture, it became clear how isolated from the national populations the liturgy actually was. When the presiding ministers came from the sending countries, the sharp contrast between the nationals and the missionaries became even more evident.

In the United States and Canada a clearly recognizable contrast exists between the prevailing culture and the cultures of other groups such as African-American and Hispanic. In each of these sections of North American life, particular patterns of music, speech, ceremony, and activity have become normal for the people of the churches. There is a tendency, however, for representatives of the dominant culture to assume that their music, art, and use of language are necessarily better than those of other cultures, and therefore that the dominant patterns should become the norm for excellence in all of the others.

A similar separation, although more subtly expressed, is present in places where congregations are fully identified with the national culture. Here the contrast is between the aesthetics and theology of the leaders and of the people. The situation often present is that the people's taste in religious music is a combination of nineteenth-century gospel songs and more recent popular religious music. This is the music that they are willing and able to sing and that brings tears to their eyes. This hymnody is prominently presented in hymnals published by freelance publishers. In contrast, the official hymnals have contained hymns with texts approved by theologians and tunes that match the religious and aesthetic commitments of trained church musicians. As a result, worship that is to be the work of the whole people of God becomes the work of those who understand correct theology and appreciate good music. Thus the conflict sets in. The congregants demand what is most popular, giving less attention to the adequacy of texts or sturdiness of the tunes. Pastors and musicians insist upon approved texts and music from the high culture and the people respond with passive nonparticipation. What needs to happen, if worship is to be the work of the people, is for the contrasting forms of music to be brought into a more satisfactory synthesis.

The new generation of church hymnals represents a strong commitment to creating this synthesis. Examples are *The United Methodist Hymnal* (published in 1989), *The Presbyterian Hymnal* (published in 1990), and *Chalice Hymnal* (published by Disciples in 1995). The core of all three books consists of well-known hymns from ancient, European, and North American sources, many of them adapted to conform to contemporary standards. Alongside of these materials are representative hymns and songs from the evangelical older tradition, from the recent popular repertory, from the many new hymns of England and North America, and representative hymns from African-American, Hispanic, Asian-American, and Native American traditions. These new hymnals also provide a significant number of psalms arranged for congregational singing. These newly published books for the people acknowledge the wide cultural range present in American church life and can help the people sing with renewed zeal.

Pressures always at work in congregations tend to lessen lay involvement in worship. One is the inclination to specialize labor and assign tasks according to these categories of specialization. The larger the congregation, the greater is the tendency to move away from local, volunteer leadership to highly trained and well paid professional staff, including lead singers in the choir.

In most congregations, however, the primary obstacle to the priestly ministry of the congregation as a whole exists within the people themselves rather than in doctrines of ministry and sacraments or in the practical administration of church life. A generation ago writers described the malaise of the church with lively phrases such as "God's frozen people" (the title of a book by Mark Gibbs and T. Ralph Morton; see also their later *God's Lively People*). More recently, writers have adopted a more prosaic terminology, such as "the passive church" (Schaller 1981). While differing in detail, these analyses of the churches are similar in broad outline. The people of God are passive in their churches; furthermore, they see very little relationship between their Christian faith and their lives in family, school, workplace, and wider world. Neither in church nor in the rest of their lives do they recognize the grace of God at work and their actions as active responses to that grace.

Therefore, Christian people find it difficult to offer the sacrifice of praise and thanksgiving by which their priesthood is expressed. Herein lies the challenge to help the people recover the power of religion so that they can become priests once again.

Life as the Sacrifice of Praise and Thanksgiving

Priestly activities consist primarily of offering gifts to God and one another. Therefore, if the people are to be priests, *they need to be able to offer something valuable*. If they are to be priests, *they need to believe that the making of these offerings is critical to their well being and to the improvement of life in the world*. If they are to be priests, *they must be convinced that services of worship in churches are important settings for offering their gifts*.

The gifts we offer are ourselves and the total range of activities in our daily life. We make these offerings because giving exists at the core of human personality. The primary location for this self-giving is daily life in home, school, work, and play. We become what we are supposed to be in the actual process of doing everything that we do—so long as this activity is shaped by the template of generous giving. This central focus of life is clearly expressed within the family as father and mother give themselves for the sake of their children; and these children, in turn, learn through example and imitation that this is the way that life ought to be lived. Much of the time, this same quality shows through in the other activities of natural life. All of this is true whether or not people are self-consciously religious.

Thus the question soon arises: if our true nature is expressed in the self-offering of ourselves to one another in daily life, why complicate this process with religious ceremony? *If I can be good without being religious, why be religious?* One answer to this question is that being religious helps us to be good. The theological teachings of our faith help us to be clear about life and its meaning. The ethical standards of our religious community show us how to be good to one another and to the world itself. The nurturing qualities of the religious community support us in our efforts to give ourselves in neverending love.

In a second way our religious life helps us fulfill the natural life of generous self-giving. Being religious extends the range in which we live as people whose real life is realized through giving. From earliest childhood we experience the world both as impersonal, objective reality and as personal, subjective presence. (See my *Liturgies in a Time When Cities Burn* and ideas developed by Ernst Cassirer and Susanne K. Langer.) The world as thing exists to be enjoyed through contemplation and use. The world as person exists to be enjoyed through communion and shared life. The heart of religion is communion with the Personal Presence who comes to us in our encounters with the world. It is only when we are self-consciously religious in our practice that this fuller dimension of human experience comes to full flower.

This attitude can be expressed in highly personal and very private ways and some Asian religions are built around individualized rituals of communion with the spiritual reality of the world. In contrast, one of the primary characteristics of Christianity and other Semitic religions is that life in community shapes religious experience, including the solitariness of life in the world. When we are together with others who see things the same way we do, our sense of divine presence becomes stronger than when we are by ourselves. Our life together sensitizes us to the real character of the world so that we are better able to enter into self-giving communion with everything that is.

Why do we participate in worship, offering our ritualized sacrifice of praise and thanksgiving? Because by so doing we come to understand the depth of life as Personal Presence. We learn the name of this reality, the name God. We are invited and encouraged to express our true nature, which is to give ourselves in joyful communion with one another, with the world, and with the God whose own self-giving makes possible all of our giving in the rest of life.

A Course of Action

This diagnosis of church life naturally leads to a prescription for action. The most important steps are those that affect the people of the congregation, helping them move from passivity to active engagement in the Christian life. In addition, there are steps to be taken that relate specifically to the professionals—to pastors and musicians. In one sense, however, everything relates to the professionals since they are the people who by virtue of their position in liturgical activity determine most of what happens.

The first step is *to highlight life in the world as the offering of praise.* If it is true that people in the churches are but dimly aware of this theology of the Christian life, every possible action must be undertaken to help them come to this understanding of things. This theme deserves prominence in activities that prepare people for baptism into Christ and membership in the church. It needs to be reinforced regularly in the educational program of the congregation and in sermons. The interpretations given to the offering in worship services can affirm that all of life is this giving of oneself to God and to one another in gratitude for life itself.

This attitude can also characterize the approach to church program and local outreach. There even is a scriptural precedent for this way of thinking about the church and its life. Paul's instructions to the church in Rome (Romans 12:3–8) are based on the fact that God blesses each Christian in a distinctive way, and that the effective life of the church depends upon the full functioning of all of its members with these many different gifts. He then encourages the people to exercise their various gifts fully. A similar way of organizing and administering congregational life is widespread among many churches today. (See *Leading and Managing Your Church* by Carl F. George and Robert E. Logan.) Members are helped to discover the combination of ability, opportunity, and interest that constitute their gifts. They are encouraged to find ways in the church and in the rest of life to express these gifts, all to the glory of God and the blessing of the people around them. Life lived this way becomes increasingly effective. People are happy with what they are doing, and they find themselves fulfilled by their labor. Because they continually give of themselves in ways that satisfy their innermost being, they gain strength from what they do.

This kind of life leads to full-throated, full-bodied participation in worship. What happens on weekdays is recognized as directly related to what is done in church on Sundays. By praising God for their gifts, and asking for new power to exercise them, worshipers are renewed for their continuing work of being Christian in all that they do.

A second step is *to provide an adequate opportunity for liturgical expression of this attitude toward life*. The most important places are the congregational prayers, the bringing of gifts that prepare for the celebration of holy communion, and special acts of commissioning people for their participation in their work. The liturgical function of the prayers and the offertory have already been discussed (in Chapter 7). In this chapter the ecclesial and missional character of these actions is the focus of attention. Many of the recent experiments in extemporaneous and dialogical prayer have been prompted by the desire to include the regular life of the people in the contents of what the church offers to God in prayer. The idea is that when the people themselves initiate both the topics and the wording, the prayers becomes theirs. Their life is now the substance of the liturgy. Life in the world and life in the church are intertwined as one complex offering of praise to God. Similarly, the inclusion of the people in the offering is intended to give them this strong sense of interconnection.

Even these well-intentioned liturgical actions, however, need to be kept in mind, and frequently revised in form and contents if worshipers are to be fully and continuingly aware of the meaning of what they are doing. One of the most useful functions of a worship committee in the congregation could be to review the liturgy periodically in order to assess the strength of the people's participation in prayers and offering. More than the pastoral and music staff, the lay members of the worship committee can reflect how congregants experience the various parts of the service.

The Ministries of Liturgical Leadership

The popularizing of the liturgy raises serious questions for the ministers and musicians. The discussion so far in this chapter could lead to the conclusion that the theological and musical training of leaders is of little value in their work on Sunday morning. Many musicians, for example, have commented that they might just as well never have gone to music school for what little good their training does them. Similarly, preachers sometimes wonder what good seminary was if they can't preach the theology they have learned through much hard study.

The answer may be easier for preachers than for musicians. For them the way to popularize is to deal with the most profound questions of human existence, but to do so with vocabulary, illustrative material, and speech techniques that are adapted to the experience, expectations, and capabilities of the people to whom they preach. What they have to give up is not their theology, but only their technical speech. What many preachers have discovered is that the simpler the form of discourse, the greater the rhetorical challenge. As time goes on, the capacities and experiences of the congregation increase; and the preacher becomes ever more sensitive and skillful in communicating. Thus preaching grows stronger over time.

A similar solution can be suggested for the aesthetic issues involved in music and other forms of artistic experience. Part of the solution to this problem is the fact that most people enjoy a fairly wide range of music, and they appreciate music that is performed with intensity, energy, and artistry. Thus musicians, like their preacher counterparts, must work to discover the range of music that is possible with a particular congregation. Their first goal, then, should be to select from within that range music that is not only satisfying to worshipers but also appropriate to the content of the liturgy at that point, and interesting to the performers. This music needs to be performed in as powerful a way as possible. As trust and experience with one another are established, then it becomes possible to broaden the range of music that comes into use in worship. No two congregations will come to the same synthesis of forms and styles of music, but they can all move toward a range that more fully encompasses the scope of liturgical music available to congregations today.

What then are the specific tasks of musicians and ministers in the liturgical assembly? They are, first, to preside with sincerity and strength, doing their parts well. There is no excuse for musicians to come in at the last minute, scurry around to find their music and set it up, and then sightread their way through a service. Nor is there any excuse for liturgical leaders who improvise because they don't take time to prepare, and bluff their way through the service. Leaders are to be in their best form for each occasion. Ministers and musicians are, second, to keep the liturgy in focus and on time. The congregational tendency to drag while singing hymns is well known; and the song leader or accompanist bears responsibility to keep the tempo where it needs to be. Spoken and acted parts of the liturgy also need to move along with a rhythm that matches their place and importance. Here ministers have a special responsibility because they largely control the pace by which part succeeds part. Focus is achieved by the pattern of intensity with which a service is conducted. Public reading, for example, can be done in a way that blurs the story line or the idea that is expounded; or the text can be read so that hearers are able to follow the ideas, feel the texture, grasp the feeling tone of the reading.

The ministers and musicians in a congregation, third, represent continuity. They are always there, thus conveying a sense of stability that helps other worshipers do their parts of the service with confidence. Fourth, the leaders represent the larger liturgical tradition of the church. Usually they come from somewhere else and have been trained with people from other places and with other experiences. Part of this training includes ideas and standards that are held by the church in its broader manifestations. In their work with their congregations musicians and ministers try to bring the local community and the wider world into a fruitful relationship.

Fifth, ministers and musicians have administrative responsibility to take the lead in planning, enlisting, instructing, and supporting other congregants as they share worship leadership. In part, this administrative work results from the fact that they are a congregation's staff, charged with similar responsibilities across the entire range of a congregation's life. In part, their supervision of worship grows out of the need to maintain a balance between representativeness and competence. Someone needs to see that both women and men are regularly involved in speaking roles, that various age groups are represented, and that other constituencies, such as language or racial groups, in a congregation are also given appropriate places in leading worship.

One way of summing up this discussion of the work of ministers and musicians is to say that in worship they are both recitalists and conductors. There are parts of the service that they do themselves, and here they must always seek to work at the top of their form. There are other parts of the service where they are conductors, bringing in other parts of the congregation, giving cues to other leaders, and setting the pace for the performance. Both kinds of leadership are important; and the people of God, as they perform their priestly work at the table, depend upon their leaders.

The Meaning of Ordination

The distinction between the people and their liturgical leaders is partly functional, as this chapter has so far indicated. The distinction also is theological, as is indicated by the fact that some are given sacramental leadership through the laying on of hands and prayers that constitute the heart of ordination. Most churches do, in fact, ordain their ministers. Although their explanations of this act differ, two elements are usually part of the systems of explanation.

The first is *authorization*. Ordination is an especially solemn act of public recognition and transmittal of public authority. It acknowledges the character and competency of the ordained to be religious leaders and also the readiness of the church to accept that leadership. Thus ordination regularizes the oversight of the church's sacramental life. The second factor in most doctrines of ordination is *empowerment*. Here theologies differ extensively. Some stress charismatic power—an infusion of the Holy Spirit that enables ministers to do the "mightier works than these" that Jesus mentioned to his disciples (John 14:12). Other churches describe power in a more organic way, referring particularly to the God-given capability of leading the sacraments so that their character is transformed. In these churches sacraments conducted by the unordained are thought to resemble true sacraments but their true, inner reality is not thought to be present.

In the past these doctrines of ministry have been major factors in the alienation of churches from one another. Unwilling to acknowledge the authenticity of one another's ordinations, they were unable to offer or enjoy hospitality at one another's eucharistic tables. Fortunately, in our time these barriers have been partially breached. Churches are affirming that the apostolic faith is present in the many churches even though it has been preserved and handed down in differing ways. Furthermore, the churches are affirming that one another's churches do participate in the one, holy, catholic, and apostolic church, which means that the rites and ceremonies, including ordination, in one another's churches are in some important ways valid and efficacious. Another basis for closer relations is the frank acknowledgment that what we do in our churches is clearly blessed by God and therefore has to be recognized by everyone.

While the theological barriers that have separated our churches are being broken down, the disciplines and customs that keep us apart still function effectively. Thus we find it difficult to live the Christian life in close companionship with one another. Gradually, however, we are discovering that what binds us together in Christ is more important than the experiences of history that have separated us into competing institutions.

Whatever else ordination may mean in the many churches, these two elements are present across the entire Christian world. Back of the religious ceremony is the experience of being called by God to be a leader in the church's life and mission. The people who come to this conviction about their vocation before God then offer themselves to the church as its servant-leaders. The church receives this offer of a life and helps the person find the appropriate way to fulfill this calling. In our time, the majority of these people are received into leadership in the church's public life, and especially as leaders of Word and sacrament. Ordination affirms the call, expresses the church's acceptance of this gift of life, asks God to bless this person and the ministry that will follow, and authorizes the person to continue among its corps of significant leaders.

The ceremony in which this takes place calls for the public examination of the candidates for ordination. Already, of course, there will have been extensive preparation by the candidate and evaluation of suitability and readiness for ministry. The public examination summarizes what has taken place already and, in a sense, makes it all part of the public record. There are prayers for the candidate and the church, calling upon the Holy Spirit to come with the gifts of ministry. The dramatic action at the heart of the service is the moment when representatives of the church's spiritual leadership place their hands upon the head and shoulders of the person being ordained, thus making use of one of the oldest religious signs described in the Bible. A prayer is closely associated with this laying on of hands, a prayer that asks God to give to this person the power needed to do the work of the ministry. From that time onward, the persons ordained are looked upon by the church as God's people, ready to preach the gospel, administer the sacraments of grace, and lead the church in its full life and program.

Encouraging the Conversation

One way to get into this chapter is by taking up the division of labor between the leaders of worship and the people of the congregation. In the church where you worship:

- What parts of the service do the people of the congregation do?
- What parts are done by ministers, musicians, and leaders?
- Is this division of labor consistently maintained, or does it change from Sunday to Sunday, or from season to season?
- What is the basis for this division? Theology? Local custom? Other considerations?

This chapter uses the offering of life as the theme that connects daily life and worship. As you think about your experience and your church, in the light of this chapter, would you say that most people would agree? Would worship be enlivened and life energized if they did?

13

For the Life
of the World

This final chapter picks up a theme that was announced early in the book but has been largely silent through the intervening chapters. It is that the recovery of eucharistic worship can have a strong and good impact upon congregations, their members, and their mission in the world. Here, as in earlier chapters, *eucharistic worship* is used in two ways: to describe an attitude of thankful praise that generates and permeates all of the churches' ceremonial actions, and also to name the preeminent act of worship, the celebration of the Lord's supper. Throughout the following pages these two meanings are intertwined. Sometimes the broad attitude is intended and sometimes the more specific liturgy of Word and Table.

By this time the reasons for the intertwining should be clear. This book recommends a way of worship that is table-centered in principle even when the people of God conduct other liturgies. The life of some families is similar. Whatever else they may do, these families are most fully themselves when they gather around the supper table evening by evening, or at picnic tables as they travel, or for parties with food at the festal moments in one another's lives. Their meal fellowship makes them what they are. So too in some churches. Congregations that are constituted by the communion table carry those eucharistic qualities into everything else that they do.

What kind of life is shaped by eucharistic worship? What kind of people develop in a church whose whole life is infused with thankful praise? What sort of community is created by this table friendship? What does their world become? These are the questions that this chapter explores.

Congregational Life

These questions can be sharpened. Most congregations that be-come eucharistic in their worship as this book recommends previ-ously will have been word-centered in their worship. When the change to sacramental worship takes place, what is the impact upon their church?

During the middle years of the century an answer developed in several churches in Europe and North America. Their claim was that the recovery of sacramental worship, celebrated in a strongly par-ticipatory mode, leads to church renewal at a depth level. One of the strongest spokespersons for this point of view was Alfred R. Shands, an Episcopal priest, who studied church renewal movements, both Protestant and Catholic, giving special attention to the renewal of sacramental worship in Protestantism. He mentions the Swedish Lutheran Church and the Iona Community of the Church of Scot-land, calling attention to the fact that in both settings Christians were becoming aware of the "social significance of the sacraments." Speak-ing of Iona, Shands comments: "This group discovered anew the role of the sacraments in community life" and helped convince Protes-tant churches "that the Liturgical Movement is not a subtle effort to compromise the principles of the Reformation" (Shands 1965, 29).

By emphasizing renewal at the depth level, Shands distinguishes the quality of church renewal achieved by the liturgical movement from the renewals achieved by other movements such as the recov-ery of evangelistic preaching or Christian social witness. He cites T. O. Wedel's description of the religion of the average person: "Golden Rule Idealism," which is "a rather shallow understanding of doing to others what you would have them do to you. The religion of the majority today is 'a sincere acceptance of the moral ideals of Christ.'" In order for churches to become strong and vital, members need to be challenged away from their religion of moralism to a religion of life in the Body of Christ (Shands 1965, 34). Shands states that this self-understanding leads to mission: "When we realize that we have been joined together to embody the self-offering of Christ as exem-plified in the liturgy, then mission begins" (Shands 1965, 35).

Some pastors who have more recently made the change from pulpit-centered to table-centered worship confirm the general lines of Shands' argument by identifying five changes in congregational life. Added together they constitute renewal at the depth level.

The first change is that *a new character is given to preaching*. In eucharistic worship sermons prepare the people to bring their sacri-fice of praise and thanksgiving and to receive God's self-offering through the meal of bread and wine. Regardless of the main theme of the discourse, the preacher has to bring it around so that worshipers are introduced to the Good Shepherd. Regardless of the style of the exposition, its remoteness to the people or its immediacy, the sermon fails unless it concludes with a word about the suffering Savior that people can understand. In some churches, the normal service has celebrated the Lord's supper in the early part of the liturgy, with the sermon following. When the order is rearranged, with the sermon regularly coming before communion, preachers find that both the style and content of their preaching change. Preaching is focused more on the gospel, more on the fact that God forgives sinners and transforms life, more on the promises of the gospel and less on its demands. Yet, the results are that hearers are more often persuaded of the gospel expectations and energized to be faithful to these expectations in their lives.

Contrary to what some might expect, sermons in the context of the eucharist are not constricted into a narrow range of topics. The entire range of religious themes can and need to be expounded—so long as they make it possible for the sermon always to bring people to the table of thanksgiving. To put it simply: eucharistic worship provides the context for coloring all doctrinal and ethical instruction with the blood of Jesus Christ.

Furthermore, preaching in this context is strengthened because it is followed by liturgical actions that the people need in order to complete their encounter with the living Word of God. In eucharistic worship the people are provided ways of responding through intercessions and offering. Thus their lives outside of the sanctuary are interpreted and reformed according to the gospel. Further, the eucharist itself provides a ratification of the covenantal agreement with God. As Webber points out, in the Old Testament God used a blood sacrifice to demonstrate the sealing of God's covenant with the worshipers. After Jesus' sacrifice, the Lord's supper is the sign of that covenant between God and the church (Webber 1982, 25).

Many of the congregations built around a powerful pulpit are large and strong. When this preacher is in the pulpit, attendance is very good; and it seems clearly to be the case that the congregation's capacity to draw members is built around the preaching skills of the strong voice who proclaims the word most Sundays. Most congregations of this type feature a service of the Word, culminating on most Sundays in the sermon. These churches are examples of Webber's claim that worship in evangelical churches, "for the most part, centers on the preacher. What he says to us, how he says it, and what effect his words have on us appear to be paramount" (Webber 1985, 42). The anomaly in such churches is that the theology that they teach is focused upon Christ as the revelation of God and reconciler of humankind to this God. Yet, says Webber, worship in the pulpit-centered form of worship teaches about God more than it leads to experiencing God. What Webber says about evangelical churches is also true in pulpit-centered churches in mainline denominations. The theological line probably differs as do the music and other art forms, yet the liturgical form is essentially the same—instruction, emotion, and sacred concert, dominated by musicians and preacher.

What would happen if these congregations were to focus their entire life upon the thankful praise of God, with the communion table at the center of all they do? Many suspect that the results would be one or the other of the following—that the attendance would tail off fast, or that the membership would change significantly, with one group of people dropping out and another group taking their places. A third possibility, however, is possible when the preacher believes in the change from pulpit-centered to table-centered worship and alters the character of preaching. Sermons can still be extended in form, diversified in content, and emotionally powerful even when they are followed by the celebration of the Lord's supper. Indeed, the stronger the preaching, the greater is the desirability that people have an expressive mode of response that channels their deep feelings into a praise-filled and consecratory giving of themselves to God. The eucharist is exactly that kind of group response to the powerful proclamation of the Word of God. Furthermore, even powerful preachers are sometimes absent from their pulpits and sometimes fall short in their preaching. A strong liturgy, with the high point in the eucharist, provides a means of holding things together even on these homiletically less powerful occasions.

This description of the eucharist as the congregation's response to strong preaching leads naturally into a second effect of eucharistic worship upon congregations. *Congregants experience one another in a new way.* Meeting one another at a table is quite different from sitting side by side listening to a talk. In both associations people are aware of one another, but eating and drinking are expressions of life at a more basic level than is giving attention to the proclaiming of a message, and therefore the connection between participants is at a more primal level of their lives. It is possible to sit at table and avoid one another, but the strain is intense and cannot long be sustained. Either the physical proximity must be discontinued or one another's presence be recognized. When we eat together, the social distinctions that ordinarily separate us into groups and categories diminish in their importance and power.

This point can be made another way. The relationships formed at the table are marked by immediacy and intimacy that do not depend upon family ties or social compatibility. This is well illustrated when the eucharistic liturgy invites people to greet one another with the peace of Christ and when they go from their seats to a place where the communion elements are distributed to them one by one. In these circumstances people reach out to others and are physically touched themselves, which for many people in contemporary society rarely happens in other contexts. In some celebrations they are called by name, and this in a context that is highly charged ceremonially. Again, the sense of intensity is prominent.

Third, *people are linked across generations and the many critical experiences of life are incorporated into a new fabric of meaning.* In some liturgical traditions the eucharist is frequently part of weddings, funerals, and certain other turning points in life. In these churches the likelihood is especially strong that when people come to the table they recall a montage of other occasions when they have been guests at that place and met their family members and friends. Even when the eucharist is ordinarily not celebrated other than on Sunday morning, the "great cloud of witnesses" still comes to consciousness.

Fourth, *eucharistic worship affects the character of pastoral leadership.* Congregants report that during the communion service the pastor's voice takes on a warmer, more human character than at any other time—which is one of the reasons why many of them appreciate those Sundays of the year. Preaching is a form of liturgical activity that invites strong, sometimes strident tones and tempts preachers to become the representatives of moralistic and organizational norms and expectations. At the eucharistic table, however, the natural character of leadership pushes toward hospitable and nonauthoritarian modes. Furthermore, sacramental leadership can lead to a greater sense of humility among pastors. In preaching, the people's response responds directly to the self-presentation of the preacher. In administering the sacraments, however, the personality of the pastor is less evident; the power inherent in the sacraments is more evident.

The conclusion toward which these ideas move is that eucharistic worship is the process of maturation whereby the Christian community becomes what it was born to be in baptism. The letter to the Ephesians refers to the one baptism and the one hope of the church's calling. It speaks of the gifts that Christ gives to the various members of the church and then states the goal: "to equip the saints for the work of ministry, for building up the body of Christ" (Ephesians 4:12). The passage alternates between references to individual members and to the church as the one body of Christ. Clearly, the *member in community* is the focus of attention, and the passage firmly points toward continued growth to the full stature of adulthood in Christ. The epistle continues with encouraging exhortations and moves into a description of early Christian worship, implying that this worship is both the cause of growth in grace and the result of that same growth. These Christians are to sing and make melody to the Lord, "giving thanks to God the Father at all times and for everything in the name of our Lord Jesus Christ" (Ephesians 5:15–20). This verse certainly refers to the general spirit of all Christian activity, but it also implies the more specific offering of praise when the church gathered for worship. Growth into full stature as Christ's body happens in the eucharistic life of the community of faith.

The Individual

Congregations consist of individual worshipers, and the impact of sacramental worship upon people one by one also needs to be considered. Some of these influences have been implied in the previous discussion, but they need to be noted from the standpoint of individuals. One effect upon individuals is that *sacramental worship intensifies and energizes the evangelical center of their faith*. A series of personal accounts assembled by Robert Webber speaks eloquently of what some people have experienced as they have moved from worship that focuses upon the pulpit to worship that focuses upon sacramental signs and especially the celebration of the eucharist. One writer (James Johnson) makes his most explicit statement as he describes participating in an Ash Wednesday liturgy that included being marked on the forehead with ashes. He had entered for the first time "into the sorrows of Christ, sorrows he took for me." No one was preaching, nor testifying to the truth of the story, nor "manipulating that truth through dramatic atmosphere. It had all come through the sense of his presence via the palpable symbol of darkness" (Webber 1985, 111; see also Ranaghan's description of the liturgical renewal at Oral Roberts University, Ranaghan 1973, 122-136).

Webber generalizes upon such experiences and shows how they reach their fullness in eucharistic worship. "As I eat the bread and drink the wine," he says, "the mystery of what Christ did for me on the cross reaches into my inner person in a way that I cannot describe." The bread and wine, he continues, speak of his sin and of justification and sanctification, but what is more important, they communicate the saving reality of Christ. "I am caught up in its power and cleansed by the fresh work of the Holy Spirit which I continually experience at that Table of Communion" (Webber 1985, 84).

A second impact upon the individual is that *sacramental worship provides a clear focus for modeling one's life*. Several passages of scripture suggest that Jesus Christ is the model for how people should live. One such time was the occasion late in his ministry when Jesus was asked to give James and John favored places in his commonwealth. In response to the anger of the other disciples, Jesus stated that leadership in his service was different from that in the world. In the realm that he would establish greatness was measured by service and highest position was ascribed to slaves. Jesus then gave himself as the example for he had come "not to be served but to serve, and to give his life a ransom for many." (Matthew 20:20–28) A similar spirit is expressed in Paul's farewell to the Ephesian elders. After citing his own pattern of devoted labor in their midst and encouraging them to "support the weak," he concludes with the words of Jesus: "It is more blessed to give than to receive." (Acts 20:35)

Jesus' full life and ministry are appropriately held out to people as the model for life. Yet, most people are unlikely to duplicate the details of that model—celibacy, homelessness, itineracy, teaching, and healing. His commendation of a ministry of healing and liberation, as reported in the sermon at the Nazareth synagogue (Luke 4), provides a way of creating a model of his life without making it a template for exact reproduction. These very qualities are highlighted in a eucharistic prayer developed by the United Methodist Church:

> Holy are you,
> and blessed is your Son Jesus Christ.
> Your Spirit anointed him
> to preach good news to the poor,
> to proclaim release to the captives
> and recovering of sight to the blind,
> to set at liberty those who are oppressed,
> and to announce that the time had come
> when you would save your people.

Later the prayer asks that the people who at this table receive Christ's body and blood, and thus become the body of Christ for the world, may by the Spirit be made "one with Christ, one with each other, and one in ministry to all the world" (*Holy Communion* 1987, 12, 13).

Even this guidance may be too detailed to use as general principles. Thus a more broadly defined set of ideas can become the principles that can shape the lives of all Christians. Here the words in Philippians 2 come to mind even though their first application is to the congregation rather than to the individual. Jesus provides the example of *obedience to God* and *suffering for the sake of the world* as the preeminent marks of faithfulness. Both words need to be understood carefully, especially in light of the critique of these very ideas in contemporary social analysis. Obedience is the self-chosen act of persons who are free to do something else. It is the voluntary yielding of position or power in order to contribute to the achieving of goals desired both by those who obey and those who command. Thus, marchers in a civil rights demonstration obey the commands of leaders of the march. The energies of the people are compressed, channeled, and released in ways that are far more effective than can result from uncoordinated, undisciplined modes of public witness. Part of the decision that free people make is the extent to which their obedience will extend. Will they do the march only as long as the day is sunny and the breeze refreshing? Will they continue when the sun blazes down upon them? Or when the cold rains drench them? How will they respond to opposition? Will they persist until the shedding of blood? Or cease when the danger level mounts?

In the eucharistic meal the entire life of Jesus, and all of his redemptive work, are concentrated and focused, as the light of the sun is focused and concentrated by a prism. By their regular participation in this sacrament, Christians continually encounter the suffering and obedient love that is to be the center of their lives, too. They then are able to move into their own life circumstances, which are totally different from those that Jesus lived, and find their own ways of obeying God even to the point of suffering. By their obedience, they enter into God's continuing effort to redeem the world "groaning in travail." By their willingness to suffer, they press past the resistance they encounter and break through to new possibilities for the world around them.

A third effect upon the individual is that *it connects them with a community whose objective base overcomes some of the limitations that are present when community is subjectively based.* The command of the gospel is that we *love* one another, not that we *like* one another. The contrast can be seen in the extending of the peace of Christ during the liturgy is compared with the coffee hour afterwards. Some congregations extend the peace of Christ in ways that are expressive and inclusive. Congregants have learned to cut through social convention and for a few moments to encounter one another in a direct way. By firm hand clasps, eye contact, and direct address, they extend the peace of Christ. The stylized language of the address and the immediacy of the personal approach transcend autobiographical detail so that the soul of one, in a relatively unprotected mode of self-presentation, reaches out to the other. The foundation is the love of Christ shining from one and being received by the other. As a stranger in services, I can testify to the reality of this objective community that sometimes occurs.

All of us also need to experience community in ways whereby the autobiographical detail is important. We need lovers, confidants, cronies, morning coffee conversation partners, people with whom we are bound by all manner of likes and dislikes. Yet subjectively based relationships are limited in their extent. We can be autobiographically present to a relatively small number of people, and the strain upon our psychic energy is great. In contrast the objective community that disregards autobiographical detail in order to emphasize the connections based upon common elements—our humanity, our peoplehood, our faith, our nationality—relaxes consciousness and relieves strain. We are accepted not because of what we can do, but because of what has been done to us by the outside forces of procreation, enculturalization, and conversion. A worshiping congregation is not a family; it is a pilgrimage of people moving from the commonwealth of this world to the commonwealth of heaven that is to come.

A fourth impact of eucharistic worship is that *people who have trouble listening can still participate*. Much of the service of worship is aggressively verbal and intellectual. It enters the worshiper by the ear and mind. For some worshipers, however, these channels of divine grace are obstructed. Because of age, illness, or some other condition in life, some can't hear or can't understand. For many of them, the fact that the eucharist uses the eyes, nose, and tongue more than the ears opens to them a mode of experiencing God's love and perhaps even of coming to understand it and to love God in return. Because of its value to these people, eucharistic worship can be highly influential in their nurture and maturation.

These influences of eucharistic worship upon individuals can be summed up by saying that coming together in the Lord's supper continues in the lives of Christians the power that was given them in their baptism. At baptism their sins are forgiven, but inevitably they continue to sin. Baptism is part of their conversion to Christ, but that conversion is partial and continues throughout life. Baptism commissions them for ministry in the world in the name of Jesus, but they need constant renewing of power with which to do that ministry. All of these continuing needs are met by the regular meeting with Christ and one another at the table. Here the forgiveness of sins is renewed, their conversion to Christ deepened, and their power for ministry restored after its depletion by their work in Christ's name.

Impact upon Life in the World

Worship always has an impact upon the church's relationship to the life of the wider community. Therefore, we must now consider the effect of eucharistic worship upon this public witness of churches. The framework for this discussion is the typology developed by Roozen, McKinney, and Carroll, which consists of four modes of religious presence by churches and synagogues. *Activist* is the name they give to a mode in which leaders and congregations devote their energies to direct action in the world, seeking to accomplish specific goals for transforming life. *Citizen* is the name they give to a mode of public presence in which the major emphasis is upon theological and ethical instruction rather than upon direct action. It is assumed that members of these congregations will use their religious understandings in their own activities and modes of participation in both the private and public spheres of life. *Sanctuary* is the name given to a mode of presence that perceives the congregation as a respite from vigorous engagement in life. Here, people find healing and strength, and as whole persons are enabled to develop their own ways of understanding the wider world, God's claims over it, and their own ways of working within it. *Evangelist* is the name given to the fourth type of engagement. In this mode, the major emphasis is upon bringing people into life in the congregation, with the assumption that converted people will become active in converting the world (Roozen, McKinney, and Carroll 1984).

Christian congregations of all four types include the eucharist in their liturgical system. The Lord's supper, however, bears a strong affinity to two of these modes—sanctuary and activist. The eucharist and the sanctuary mode of presence easily become partners. Eucharistic worship points to the past action of God in Christ and to the future action in the consummation of all things. These ideas often lead to quietism with respect to life right now. Thus, the eucharist becomes an especially potent mode of experiencing respite from this world and receiving energy for the trans-historical world still to come. Because of its emphasis upon a theology of incarnation, however, eucharistic worship also can lead to active participation by leaders and congregations in mission in the life of the world. Rafael Avila states this idea clearly and energetically. After referring to the Passover as the celebration of "the liberation of the Jewish people," he affirms that the eucharist "is the banquet of the liberty of the children of God." The eucharist, he continues, "obliges us to review and renew the commitment we have made to Christ to collaborate with him in the total liberation of all human beings" (Avila 1977, 82).

These two patterns of public presence can and should exist in a relationship that is reciprocal rather than antagonistic. When functioning fully, congregations and church members move back and forth between intensely experienced relationships with God and fully engaged interaction with the world around them. In the church as sanctuary, they see the Holy One "high and lifted up." Their eyes are opened to their own moral condition in the light of God's radiant goodness, and they are convicted. Yet, they also experience the grace of divine forgiveness, with the result that they are cleansed, renewed, and encouraged once again to move into all of the world in the name of Christ. Being removed from battles in the world is not blameworthy, unless that removal is habitual and constant.

Furthermore, they find in the eucharist as sanctuary an experience of the human community God intends for all of the world. Brian Wren's eucharistic hymn "I Come with Joy" states this function of sanctuary well. At this table, "as all are fed," we find "the new community of love in Christ's communion bread." Each "proud division

232 The Great Thanksgiving

ends," and because Christ's love makes us all one "strangers now are friends." This hymn also states the reversing of the current. "Together met, together bound, we'll go our different ways." As Christ's "people in the world we'll live and speak his praise."

Part of the dynamic in this reciprocating movement is the dissonance between the vision of God's commonwealth and knowledge of the world as it is. While the harmonies of heaven may resound in the house of worship, the rest of life is blasted with raucous noise and cries of anguish. The positive relations with one another expressed by the liturgical exchange of peace contrast sharply with the hostile and often destructive associations that worshipers frequently meet in their work and sometimes in their homes. In church it is relatively easy to believe in the peaceable kingdom that the prophets proclaim. Outside of church, Luther's phrase is more easily believed, that the whole world is "with devils filled."

This dissonance cannot long be sustained. Some people suppress it, refusing to acknowledge that the world outside is as bad as it seems. Some people separate the two spheres of their lives, in which case the church as sanctuary is in fact the place where they escape from the realities of life. The better response, however, is to face the contrast directly and work to make life in the larger world conform more closely to life in the more intimate world of the eucharistic assembly. In this way, the church and its people move back and forth between the retreat mode and the activist mode of engagement. The clearer their vision of what God really wants, the stronger their sense of divine calling for their lives, the more confident they are of their place in a community of love, the greater is the likelihood that worshipers can move forward into the world, working with God to bring it to its completion.

This movement into the world is also empowered by the meal in the sanctuary. Thus the eucharist becomes rations for the hard work that is to come. Marathon runners and long-distance bicyclists know the importance of continually taking in new supplies of energy if they are to be strong until their event is completed. With nourishment, they remain strong even though they tire from the constant exertion. Without nourishment, their bodies are depleted and they "hit the wall," no longer able to push through their fatigue to the final effort that brings them to their destination. So the eucharist week after week is that bread of heaven and water of life that quenches thirst forever.

Works Cited

Anaphora of Addai and Mari. See Deiss 1979.

Avila, Rafael. 1977. *Worship and Politics*. Maryknoll, NY: Orbis Books.

Babin, David E. 1976. *Week In—Week Out: A New Look at Liturgical Preaching*. New York: The Seabury Press.

Baptism and Belonging. Edited by Keith Watkins. 1991. St. Louis: Chalice Press.

Baptism, Eucharist and Ministry. 1982. Geneva: World Council of Churches.

Bartow, Charles L. 1988. *Effective Speech Communication in Leading Worship*. Nashville: Abingdon Press.

BAS. See *The Book of Alternate Services...* 1985.

BCP 1928. See *Book of Common Prayer...* 1928.

BCP 1979. See *The Book of Common Prayer...* 1979.

BCW. See *Book of Common Worship*.

BEM. See *Baptism, Eucharist and Ministry*. 1982.

The Book of Alternative Services of The Anglican Church of Canada. 1985. Toronto: Anglican Book Centre.

Book of Common Prayer, According to the Use of the Protestant Episcopal Church. 1928. New York: Oxford University Press.

The Book of Common Prayer, According to the Use of the Episcopal Church. 1979. New York: The Church Hymnal Corporation.

Book of Common Worship. 1993. Prepared by the Theology and Worship Unit for the Presbyterian Church (U.S.A.) and the Cumberland Presbyterian Church. Louisville: Westminster/John Knox Press.

The Book of Occasional Services. 1979. New York: The Church Hymnal Corporation.

Book of Worship: United Church of Christ. 1986. New York: United Church of Christ Office for Church Life and Leadership.

Brilioth, Yngve. 1956. *Eucharistic Faith and Practice: Evangelical and Catholic*. London: SPCK.

Bronstein, Herbert, ed. 1982. *A Passover Haggadah*, 2nd revised ed. New York: Central Conference of American Rabbis and Penguin Books.

Bruce, F. F. 1990 *The Acts of the Apostles*. 3rd revised and enlarged ed. Grand Rapids: William B. Eerdmans Publishing Company.

BW. See *Book of Worship...* 1986.

Cartwright, Colbert S. 1992. *Candles of Grace: Disciples Worship in Perspective*. St. Louis: Chalice Press.

Casel, Odo. 1962. *The Mystery of Christian Worship and Other Writings*. Edited by Burkhard Neunheuser, O.S.B. Translated by I. T. Hale. Westminster, MD: Newman Press.

Cassirer, Ernst. 1953. *Language and Myth*. Translated by Susanne K. Langer. New York: Dover Publications, Inc.

CCT. See Consultation on Common Texts.

Chalice Hymnal. 1995. St. Louis: Chalice Press.

Church, F. Forrester, and Terrence J. Mulry (eds.) 1988. *The Macmillan Book of Earliest Christian Prayers*. 1988. New York: Macmillan.

Church of South India. 1963. *The Book of Common Worship*. London: Oxford University Press.

COCU. See Consultation on Church Union.

Commentary on Prayer Book Studies 30 containing Supplemental Liturgical Texts. 1989. New York: The Church Hymnal Corporation.

Constitution on the Sacred Liturgy. 1963. Washington: U.S. Catholic Conference.

Consultation on Church Union. 1968. *An Order of Worship for The Proclamation of the Word of God and The Celebration of the Lord's Supper With Commentary.* Cincinnati: Forward Movement Publications.

_____. 1973. *An Order for the Celebration of Holy Baptism With Commentary.* Cincinnati: Forward Movement Publications.

_____. 1978. *Word Bread Cup.* Cincinnati: Forward Movement Publications.

_____. 1985. *The COCU Consensus: In Quest of a Church of Christ Uniting.* Princeton.

Consultation on Common Texts. 1988. *Praying Together.* Nashville: Abingdon Press.

_____. 1992. *The Revised Common Lectionary.* Nashville: Abingdon Press.

Cope, G., J. G. Davies, and D. A. Tytler. 1958. *An Experimental Liturgy.* Richmond: John Knox Press.

Crockett, William R. 1989. *Eucharist: Symbol of Transformation.* New York: Pueblo Publishing Co.

Cullmann, Oscar. 1953. *Early Christian Worship.* London: SCM Press.

Cuming, Geoffrey, "Four Very Early Anaphoras," *Worship* 58 (1984), 168-172.

Davies, Horton. 1970. *Worship and Theology in England: From Cranmer to Hooker, 1543-1603.* Princeton: Princeton University Press.

_____. 1990. *The Worship of the American Puritans, 1629-1730.* New York: Peter Lang.

Deiss, Lucien C.S.Sp. 1979. *Springtime of the Liturgy.* Collegeville, Minn: The Liturgical Press.

Di Sante, Carmine. 1991. *Jewish Prayer: The Origins of Christian Liturgy.* Translated by Matthew J. O'Connell. New York: Paulist Press.

Dix, Gregory. 1945. *The Shape of the Liturgy.* London: Dacre Press.

Duck, Ruth. 1991. *Gender and the Name of God.* New York: The Pilgrim Press.

Falla, Terry C. (ed.) 1981. *Be Our Freedom, Lord.* Grand Rapids: William B. Eerdmans Publishing Company.

Fenwick, John. 1991. "Some Ecumenical Considerations," *Liturgy for a New Century,* ed. by Michael Perham. London: SPCK / Alcuin Club.

Finn, Peter C. and James M. Schellman, eds. 1990. *Shaping English Liturgy.* Washington: The Pastoral Press.

The Funeral: A Service of Witness to the Resurrection. 1986. Philadelphia: The Westminster Press.

Gates of Prayer: The New Union Prayerbook. 1975. New York: Central Conference of American Rabbis.

George, Carl F., and Robert E. Logan. 1987. *Leading and Managing Your Church.* Old Tappen, NY: Fleming H. Revell.

Gibbs, Mark, and T. Ralph Morton. 1965. *God's Frozen People.* Philadelphia: The Westminster Press.

_____. 1971. *God's Lively People.* Philadelphia: The Westminster Press.

Herzog, Frederick. See Shepherd 1963.

Hoffman, Lawrence. 1987. *Beyond the Text: A Holistic Approach to Liturgy.* Bloomington: Indiana University Press.

Holeton, David R. 1988. "Changing the Baptismal Formula: Feminist Proposals and Liturgical Implications," *Ecumenical Trends* 17:5 (May).

Holy Baptism and Services for the Renewal of Baptism. 1985. Philadelphia: The Westminster Press.

Holy Communion: Supplemental Worship Resources 16. Nashville: Abingdon Press.

The Hymnal 1982. 1985. New York: The Church Hymnal Corporation.

Interpretation 31. 1977.

Jasper, R. C. D. and Cuming, G. J., eds. 1987. *Prayers of the Eucharist: Early and Reformed.* 3rd revised ed. New York: Pueblo Press.

Jungmann, J. A. 1951. *The Mass of the Roman Rite.* Translated by F. A. Brunner. New York: Benziger Brothers.

Kavanagh, Aidan. 1978. *The Shape of Baptism: The Rite of Christian Initiation.* New York: Pueblo Publishing Company.

Kirby, John. 1969. *Word and Action: New Forms of the Liturgy.* Toronto: The Anglican Church of Canada.

Kol Haneshamah: Sabbat Eve. 1989: Wyncote, PA: The Reconstructionist Press.

Langer, Susanne K. 1951. *Philosophy in a New Key.* New York: A Mentor Book.

_____. 1953. *Feeling and Form.* New York: Charles Scribner's Sons.

_____. 1964. *Philosophical Sketches.* New York: A Mentor Book.

LBW. See *Lutheran Book of Worship.*

Lindars, Barnabas SSF. 1991. *The Theology of the Letter to the Hebrews.* New York: Cambridge University Press.

Link, Hans-Georg, ed. 1984. *Confessing Our Faith Around the World. Vol. III.* Geneva: World Council of Churches.

Lohmeyer, Ernst. 1962. *Lord of the Temple.* Richmond: John Knox Press.

Lowery, Richard H. 1993. "Sabbath and Survival," *Encounter* 54 (Spring).

Lutheran Book of Worship. 1978. Minneapolis: Augsburg Publishing House.

Marshall, I. Howard. 1973. "Meaning of the Verb 'to Baptize,'" *Ecumenical Quarterly* 45 (July-September).

Martos, Joseph. 1981. *Doors to the Sacred Garden.* Garden City, NY: Doubleday. An expanded version is printed in Kieran Scott and Michael Warren, eds. 1993. *Perspectives on Marriage: A Reader.* New York: Oxford University Press.

Mass. See *The New American Sunday Missal.*

Mettinger, Tryggve N. D. 1988. *In Search of God: The Meaning and Message of the Everlasting Names.* Translated by Frederick H. Cryer. Philadelphia: Fortress Press.

Mitchell, Leonel L. 1985. *Praying Shapes Believing.* Minneapolis: Winston Press.

Mitchell, Nathan. 1982. *Cult and Controversy: The Worship of the Eucharist Outside of Mass.* New York: Pueblo Publishing Co.

Morley, Janet. 1988. *All Desires Known.* London: Movement for the Ordination of Women.

The New American Sunday Missal. 1975. Edited by Bernard Beniziger. Cleveland: Collins World.

A New Dictionary of Liturgy and Worship. 1986. Edited by J. G. Davies. London: SCM Press.

A New Zealand Prayer Book: He Karakia Mihinare o Aotearoa. 1989. The Church of the Province of New Zealand. London: Collins Liturgical Publications.

NZPB. See *A New Zealand Prayer Book.*

Old, Hughes Oliphant. 1984. *Worship.* Atlanta: John Knox Press.

Osborn, G. Edwin, ed. 1953. *Christian Worship: A Service Book.* St. Louis: Christian Board of Publication.

Pannenberg, Wolfhart. 1983. *Christian Spirituality.* Philadelphia: The Westminster Press.

Petuchowski, Jakob J., and Michael Brocke, eds. 1978. *The Lord's Prayer and Jewish Liturgy.* New York: Seabury Press.

PH. See *The Presbyterian Hymnal.*

The Presbyterian Hymnal. 1990. Louisville: Westminster/John Knox Press.

Ranaghan, Kevin M. 1973. "The Liturgical Movement at Oral Roberts University," *Studia Liturgica* 9.

Roozen, David A., William McKinney, and Jackson W. Carroll. 1984. *Varieties of Religious Presence: Mission in Public Life.* New York: Pilgrim Press.

Schaller, Lyle B. 1981. *Activating the Passive Church.* Nashville: Abingdon Press.

Schillebeeckx, Edward. 1963. *Christ the Sacrament of the Encounter with God.* New York: Sheed and Ward.

_____. 1968. *The Eucharist.* New York: Sheed and Ward.

Schmemann, Alexander. 1973. *For the Life of the World: Sacraments and Orthodoxy.* Crestwood, NJ: St. Vladimir's Seminary Press.

Schmidt, Leigh Eric. 1989. *Holy Fairs: Scottish Communions and American Revivals in the Early Modern Period.* Princeton: Princeton University Press.

Searle, Mark. "The Opening and Closing Rites of the Mass." See Finn and Schellman, 1990.

Senn, Frank C., ed. 1987. *New Eucharistic Prayers.* New York: Paulist Press.

Shands, Alfred R. 1965. *The Liturgical Movement and the Local Church.* Revised edition. New York: Morehouse-Barlow Co.

Shepherd, Massey Hamilton, Jr. 1950. *The Oxford American Prayer Book Commentary.* New York: Oxford University Press.

_____ (ed.) 1960. *The Liturgical Renewal of the Church.* New York: Oxford University Press.

_____. 1963. *Worship in Scripture and Tradition.* New York: Oxford University Press.

Shorter, Aylward. 1973a. *African Culture and the Christian Church.* Maryknoll: Orbis Books.

_____. 1973b. "Three More African Eucharistic Prayers." *Afer* 15.

Smallzried, Kay. 1964. *Spilled Milk: Litanies for Living.* New York: Oxford University Press.

Smart, James D. 1954. *The Teaching Ministry of the Church.* Philadelphia: The Westminster Press.

Taizé. 1962. *The Eucharistic Liturgy of Taizé.* With an introductory essay by Max Thurian. Translated by John Arnold. London: The Faith Press.

Taylor, Edward. 1960. *Poems.* Edited by Donald E. Stafford. New Haven: Yale University Press.

_____. 1962. *Christographia.* Edited by Norman S. Grabo. New Haven: Yale University Press.

Thankful Praise. 1987. Edited by Keith Watkins. St. Louis: CBP Press.

Thompson, Bard. 1961. *Liturgies of the Western Church.* Cleveland and New York: Living Age Books.

Thurian, Max and Geoffrey Wainwright, eds. 1983. *Baptism and Eucharist: Ecumenical Convergence in Celebration.* Grand Rapids: William B. Eerdmans Publishing Company.

Toulmin, Stephen. 1990. *Cosmopolis: The Hidden Agenda of Modernity.* New York: The Free Press.

Turner, Victor. 1967. *The Forest of Symbols.* Ithaca, NY: Cornell University Press.

_____. 1974. *Dramas, Fields, and Metaphors: Symbolic Action in Human Society.* Ithaca, NY: Cornell University Press.

UMH. See *The United Methodist Hymnal.*

The United Methodist Hymnal. 1989. Nashville: The United Methodist Publishing House.

Uzukwu, E. E. 1991. "African Symbols and Christian Liturgical Celebration," *Worship* 65 (March).

Watkins, Keith. 1969. *Liturgies in a Time When Cities Burn.* Nashville: Abingdon Press.

_____. 1991. *Celebrate with Thanksgiving.* St. Louis: Chalice Press.

Webber, Robert E. 1982. *Worship Old and New.* Grand Rapids: Zondervan Publishing House.

_____. 1985. *Evangelicals on the Canterbury Trail.* Waco: Word Books.

Werner, Eric. 1959. *The Sacred Bridge: The Interdependence of Liturgy and Music in Synagogue and Church during the First Millennium.* New York: Columbia University Press.

White, James F. 1989. *Protestant Worship: Traditions in Transition.* Louisville: Westminster/John Knox Press.

Word and Sacraments. 1987. Toronto: Board of Congregational Life, The Presbyterian Church in Canada.

Worship for the Way: Prayers and Services for the Life Journey. 1988. Toronto: Board of Congregational Life, The Presbyterian Church in Canada.

The Worshipbook. 1970. Philadelphia: The Westminster Press.

Young, Robert D. 1980. *Be Brief About It.* Philadelphia: Westminster Press.

Index of Subjects

Anamnesis 141-43
Anaphora 146
Baptism 153-87, 198, 226
  and confirmation 173
  and Donatist controversy 156
  and eucharist 158, 166-67
  by immersion 161, 170-71, 180-81
  ecumenical consensus on 159-64
  in early church 155-56
  in New Testament 153-55, 156-57, 179
  in Reformation 157-58
  laying on of hands 157, 181-83
  of believers 158-59, 160-61
  of infants 157-59, 160, 164-65
  rebaptism 184-85
  renewal of vows 164, 185-86
  thanksgiving 176-79
  welcoming after 183-84
Bible, in worship 101-05, 111-13
Blessing 41-43, 174
Care for the dying 200-201
Congregation 98-99, 125, 207-11, 223-32
  as community 226-27, 229-30
  as royal priesthood 208-11
Entrance rites 97-101
Epiclesis 143-45, 146-47
Eucharist
  and baptism 158, 166-67
  as center of worship 4, 7-10, 17-40, 54-59, 222, 224-25
  as communion 23-24, 49, 122-27

as remembrance 141-43
as sacrifice 19-21, 26, 122, 143
as sanctuary 231-32
as thankful praise 4, 41, 43, 136-39
defined 3-4
eucharistic prayers 46, 129-49, 228
frequency of 8
in early church 18-23, 45-47, 58, 85, 122, 132-33
in Reformation 7-8, 27-28, 133-34
meaning of 23-25
theologies of 25-33, 138
Funerals 188-89, 196-204
  care for the body 201-202
  memorializing the deceased 202-03
Gathering 97-101
Holy Spirit, invocation of 143-45
Invitation to discipleship 109
Last Supper 18-19
Leadership
  liturgical 217-21
  pastoral 226
Lectionaries 102-05, 107-08
Liturgies 28-29, 33-39
  baptismal 160-61, 170-87
  Church of South India 33
  Consultation on Church Union 34-35, 37, 160-61, 163-64
  Episcopal 64, 147-48
  Lima 35-36
  Methodist 64-65
  Presbyterian 65, 171
  Taizé 34